I0834097

GENEALOGY

OF

WILLIAM ALLIS

OF

HATFIELD, MASS.

AND

DESCENDANTS

1630-1919

By

HORATIO D. ALLIS

Hartford, Conn.

Printed by

Art Press, Hartford, Conn.

Notice

In many older books, foxing (or discoloration) occurs and, in some instances, print lightens with wear and age. Reprinted books, such as this, often duplicate these flaws, notwithstanding efforts to reduce or eliminate them. The pages of this reprint have been digitally enhanced and, where possible, the flaws eliminated in order to provide clarity of content and a pleasant reading experience.

Originally published
Hartford, Conn.
1919

Reprinted by:

Janaway Publishing, Inc.
732 Kelsey Ct.
Santa Maria, CA 93454
(805) 925-1038
www.JanawayGenealogy.com

(1919), 2018

ISBN: 978-1-59641-426-6

Made in the United States of America

PREFACE.

This book is the result of my desire to know something in regard to my own ancestors. Its production has largely been possible because of the efforts of my predecessors, and I desire to acknowledge my indebtedness to those who have heretofore had a share in this work, and to the host of correspondents who have for the most part so heartily responded to my inquiries.

Among the first to desire a genealogy of the family was Waitstill H. Allis of Springfield, Mass. He was much interested in the work of collecting data and historical documents and he gathered together a great many facts of value. He sent out invitations to attend a convention at Saratoga Springs, N. Y., on September 6th and 7th, 1882, for the purpose of forming the Allis Historical Association, the object being to interest all living descendants of William Allis in the task of securing data for the publication of an "Allis Memorial." Delegates were present from several states, and although no definite plans were made the occasion was a very enjoyable one. Nothing further seems to have been done relative to the association, but the data which Waitstill H. Allis accumulated was passed along and is included in this book.

The next one to actively take up this work was Hubbard S. Allis of Whately, Mass., and Prattsburg, N. Y. He spent a great deal of time in looking up and arranging facts relative to the family, and was assisted in no small way by his daughter, Mrs. Gertrude A. Billings of Whately, Mass. I have been fortunate in having her assistance also. While a resident of Prattsburg, N. Y., Hubbard S. Allis had a leaflet printed covering his own branch of the family as of June 1st, 1890, and stating that the information would be passed on to Charles Allis of Milwaukee, Wis., who would publish a more complete book.

On May 4th, 1893, Charles Allis sent to many living descendants his booklet entitled the "Allis Genealogy", with the idea of interesting them and securing from them information that would enable him to complete the unfinished and missing lines and make possible the publication of a correct and up-to-date genealogy.

I became interested in this work in the fall of 1911, when I saw for the first time the booklet published by Charles Allis, and after looking up some facts about my own line I decided to take up other lines as well, and the work from a small beginning soon grew to be quite an undertaking. It is to be regretted that some family lines are still incomplete, but after an investigation I feel sure that a part of the information is not obtainable. I have not relied on tradition in this work but have depended upon recorded facts, and hope the book will be found fairly accurate.

Again I wish to thank those who have aided in making this genealogy possible and express the hope that it will give us a better knoweldge of our ancestors and enable us to become better acquainted.

HORATIO DANA ALLIS.

INTRODUCTION.

Nearly all of the Allises in this country are descendants of William of Hatfield. It is to be regretted that he left no record of his parents or clue that would help to clear up the obscure period of his history before 1630, the year in which he sailed from England. It is recorded that a Richard Allis took the oath of allegiance in England on June 22, 1632, before embarking in the "Lion", which arrived at Boston on September 16, 1632, but where he lived here is unknown as no later trace of him can be found. It is possible that they were brothers, but as Richard also left no clue as to his ancestry we can only surmise this to be so.

It is a reasonable probability that we are descendants of the William Alis referred to in the "Domesday Book", which is the ancient record of the survey of lands of England completed by William the Conqueror in 1086. It is recorded therein that William Alis held Ellatune, co. Hants (now Allington, Hampshire), as tenant-in-chief of the king. There is no doubt but that he took part in the invasion and conquest of England by William, Duke of Normandy (called the Conqueror), in 1066-1071, and received this large grant of land from him, which rated about 360 acres and included a church and two mills. He was undoubtedly connected with the Parish of Alisay (formerly Alis), a pretty village near Paris, France, and Geoffrey Alis, possibly a brother, went to the Holy Land as a crusader with Robert, Duke of Normandy (son of William the Conqueror) in 1096. It is recorded that a Sir William Alis, with nine other knights, was taken prisoner when fighting under the banner of the Earl of Bretton in 1091 near Yvery, Normandy. (7 Collins Peerage, 541.)

It is clearly shown by several old English records that William Alis, the owner of Ellatune, was the ancestor of Roger Alis (1161), Sir William Alis (1184), Walter Fitz Alis, Sheriff of London in 1201, Martin Fitz Alis, Sheriff of London in 1213, Sir Roger Alis and Sir Thomas Alis (in the time of Henry III, 1216-1272), William Alis (in the time of Edward I, until about 1303), and Roger Alis, Sheriff of London in 1395.

The next descendant of whom we have a record is Geoffrey Allis in 1454, whose name appears in the church records of London published by the Harleian Society. After that date the family seems to have spread out from London and the name appears in the records of various places. A record of Chichester wills shows the name of William Alys of Felpham in 1535, and a Richard Allis of Lincolnshire was one of the men eligible to serve in the wars in the time of Queen Elizabeth in 1558-1563, The descendants of Richard Allis have apparently lived in Lincolnshire ever since that time and can be found there to-day. Of principal interest among the names shown in the Lincoln records are Thomas Allis (1538-1540), Joseph Allis (1558), William Allis (1591) and Robert Allis (1620).

The Allis family in London was quite a large one until the great plague of 1665, during which it was nearly exterminated. One family lost seven members in two days, and a reference to the burial registers will show why the name is now so rare there. Most of the entries after 1665 in the records of the Harleian Society are of the Essex Allises, which include Edward Allis, Chingford, in 1675, and John Allis, Woodford, in 1685.

It is of course impossible to establish a continuous line of descent from William Alis of Ellatune up to the present time, but after studying certain authorities on surnames and noting the regular use of the original Christian names from generation to generation it would seem to be a fact that we are his descendants.

The first record of the coat of arms is that borne by the last of the Roger Alis line when he was made Sheriff of London in 1395. Undoubtedly the coat of arms was worn by Sir Roger Alis, who was a crusader in the time of Henry III and received a grant of Hampshire land for his services from Isabella Mortimer in 1217 (Rot. Lit. Claus, p. 305; Testa de Nevill, p. 230). It is a regular crusader's arms, viz. "Or, on a cross sable, five crescents argent" (Her. Col. 19 R), that is, a black cross on a field of gold with five silver crescents.

It is interesting to note the different spelling of the name in various English and Colonial records, for instance, Alis, Alys, Allis, Allise, Allice, Alyes, Ellice and Ellis. There are at least two cases where after a change of residence the name was recorded Ellis, although originally Allis, namely the families of Thomas Allis of Guilford, Conn., and Abel Allis of Kensington, Conn. It is possible there are other similar cases.

1. WILLIAM ALLIS was born between 1613 and 1616, probably in Essex or London, England, and came to this country with Winthrop's fleet in 1630. The fleet consisted of eleven vessels: Arabella, Talbot, Ambrose, Jewel, Charles, Mayflower (third voyage), William and Francis, Hopewell, Whale, Success and Trial.

1 Bancroft's History of U. S., ed. 1890, 230-4.
Barry's History of Massachusetts.
1 Winthrop's Journal, Hosmer's edition, 24.

In the Winthrop colonists, consisting of 700 immigrants, there were three distinct communities represented: (1) those from Dorset and Devon, known as the Dorchester men, who first settled in Boston a number of years before it received that name, (2) those from Lincolnshire, who were properly called Boston men and had determined upon the name of Boston for the new settlement before they left England, (3) those from London and Essex.

1 Winsor's Mem. History of Boston, 90.

William Allis came with the last named company and was no doubt one of the 39 men on the Mayflower (third voyage). They first touched at Salem, but landed at Charlton Harbor, Boston (then called Trimountain), July 1, 1630.

1 Bancroft's History of U. S., 228-9, 235-7.
1 Winthrop's Journal, Hosmer's edition, 24.
1 Winsor's Mem. History of Boston, 82, 85, 90.

The Mayflower brought what was called the Braintree Company, which included with William Allis, Thomas Graves and Thomas Meekins, all of whom played an important part in the first generation of our family. Our ancestor was associated with Graves from the start, always lived at the same place, and the families eventually intermarried. They were both surveyors and laid out the town or fort of Charlestown, the first regular settlement of the Massachusetts Bay Colony.

1 Winsor's Mem. History of Boston. 225-9.
1 Barry's History of Massachusetts, 187-192.

The first trace of William Allis after landing was in Mount Wollaston (afterward Braintree) in 1632. That town, comprising 50 square miles, was surveyed and laid out by him before 1634, and during that year, by order of the General Court, it was annexed to Boston. Large tracts of land were granted to certain inhabitants to settle in Mount Wollaston and William Allis received 12 acres on February 24, 1640. On May 13, 1640, the inhabitants of Mount Wollaston were incorporated as the town of Braintree and, with Dorchester, Dunham, Hingham, Natasket and Roxbury, were incorporated to form the city of Boston.

Drake's History of Boston, 250.
Pattee's Braintree & Quincy, 11.
Massachusetts Rec., vol. 1, 291.
Winsor's Mem. History, 116, 217, 234.

On that date William Allis was made a freeman. Only those who were members of the church were allowed to take the Freeman's Oath, which gave them the right to vote and hold office. Several historians have apparently been misled by the records of the Massachusetts Bay Colony into stating that the first knowledge of William Allis was on May 13, 1640. The reason for the error was that the official records of Braintree were first instituted on that day. He was made a freeman then because Braintree was incorporated in the city of Boston.

In 1641 William Allis married Mary —— and their eight children were born in Braintree:

2. John, b. March 5, 1642; *
3. Samuel, b. February 24, 1647; *
4. Josiah, b. in 1649; died October 25, 1651.
5. Josiah, b. October 20, 1651; no further record.
6. William, b. January 10, 1653; died in July, 1653.
7. Hannah, b. in 1654; married William Scott of Hatfield on January 28, 1670, and died in 1718. Their children were:

Josiah,	b. June 18, 1671.	John,	b. July 6, 1684.
Richard,	b. Feb. 22, 1673.	May,	b. in 1686.
William,	b. Nov. 24, 1676.	Mehitable,	b. Sept. 9, 1687.
Hannah,	b. Aug. 11, 1679.	Jonathan,	b. Nov. 1, 1688.
Joseph,	b. March 21, 1682.	Abigail,	b. Nov. 23, 1689.

8. William, b. October 11, 1655; killed by the Indians in the battle at Great Falls (now Turner's Falls) on May 19, 1676.
9. Mary, b. in 1657; died, unmarried, in February, 1690.

Our ancestor was a well-educated, capable man, and well fitted to take his place among the Puritan settlers. He was not only an experienced surveyor but also a successful farmer in Braintree. He was a prominent citizen of the town, being one of its selectmen, and had the supervision of building a road from Boston, Mass., to Providence, R. I. He lived in Braintree until 1658 and then emigrated to Wethersfield, Conn., in the fertile Connecticut valley. At that time the Massachusetts Bay Settlement was becoming somewhat crowded, and as a result the colonists left there from time to time for Connecticut, settling the towns of

Windsor, Wethersfield and Hartford in the order named. Most of the settlers made the trip afoot through the wilderness and brought with them only such things as they needed most, leaving the remainder of their possessions to be brought around from Boston and up the Connecticut River by boat.

Stiles History of Ancient Wethersfield, 162-4.

All went well until there arose a difference of opinion among the settlers of these three towns in regard to church government and ordinances. A crisis was reached in 1660 and a meeting was called at which a committee was appointed to go up the Connecticut River and view the lands east and north of Northampton, Mass., which had been purchased from the River Indians through Major John Pynchon of Springfield, Mass. A favorable report was made by the committee and about 60 men, 20 of whom lived in Wethersfield, agreed to move with their families to that very attractive place, and the land was shared between them and a lot assigned to each one. In that way Hadley was settled by the English from Wethersfield, Hartford and Windsor, William Allis being one of the number.

Judd's History of Hadley, 11, 23.

It is claimed that William Allis and Thomas Meekins, with several others, made the journey by way of the cart path through Westfield in 1661, in which year the first of the English settled in Hadley. The journey was a difficult one on account of the wilderness, the many streams to be bridged or forded and the impassible swamps, and with their heavily loaded carts, women and children, personal effects and live stock of various kinds, it took them ten days to make the trip of about 50 miles.

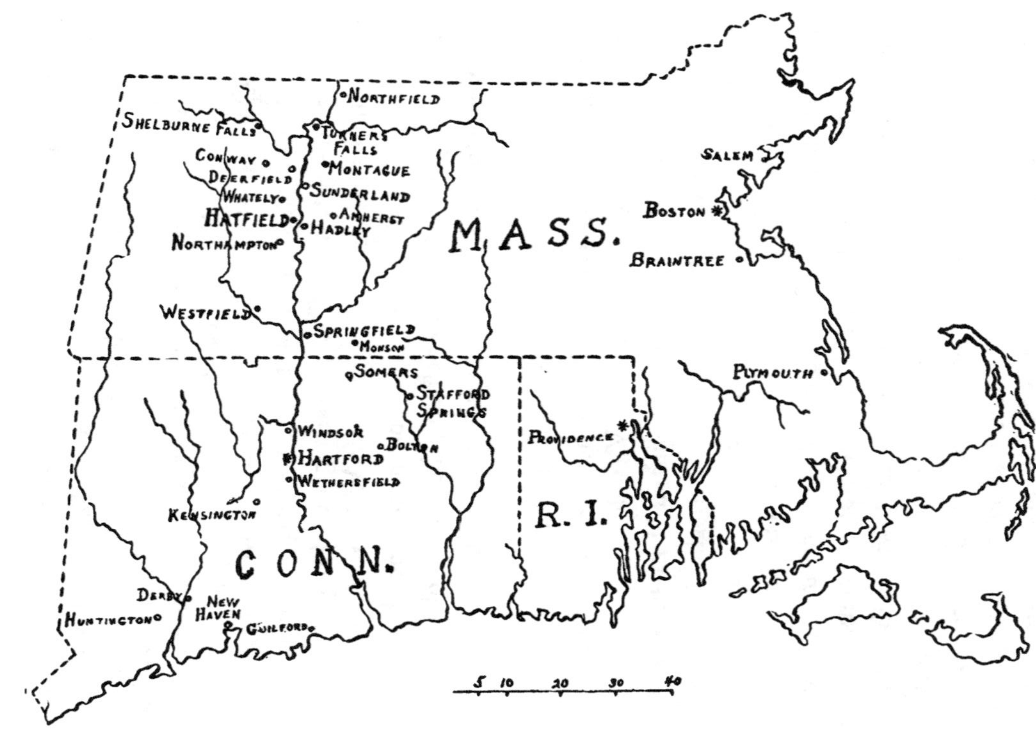

MASS.
CONN.
R. I.
SHELBURNE FALLS
NORTHFIELD
TURNERS FALLS
MONTAGUE
CONWAY
DEERFIELD
SUNDERLAND
WHATELY
AMHERST
HATFIELD
HADLEY
NORTHAMPTON
WESTFIELD
SPRINGFIELD
MONSON
SOMERS
STAFFORD SPRINGS
WINDSOR
BOLTON
HARTFORD
WETHERSFIELD
KENSINGTON
DERBY
NEW HAVEN
HUNTINGTON
GUILFORD
SALEM
BOSTON
BRAINTREE
PLYMOUTH
PROVIDENCE
5 10 20 30 40

The Hadley lands were on both sides of the Connecticut River and had been partly cleared by the Indians. The house lots of eight acres were laid out on each side of the main street, which was ten rods wide and extended a mile north and south. Hadley was laid out somewhat after the fashion of English towns and was named after Hadleigh, Suffolk County, England.

Our ancestor's home lot was on the west side of the main street in the center of the settlement. The present meeting house, town hall and Congregational parsonage are all on the lot which was assigned to William Allis. The main street was surrounded by a continuous line of palisades during King Philip's war, enclosing the houses of the original proprietors, and those who settled later were outside the palisades.

On May 31, 1670, that part of Hadley became the town of Hatfield, and in 1771 the northern part of Hatfield was incorporated as the town of Whately.

William Allis was a leading citizen of Hatfield and a trusted lieutenant of John Pynchon of Springfield. He held the offices of deacon, justice of the peace and selectman, was often on advisory committees with prominent men of that section and in 1672 was one of those commissioned to lay out Squakeage (Northfield). He was a member of the committee which was appointed by the town on March 7, 1673, and authorized to say who should be the inhabitants of Deerfield by right of purchase or otherwise, to regulate the herding of cattle, to advise about the institution of a church and secure a good orthodox minister, etc. At a later date, namely May 7, 1673, the Great and General

Amt. Estate	Amt. Acres		Rods Wide
	4	John Hawks	16
		Middle or Mill Lane	8
	4	Samuel Kellogg	6
	4	Obadiah Dickinson	6
	8	John Allis	12
£100	8	Samuel White, Jr.	12
200	8	William Allis	12
200	8	Thomas Meekins	12
50	4	Eleazer Frary	6
100	8	John Graves	12
150	8	Isaac Graves	12
50	8	Stephen Taylor	12
100	8	Ozias Goodwin	12
125	8	Zachariah Field	12
		Highway to Northampton	
150	8	John Cole	
100	8	Richard Fellows	

Rods Wide		Amt. Acres	Amt. Estate
16	Philip Russell	4	
16	Samuel Gillett	4	
18	John Wells	4	£100
16	John Coleman	4	100
16	Samuel Belding	8	100
16	William Gull	8	100
16	Samuel Dickinson	8	100
16	Edward Benton	8	100
16	John White, Jr.	8	100
16	Nat'l Dickinson, Jr.	8	150
16	Richard Billings	8	100
16	Daniel Warner	8	100
16	Thomas Bull	8	125

Plan of the house lots in Hatfield, Mass., laid out 1661-1670. The enclosure shows line of the first stockade built in King Philip's War.

Court appointed him one of a committee of six to act in all respects, to lay out the farms and to admit inhabitants to Deerfield, and in 1674 was one of those commissioned to lay out Swampfield (Sunderland).

During these years, as the Indians had been fairly dealt with by the settlers, peace existed between them until war was incited by King Philip. On October 19, 1675, the Indians numbering about 800 attacked Hatfield with the intention of destroying the town and slaying the inhabitants, as they had at the neighboring towns of Northfield and Deerfield, but they were expected by the settlers and beaten off with but small loss to Hatfield.

The Indians then assumed a defiant attitude. They stole cattle and horses from the English and appropriated a number of the outlying farms. As a result the settlers decided to take the offensive and the battle at Great Falls (now Turner's Falls) resulted. The men from the different towns to the number of 150 started from their homes on May 18, 1676, and assailed the Indians at the Falls early in the morning of the 19th, when they were asleep, killing about 175 of them with practically no loss to themselves, but when they began their homeward march this success was turned into a defeat. The Indians attacked them in the rear, and a panic was created among the English by the report that a thousand warriors under King Philip were at hand. The men were scattered, and although the retreat was conducted with bravery and skill 38 of the settlers were killed, and some became lost and wandered around in the woods for two or three days before reaching their homes.

William Allis was a captain in the fight at Great Falls and had with him in the engagement three sons, one of whom, William Allis, Jr., was killed.

The settlers now saw the need of a larger force to cope with the Indians. A cavalry regiment called the Hampshire Troop, under command of Maj. John Pynchon, was recruited from the different towns.

William Allis was at first Coronet and later Lieutenant of the mounted troops. Garrisons were established in the various towns, that of Hatfield being made up of 36 men under Lieutenant William Allis, and he was in charge of the fortifying at Hatfield in the winter of 1677-78.

For a while after the Falls Fight there was an occasional plundering expedition by the Indians, but they became scattered by famine and disease and by the English troops, and the death of King Philip on August 12, 1676, appeared to put an end to the war. Nothing more was seen of the Indians until September 19, 1677, when 50 of them from Canada, led by their chief Ashpelon and encouraged by the French, attacked Hatfield without any warning. They entered the town when most of the men were harvesting corn in a distant field, set fire to many buildings, killed 12 and captured 17 of the English, and immediately started for Canada with their captives. Mary ——, the wife of William Allis, was one of those killed in the massacre, and Abigail Allis, his granddaughter, was one of those taken captive. The suddenness of the attack seemed to paralize the settlers and apparently no effort was made to rescue their relatives and friends. Perhaps they feared that the captives might be tomahawked, if pursued, and hoped they might be spared if unmolested. The prisoners, upon their arrival in Canada, were turned over to the French, and those who survived did not again see their homes until eight months afrerward.

On June 25, 1678, Lieutenant Allis married Mary, daughter of John Bronson and widow of John Graves of Hatfield, Mr. Graves having lost his life in the Hatfield massacre. She was also the widow of John Wyatt of Haddam, Conn., before she married John Graves of Hatfield. On March 16, 1681, after the death of Lieutenant William Allis, she married Samuel Gaylord.

Lieutenant William Allis died on September 6, 1678. He was evidently a prosperous man in his day and at the close of his life he had accumulated quite an estate. The inventory of his property, which was taken September 18, 1678, was as follows:

Item	£	s	d
In purse and apparel	£ 9	13	0
Arms and ammunition	6	1	0
Beds and other furniture	9	5	0
Napkins and other linen	2	1	0
Brass and pewter pieces	5	10	0
Iron utensils	2	11	6
Cart, plow irons, chains, stilliards	7	15	0
Tables, pitchforks, cushions, scythe	1	19	0
Barrels, tubs, trays	3	9	6
Woolen and linen yarn	0	18	6
Several sorts of grain, flax	11	12	0
2 horses	7	0	0
3 cows, 2 steers, 2 calves, 1 heifer	20	0	0
Swine and sheep	10	8	0
Houses and home lot	100	0	0
Land in South Meadow	114	0	0
Land in Great and Little Meadow	136	0	0
Land in Plain and Swamp	20	0	0
Land in Quinepiake	28	13	0
	496	6	6

SECOND GENERATION

2. JOHN ALLIS was born in Braintree, Mass., on March 5, 1642, and died in Hatfield in January, 1691. He married on December 14, 1669, Mary, daughter of Thomas Meekins and widow of Nathaniel Clark. She married Samuel Belden of Hatfield about a year after

the death of John Allis and died in 1704. She was the mother of two children by Nathaniel Clark and twelve by John Allis, the Allis children being:

10. Joseph, b. Nov. 11, 1670.*

11. Abigail, b. Feb. 25, 1672. She was taken by the Indians on September 19, 1677, but later restored. She married Ephraim Wells on Jan. 23, 1696, and had the following children:

Ephraim,	b. prob. 1696-7		Sarah,	b. prob. 1706
Abigail,	" 1698		Elizabeth,	" 1708
Thomas,	" 1700		Hannah,	b. Jan. 22, 1709-10
Mary,	" 1702		Lydia,	b. Jan. 18, 1711-12
Joshua,	" 1704		Rebecca,	b. Sept. 1, 1715

12. Hannah, b. Oct. 9, 1673; married John Broughton of Deerfield on November 19, 1691, as his 2nd wife, and had at least two children:

Mary, b. Oct. 25, 1693 Hannah, b. April, 1695

13. Ichabod, b. July 10, 1675.*

14. Eleazer, b. July 23, 1677.*

15. Elizabeth, b. April 4, 1679; married James Bridgman on July 13, 1704. They lived in Sunderland and Hatfield and had 10 children:

Jonathan,	b. Feb. 1, 1706	Elizabeth,	b. Nov. 7, 1714
Mary,	b. Oct. 21, 1707	Lydia,	b. Sept. 14, 1716
John,	b July 22, 1709	Sarah,	b. Sept. 3, 1718
Ruth,	b. Feb. 25, 1711	Samuel,	b Dec. 26, 1720
Abigail,	b. Sep. 19, 1712	Sarah.	b. Oct. 28, 1722

16. Lydia, b. Aug. 15, 1680; died Aug. 31, 1691.

17. John, b. May 10, 1682.*

18. Rebecca, b. Apr. 16, 1683. married Nathanel Graves of Hatfield on Apr. 30, 1702, and had 8 children:

Rebecca,	b. Oct. 25, 1703	Eleazer,	b. Dec. 12, 1711
Mary,	b. Feb. 22, 1706	Israel.	b. June 23, 1716
Nathaniel,	b. Nov. 16, 1707	Martha,	b. Oct. 29, 1718
Ruth,	b. Aug. 16, 1709	Oliver,	b. Aug. 6, 1725

19. William, b. May 16, 1684.*

20. Nathaniel, b. 1685.*

21. Mary, b. Aug. 25, 1687; died April 20, 1688.

John Allis resided in Hatfield, near his Father William, owning a lot on the same side of Hatfield street, and was one of the prominent citizens of that town. He was a millwright and carpenter of note. He built many churches and was erecting the first corn mill at Mill River when he died. He was the first town clerk of Hatfield, and was one of a committee of six appointed to make a survey of and lay out highways between Hadley and Windsor, Conn. He served in King Philip's War and was in the fight at Great Falls on May 19, 1676. Afterwards he was a captain in the militia.

At the time of the Hatfield massacre on September 19, 1677, the mother of John Allis was killed, his barn burned, and his six-year-old daughter Abigail carried away to Canada by the Indians, being one of the seventeen prisoners taken. On the same day the Indians went north to Deerfield, where they killed one and captured four men, and then went across the country to Lake Champlain and Canada. During the march to Canada one of the men was burned at the stake and two other captives were killed, and all endured much suffering. The trip through the wilderness was a most difficult one.

The prisoners were held in Canada by the French until ransomed eight months later through the efforts of two of the Hatfield settlers, Benjamin Waite and Stephen Jennings, whose families were among the captives. They were young men, experienced in woodcraft and familiar with Indian customs, and they determined to ascertain the fate of their relatives and friends and redeem them if found alive.

On October 24, 1676, with a commission from the Massachusetts government, they left Hatfield for Albany by way of Westfield, that being the only travelled route to Canada. They reached Albany, but the authorities were unfriendly and sent them to New York on a false pretense. After a time they were sent back to Albany with a pass, but it was December 10 before they were able to resume the journey to Canada. They first hired a Frenchman as a guide, who deserted them, and then hired a Mohawk Indian, who remained with them. In the face ot many trials and discouragements, and at times without food, they finally reached the captives at Sorell, Canada, but they were unable to secure all of them without the help of the French authorities, and therefore went on to Quebec. They were successful in their mission and were also assigned a guard of 11 soldiers to Albany. They left Quebec on April 19 and Sorell on May 2, having redeemed all of the captives. The ransom cost about £200, which was made up of contributions from the English. The party reached Albany on May 22 and eventually arrived a Hatfield safely.

3. SAMUEL ALLIS was born in Braintree, Mass., on February 24, 1647, and died in Hatfield on March 9, 1691. He married in 1675-6, Alice ——, and after his death she married Sergeant John Hawks on November 20, 1696. She was killed at Deerfield on February 29, 1703-4, during the attack by the French and Indians, at the time that her son Samuel was killed and two of her daughters (Mary and perhaps Rebecca) were captured.

Samuel Allis was a carpenter and builder of Hatfield and resided on the east side of Hatfield street. Seven children:

22. Mehitable, b. July 2, 1677; married Benoni Moore of Hatfield and Northfield on December 13, 1698, and died May 8, 1757. Their 10 children were:

Elizabeth, b. Apr. 29, 1700	Hannah, b. Sep. 22, 1708
Mehitable, b. Jan 2, 1701-2	Samuel, b. May 15, 1712
Samuel, b. Jan. 2, 1703-4	Mercy, b. Sep. 12, 1713
Hezekiah, b. Jan. 18, 1704-5	Lediah, b. Feb. 28, 1715-6
Hannah, b. Dec. 25, 1706	Ruth, b. Jan. 29, 1717

23. Samuel, b. Feb. 20, 1679; killed by the Indians in the attack on Deerfield, February 29, 1703-4.

24. William, b. Oct. 19, 1680.*

25. Mary, b. July 6, 1682; was captured by the Indians at Deerfield on February 29, 1703-4, and taken to Canada, but was afterwards released. On February 3, 1710, she married Nathaniel Brooks, a fellow captive. He was first married to Mary Williams, but in the attack on Deerfield he and his wife and two children were captured by the Indians and he only returned. His wife died in Canada and the fate of his children was unknown. Mary Allis and Nathaniel Brooks had the following children:

Nathaniel,	b. Oct. 26, 1710	Aaron,	b. Oct. 17, 1717
Samuel,	b. Aug. 20, 1712	Moses,	b. Sep. 14, 1722
Eunice,	b. Nov. 22, 1714	Dina,	b. May 13, 1725

26. Thomas, b. Mar. 12, 1684.*

27. Sarah, b. in 1685; married (1st) Ebenezer Evarts of East Guilford on April 22, 1709. He died May 19, 1722, and she married (2nd) Capt. John Scranton (being his third wife) and died October 8, 1749. Sarah and Ebenezer had five children:

Hannah,	b. Oct. 30, 1710	Abigail, b. May 12, 1718
Sarah,	b. Apr. 10, 1713	Abigail, b. July 19, 1720
Mary,	b. Sep. 7, 1715	

28. Rebecca, b. Nov. 29, 1687; no further record.

THIRD GENERATION

10. JOSEPH ALLIS was born in Hatfield on November 11, 1670, and was captured and killed by the Indians on June 19, 1724, while loading hay with several other settlers three miles from town. He was a farmer and lived in Deerfield. He married Naomi —— in 1702, and their four children were:

29. Daniel, b. April 10, 1703; was drowned near the mill May 20, 1719.

30. Mary, b. 1706; married John Smead of Deerfield on September 26, 1723. He and his wife and five children were captured by the Indians on August 20, 1746, and carried to Canada, where she died March 29, 1747. He was redeemed and with the three younger children arrived at Boston August 31, 1747. Their children were:

Bathsheba,	b. Oct. 1, 1724	Reuben.	b. Apr. 13, 1735
John,	b. Dec. 18, 1726	Simon,	b.
Daniel,	b. Apr. 1, 1729	Mary,	b. about 1740
Child,	b. Oct. 16, 1731	Captivity,	b. Aug. 20, 1746
Elihu,	b. Oct. 12, 1732		

31. Thankful, b. March 11, 1711; married Jonathan Holmes of Deerfield in 1730, and died November 21, 1737. Their children were:

Child,	b. June 14, 1731	Experience,	b. Oct. 1, 1734
Joseph,	b. Nov. 14, 1737	Naomi,	b. Sept. 12, 1736

32. Experience, b. March 11, 1711; married Noah Ferry of So. Hadley, Mass., in 1736, and died in Granby, November 4, 1794. Their children were:

Noah,		Daniel,	b. Feb. 15, 1743
Charles,	b. Jan. 7, 1739	Rebecca,	b. Apr. 9, 1745

13. ICHABOD ALLIS was born in Hatfield July 10, 1675, and died July 9, 1747. He married, first, in 1698, Mary, daughter of Samuel Belden, Jr., born August 27, 1679, and died September 9, 1724. He married, 2nd, November 25, 1726, Sarah, daughter of Benjamin Waite and widow of John Belden. When she was but two years of age she was captured by the Indians and taken to Canada, but was afterwards returned.

Ichabod Allis lived in Hatfield and was a farmer and builder. He had eight children by Mary, his first wife, as follows:

33. Abigail b. Feb. 28, 1700; married Nathaniel Smith of Sunderland December 1, 1720, and died December 22, 1767. Their children were:

Mary,	b. Feb. 16, 1724	Elisha,	b. Oct. 9, 1734
Abigail,	b. Oct. 16, 1726	Martha,	b. Oct. 23, 1736
Lydia,	b. Aug. 31, 1729	Jerusha,	b. Feb. 3, 1739
Rhoda,	b. Feb. 14, 1732		

34. Lydia, b. Jan. 7, 1702; married Daniel Dickinson of Hatfield January 13, 1736, and died October 16, 1737. Dan'l Dickinson married (2nd) Ruth Bagg.

35. Martha, b. November 19, 1703; married (1st) John Wells of Hatfield. They lived in Hatfield and Hardwick, Mass. and had seven children:

John,	b. Mar. 14, 1729	Lydia,	b. Aug. 16, 1738
Martha,	b. June 12, 1731	Submit,	b. May 3, 1742
Mary,	b. Feb. 26, 1734	Elijah,	b. April 1, 1744
Lucy,	b. Mar. 7. 1736		

After the death of John Wells she married (2nd) Captain Nathaniel Hammond of Swanzey, N. H., August 6, 1746. They lived in Hardwick and had one child, Timothy, born May 13, 1748. Captain Hammond died July 19, 1758, and his widow married (3rd) Nathaniel Kellogg of Hadley and died September 13, 1764.

36. Samuel, b. Dec. 12, 1705. *

37. Sarah, b. Jan. 11, 1708; m. Joseph Miller Nov. 14, 1734.

38. Bathsheba, b. Jan. 12, 1710; married Jonathan Warner on August 8, 1733, and had ten children:

Daniel,	b. Dec. 22, 1734	Jonathan,	b. July 14, 1744
Mary,	b. Feb. 23, 1736	Bathsheba,	b. July 24, 1746
Bathsheba,	b. Oct.-Nov. 1738	Lucy,	b. May 10, 1748
Lydia,	b. Nov. 3, 1740	Rhoda,	b. Mar. 3, 1752
Sarah,	b. Nov. 1, 1742	Rhoda,	b. Nov., 1754

39. Abel, b. July 21, 1714; married on Dec. 14, 1735, Miriam, daughter of Joseph and Lydia (Leonard) Scott of Hatfield who was born Dec. 14, 1713. She married (2nd) Joseph Benton of Hartford, Connecticut, and died May 26, 1751.

40. Elisha, b. Dec. 3, 1716; *

14. ELEAZER ALLIS was born at Hatfield July 23, 1677, and died Nov. 22, 1758, age 82. He married, first, on March 17, 1720, Jemima, daughter of John and Sarah (Banks) Graves of Hatfield and widow of John Graves of Whately. She was born at Whately April 30, 1693, and died February 18, 1727. He married (2nd) November 14, 1734, Martha, daughter of John and Sarah (White) Graves of Hatfield and widow of John Crafts, who was born at Hatfield on November 4, 1689, and died June 5, 1780.

Eleazer Allis was a farmer and lived in Hatfield, and had two children by his first wife:

41. Jonathan, b. June 22, 1723; married Submit ——— and died in 1797 without issue.

42. Eleazer, b. Dec. 15, 1725. *

17. JOHN ALLIS was born at Hatfield May 10, 1682, and was twice married: first, on January 29, 1708, Mary, daughter of John and Sarah (Smith) Lawrence, who was born Nov. 1, 1688, and died Nov. 8, 1713; second, on June 23, 1715, Bethiah, daughter of John and Mary (Edwards) Field of Northampton. He lived in Hatfield and had five children.

By first wife:

43. Joanna, b. in September, 1710; died.
44. Dorothy, b. Jan. 27, 1712; no further record.
45. Daughter, b. Oct. 28, 1713; died Oct. 29, 1713.

By second wife:

46. Ebenezer, b. June 25, 1716; died April 13, 1720.
47. John, b. Sept. 18, 1718; probably married Lydia, daughter of Joseph and Lydia (Leonard) Scott of Hatfield and died in 1734-5. Lydia married (2nd) John Field Oct. 5, 1736

19. WILLIAM ALLIS was born at Hatfield May 16, 1684, and married on Dec. 15, 1709, Mary, daughter of Jacob Griswold of Wethersfield, Conn. About the time of his marriage he removed to Wethersfield, where he died in 1761. He made his will June 14, 1756, in which he gave to his grandson, Abel Allis, all his real estate, and all his personal effects that would remain after paying the other legacies named in the will.

William Allis was a farmer and a prominent citizen of Wethersfield, and held town offices of Collector in 1712, and Lister (rate-maker) and Packer (meat inspector) the following year. His five children were born in Wethersfield:

48. Mary, b. November 22, 1711; married Ebenezer Sanford of Wethersfield and had Ebenezer, born in 1739. She died and he married, second, Sarah, daughter of Robert Chapman of East Haddam, on February 14, 1740.

49. Lydia, b. September 14, 1713; married on March 8, 1739, John Collins of Wethersfield, and had Amos, born June 5, 1746, and Kezia, born in 1747.

50. Sarah, b. October 6, 1715; married on January 13, 1742, Ezekiel Kelsey of Wethersfield and had seven children:

Asahel,	b. Oct. 30, 1743	Sarah,	b. Aug. 2, 1752
Israel,	b. Nov. 20, 1745	Patience,	b. July 30, 1754
Ezekiel,	b. Dec. 22, 1747	Patience,	b. Aug. 23, 1756
Mary,	b. Dec. 30, 1749		

51. Ann, born in 1720; married Samuel Pike.

52. John, b. Sept. 11, 1726; *

20. NATHANIEL ALLIS was born at Hatfield in 1685 and died in Bolton, Conn., in February, 1750-51. He married, first, November 28, 1705, Mercy Dudley, of Guilford, Conn., who bore him twelve children. She died June 29, 1731, and he married, second, Elizabeth———,

who died in Vernon, Conn, July 6, 1774. The children were:

53. Mindwell, b. Feb. 1, 1708; died April 15, 1708.

54. Mary, b. April 25, 1709; married Benjamin Johns of Bolton on Feb. 24, 1728, and had five children:

Mary,	b. Jan. 2, 1729	Daniel,	b. Mar. 4, 1737
Benjamin,	b. Oct. 17, 1731	Naomi,	b. Mar. 4, 1740
Stephen,	b. Oct. 14, 1734		

55. Jemima, b. June 20, 1711; married Eliakim Root of Coventry, Conn., on August 15, 1731.

56. Jonathan, b. Aug. 5, 1713; married on September 3, 1741, Martha Wickham of Glastonbury, Conn.

57. Mindwell, b. May 26, 1714; married Mr. Rood.

58. Nathaniel, b. Nov. 4, 1716; *

59. John, b. Nov. 10, 1718; *

60. David, b. July 19, 1720; *

61. Mercy, b. March 17, 1722; married Mr. Coleman.

62. Naomi, b. Jan. 1, 1724; died Jan. 26, 1740.

63. Ebenezer, b. May 24, 1726; *

64. Timothy, b. Nov. 13, 1728; married Elizabeth Whitaker of Bolton Nov. 7, 1751. Removed to Stafford, Conn. and adopted two children, Dan'l Curtis and Lydia Washburn.

Nathaniel Allis settled in Bolton about the time of his marriage and was a wealthy farmer and prominent citizen of that town. His will, made in January, 1750-51, is an interesting document and is quoted herewith:

In the name of God amen. I, Nathaniel Allis of Bolton, in the County of Hartford, and the Colony of Connecticut, being under great indisposition of body, but through God's goodness of sound and disposing mind and memory, and calling to mind ye uncertainty of life, do make and ordain this my last will and testament. First and principally resigning my soule to God, the father of Eternity and my body to the earth to be decently buried, and as for those worldly goods and effects with which it has pleased God to bless me I will dispose of as followeth:

Item: I give and bequeath unto my loving wife, Elizabeth, all those movables which she bore with her at her marriage, as also provision for her maintenance as hereinafter named and provided. Item: I give unto my son, Jonathan Allis what he has already received of his brother David on account of his portion. Item: I give unto my son, Nathaniel Allis the sum of 50 pounds money old tenor, to be paid to him as is hereafter provided. Item: I give unto my son John Allis the sum of 100 pounds old tenor, to be paid to him as is hereafter provided. Item: I give unto my son Ebenezer Allis the sum of 300 pounds old tenor, to be paid him as is hereafter provided. Item: I give to my son Timothy Allis the sum of 300 pounds old tenor, to be paid him as is hereafter provided. Item: I give to my daughter Mercy Johns the sum of 50 pounds old tenor, to be paid her as is hereafter provided, besides what I have already given her. Item: I give unto my daughter Jemina Root the sum of 100 pounds old tenor, to be paid her as is hereafter provided. Item: I give unto my daughter Mindwell Rood the sum of 50 pounds old tenor as is hereafter provided. Item: I give unto my daughter Marcy Coleman the sum of 50 pounds old tenor, to be paid her as is hereafter provided.

I give to my son David Allis all my lands in Bolton with the buildings and the appurtenances thereof, to him and his heirs and assigns forever, provided that he pay and discharge all the legacies above named to the rest of my children, which legacies I do hereby order to be paid within six years after my decease, and provided also that he, the said David Allis, maintain and subsist me and my wife Elizabeth with a comfortable maintenance during the time of each of our natural lives.

My will further is that an inventory of my movable estate be taken, and that after my just debts be paid and answered that then the remainder thereof I give to my son David to enable him to pay the above legacies. My will further is that if the state of our money be altered before the said legacies be payable that then the said David shall discharge said legacies in such money as shall then be equal to the value of old tenor at this time.

Finally I hereby nominate and appoint my son David Allis to be my sole executor of this, my last will and testament, whereof I do hereunto set my hand and seal this last day of January, A. D., 1750-51.

Signed, sealed, published and declared to be his last will in presence of

NATHANIEL ALLIS

John Bissell — Benjamin Talcott

Benjamin Carpenter — Daniel Bridges

24. WILLIAM ALLIS was born in Hatfield, Oct. 19, 1680, and married Elizabeth Davis of Northampton in 1703-4. He was one of the first forty settlers of Sunderland, Mass., where he was assigned Homestead 4, East Side, and was among the first to remove to Hunting Hills (now Montague), being one of the pioneers in the Chestnut Hill District in 1738. He died in Montague, Feb. 20, 1763, and Elizabeth, his wife, died May 1, 1758. Their children, except the youngest, were born in Hatfield:

65. Mary, b. Feb. 18, 1705; married Joseph Mitchell on Nov. 2, 1726, and died Nov. 8, 1773. They had one child, Joseph, born March 3, 1727.

66. Lois, b. Jan. 13, 1708; married Gershom Tuttle on October 17, 1737.

67. Eliphalet, b. Dec. 9, 1710; *

68. Zebediah, b. Oct. 28, 1713; *

69. Elizabeth, b. May 20, 1716; married on March 29, 1744, Daniel Baker of Northampton and had four children:
Mercy, b. Dec. 30, 1744. Elizabeth, b. Dec. 2, 1749.
Daniel, b. Aug. 1, 1747. Samuel, b. May 23, 1752.

26. THOMAS ALLIS was born March 12, 1684, in Hatfield, and married about 1716 Mehitable, daughter of John and Mary (French) Evarts of Guilford, Conn., and widow of Daniel Blachley, and was born Feb. 25, 1678. He settled in Guilford about the time of his marriage and lived there until 1732, when he moved to Haddam, Conn.

It has been impossible to secure an accurate record of the children of Thomas Allis for the reason that a part of the Guilford records were destroyed by fire and the Haddam church records (where the name is given as Ellis), contain very meagre information in regard to his family. He probably had other children than those whose names are given below, but as near as it is possible to trace them the children were:

70. Sarah, b. November 14, 1717; married Stephen Johnson on September 4, 1756.

71. Samuel, b. in August, 1719; married Mary Lee of East Guilford, Conn.

72. Rebecca, b. about 1721; married David Hoyt of Guilford in 1742 and had five children:

David,	b. Mar. 9, 1743.	Rebecca,	b. about 1749.
Timothy,	b. Jan. 17, 1744-5.	Timothy,	b. Feb. 7, 1753.
Rebecca,	b. May 2, 1747.		

73. Mehitable, b. about 1723; married Samuel Brooks of New Haven on June 23, 1748.

74. Patience, b. about 1725.

FOURTH GENERATION.

36. SAMUEL ALLIS was born in Hatfield, Mass., December 12, 1705, and died in Somers, Conn., December 16, 1796, age 91 years. On November 4, 1729, he married Hannah, daughter of John and Hannah (Chapin) Sheldon of Deerfield, who was born October 1, 1707, and died July 22, 1779.

Samuel Allis was a student at Harvard University and graduated in the class of 1724 with honors. In 1725 he secured a position as schoolmaster at Northampton, Mass., which he probably held until he was ordained as the first minister of East Enfield (Somers) in 1727. He retired from the ministry in that town after many years of service, and spent the remainder of his life on the farm which had been granted to him by the town. The nine children were born in Somers:

75. Julius, b. Sept. 18, 1732; *
76. John, b. Nov. 12, 1734; *
77. Jabez, b. Nov. 12, 1734; died in infancy.
78. Samuel, b. 1735; *
79. Lucius, b. May 14, 1737; *
80. Chloe, b. Nov. 4, 1739; no further record.
81. Abel, b. Jan. 9, 1742; died Oct. 3, 1744.
82. Abel, b. Oct. 22, 1745; *
83. Lemuel, b. June 22, 1749; *

40. ELISHA ALLIS was born in Hatfield, December 3, 1716, and died there in the year 1784. He lived in Whately, Mass., and Somers, Conn., but returned to Hatfield, where he was a wealthy farmer. He married (1st) December 20, 1744, Anna, daughter of Sergt. John and Sarah (Williams) Marsh of Hadley; married (2nd) Sarah, daughter of Samuel Reade of Burlington and widow of Thomas Cutler, who died March 25, 1807. They both had large possessions and their marriage agreement, which is unique, is inserted:

"To all people to whom these presents shall come, know ye:

Whereas a marriage is intended by God's permission shortly to be had and solemnized between Elisha Allis of Hatfield, in the County of Hampshire, in New England, and Sarah Cutler of Warren, in the County of Worcester, widow. Now in case such marriage shall take effect, and for a competent jointure, the said Elisha and Sarah have covenanted and agreed as follows, viz.-

The said Elisha covenants and agrees to and with the said Sarah that in case the said Sarah shall survive him and become his widow, that as and for her dower in his estate he now has or inheritance he shall or may hereafter have she, the said Sarah, shall have the use, possession and improvement of one-third part of his real estate, whether housing or lands, for and during the full term of her natural life; and the said Elisha further covenants and agrees to relinquish, and does hereby relinquish, all claims in the personal estate of the said Sarah that she is now possessed of, except what is by this agreement or covenant specially agreed by the said Sarah he shall have, use and enjoy.

And the said Sarah Cutler covenants and agrees to and with the said Elisha Allis, that in case she shall survive him that she will accept the use and improvement of one-third part of his real estate, in manner and during the term aforesaid, in full satisfaction of her dower that she might claim by virtue of her said marriage (in case it take effect) to and in any other estate the said Elisha now has or may die siezed of; and the said Sarah further agrees to and with the said Elisha that he shall have, possess and enjoy, for and during the term of their intermarriage, her dower or thirds to or in the real estate of her late husband, Mr. Thomas Cutler, deceased, and the slaves, rent and profits arising from and out of the same by any ways or means whatsoever, to his sole and absolute use and benefit. And the said Sarah further agrees with the said Elisha that he shall have the use and improvement of her silver plate and other household goods that she now has, and shall furnish his, the said Elisha's, house withall, and also three of her cows during the time of her intermarriage, and at the end of such term he or his heirs shall have or enjoy one-third of such silver plate and other household goods and one of the said cows as his or their own estate forever, and also that he shall have the service and benefit of her negro slave named Ann during the term of ten years in case their intermarriage shall continue so long.

And the said Elisha further covenants to and with the said Sarah for himself, heirs, executors and administrators, that if she survives him she shall have two-thirds of the plate and household goods that he shall actually receive with and from her upon their marriage, or the circumstances they may then be in, without his being accountable for the wear thereof or being made worse by usage, and also two of the cows or other two of equal value, the several articles to be delivered and returned to her at his decease, she being then living; and in case of the said Sarah's decease before the said Elisha's, then two-thirds of the plate and household goods, also two of the cows or other two of equal value, shall be at her decease delivered and returned to her heirs in the circumstance and state in which they were agreed to be returned to the said Sarah had she been living. And the said Elisha further agrees that if the said Sarah survives him, or his heirs, upon the intermarriage ceasing, shall have the whole of the silver plate if 'she or they desire it, she or they allowing for one-third of the value thereof to him or his heirs, to be paid in the other household goods agreed to be returned as aforesaid. And the said Elisha further covenants with the said Sarah that he will provide suitable meat, drink and washing and lodging and apparel for two of her children, namely Bethia Cutler and Oliver Cutler, until they shall arrive respectively to the age of twenty-one years, without charging them therefor or appropriating to himself any portion there. Nevertheless, it is hereby intended and to be understood that in case of said Elisha's decease before they arrive respectively to the aforesaid age, that then they nor either of them are to receive any further support out of his estate or charges toward their maintenance; nor is the said Elisha to provide for them longer than they shall dwell with him and he have the benefit of their labor and other earnings, nor is he to be at loss or charge for them in case of sickness or any extraordinary casualties or accidents befalling them.

In Witness Whereof, We, the said Elisha and Sarah, have hereunto interchangeably set our hands and seals this fourteenth day of January, Anno Domini, 1765.

Sealed and delivered
in the presence of

Timothy Dwight, Pres. Yale College. ELISHA ALLIS

James Stone SARAH CUTLER

Elisha Allis had seven children, all by his wife Anna:

84. Elisha, b. about 1747; *
85. Anna, b. about 1749; married on July 5, 1774, Dr. Josiah Pomeroy.
86. Electa, b. about 1751; died unmarried at age 20.
87. Josiah, b. about 1754; *
88. John, b. Jan. 18, 1756; *
89. William, b. about 1758; *
90. Abel, b. about 1760; *

42. ELEAZER ALLIS was born at Hatfield, December 15, 1725, and died September 7, 1779. He married Lucy, daughter of Deacon Obadiah Dickinson of Hatfield, who was born November 20, 1731, and died March 27, 1794. They lived in Hatfield, where he kept a hotel for many years, and had six children:

91. Lucy, b. about 1753; married Joseph Nash of Whately on March 15, 1770, and had seven children: Mary, b. Aug. 4, 1779; Alpheus, b. May 25, 1781; Joseph, Jr., b. March 6, 1783; and Cotton, Lucy, Electa and David.

92. Sarah, b. Nov. 20, 1757; married Levi Morton of Whately March 11, 1777, and had eleven children:

Sarah,	b. Mar. 30, 1778.	Horace,	b. June 20, 1790.
Lucinda,	b. Nov. 11, 1779.	Justus,	b. Oct. 17, 1792.
Lucy,	b. Dec. 3, 1781.	Moses,	b. July 23, 1794.
Chester,	b. Oct. 14, 1784.	Levi, Jr.	b. Oct. 23, 1796.
David,	b. June 20, 1786.	Lucy,	b. Sep. 28, 1798.
Lucretia,	b. Mar. 13, 1788.		

93. Daniel, b. about 1763; *

94. Eleazer, b. about 1765; *

95. Jemima, b. about 1767; married on Jan. 20, 1780, Salmon Waite of Williamsburg.

96. Clarissa, b. about 1769; married on May 10, 1787, Oliver Hastings of Hatfield.

52. JOHN ALLIS was born in Wethersfield, Conn., September 11, 1726, and died May 18, 1756. In 1754 he married Zerviah, daughter of Hezekiah and Martha (Beckley) Hart of Kensington, Conn., who was born December 16, 1728. After the death of John Allis she married on October 19, 1761, David Webster of Glastonbury, Conn., and died January 17, 1786.

John Allis was a farmer and lived in Kensington, Conn. The distribution of his estate gave to Zerviah, his widow, eight acres of the home lot, a portion of the dwelling house and a portion of the movable estate, and to Abel Allis, his only child, the remainder of the home lot (sixteen acres), the remainder of the dwelling house, and various specified articles of his movable estate.

97. Abel, b. about 1755. *

58. NATHANIEL ALLIS was born November 4, 1716, in Bolton, Conn., and died in East Guilford (Madison), Conn., March 4, 1804. On November 20, 1739, he married Hannah, daughter of Captain John and Mary (Evarts) Scranton of East Guilford. She died on January 10, 1783.

Nathaniel Allis was a farmer in East Guilford, and was a Drummer in the Revolutionary War, enlisting March 22, '76, in Capt. Daniel Hand's Company, Col. Talcott's Regiment. His only child was:

98. Nathaniel, b. Feb. 23, 1742; *

59. JOHN ALLIS was born November 10, 1718, in Bolton, Conn., and died in Deerfield, Mass., in June, 1768. On February 3, 1742, he married Mary Munger of East Guilford, who was born May 13, 1723.

John Allis moved from Bolton to Hatfield at an early date, later to East Guilford, Conn., Oblong, N. Y., and Salisbury, Conn., in 1764 to Hatfield and in 1765 to Deerfield. He had nine children:

99. Abel, b. Feb. 20, 1743; no further record.

100. Eber, b. Aug. 29, 1745; *

101. Aaron, b. in 1748; married Huldah, daughter of Lemuel and Margaret Snow of Whately, Mass., on April 4, 1791. He was a farmer and a soldier in the Revolutionary War.

102. Timothy, b. Jan. 12, 1750; died Feb. 7, 1751.

103. Timothy. b. Dec. 5, 1752; *

104. John, b. Dec. 15, 1753; *

105. Daniel, b. about 1754; died in infancy.

106. Russell, b. April 28, 1756; *

107. Lydia, b. about 1758; married Bezaliel Smith and died on December 16, 1785, without issue.

60. DAVID ALLIS was born in Bolton, Conn., on July 19, 1720, and died in Vernon, Conn., April 26, 1789. He was twice married: first, to Sarah Pendal of Bolton on November 4, 1740, who died July 5, 1780, and, second, to Keziah Dewey of Lebanon, Conn., on May 31, 1783, who died June 10, 1817.

David Allis lived on his father's farm in Bolton many years, but eventually moved to Vernon, where he spent the remainder of his life. By his first marriage he had eight children:

108. Naomi, b. Dec. 2, 1742; died August 26, 1743.

109. Mercy, b. December 6, 1744; married Reuben Searls of Bolton on September 18, 1764, and had three children: David Allis, b. June 19, 1765. Reuben, b. April 14, 1769. Sarah, b. Feb. 8, 1767.

110. Hannah, b. Sept. 10, 1746; no further record.

111. Mary, b. May 17, 1748; married (1st) John Hodge of Vernon, Conn., Feb. 1, 1769, and (2nd) Nathaniel Walker of Stafford, Conn., January 30, 1772.

112. Elizabeth, b. Sept. 28, 1751; married on April 14, 1772, Elijah Hodge of Glastonbury, Conn., and died March 7, 1821. Their nine children were:

Elijah,	b. in 1773.		Esther,	b.	——
Benajah,	b. August,	1775.	Noel,	b. Mar. 21,	1792.
Elizur,	b. Oct. 15,	1778.	Sarah,	b. about	1794.
Elizabeth,	b. about	1780.	Lydia,	b. about	1796.
Burrill,	b. about	1781.			

113. Jemima, b. July 28, 1753; married John Stiles of Vernon August 3, 1784, and had several children, among whom were David Allis Stiles, b. April 19, 1792, and Timothy Stiles, b. April 15, 1795.

114. Sarah, b. May 9, 1755; married Eben Walker of Vernon on June 11, 1778.

115. Contente, b. April 13, 1757; no further record.

63. EBENEZER ALLIS was born May 24, 1726, in Bolton, Conn. On November 29, 1750, he married Experience Warner of Stafford Springs, Conn., and a few years later moved to that town. After living there a short time he and his family went to Conway, Mass. He was one of the first settlers of Conway, and was elected to town offices at the first town meeting, August 24, 1767. From Conway, Ebenezer Allis and his family moved to Shelburne Falls, Mass., where he was prominent in church and town affairs, and where he died. His children were:

116. Naomi, b. July 20, 1751; no further record.

117. Ebenezer, b. March 21, 1753; *

118. Stephen, b. March 4, 1758; *

67. ELIPHALET ALLIS was born December 9, 1710, in Hatfield, Mass. When he was about five years old his parents moved to Sunderland, Mass., and in 1738

the family settled in Hunting Hills (now Montague), Mass., where Eliphalet Allis married Mary Brooks on March 26, 1747. He was prominent in town affairs in Hunting Hills and in 1775 was elected assessor. His children were:

119. Samuel, b. Jan. 2, 1748; died Jan. 10, 1748.

120. Samuel, b. Jan. 5, 1747; died Jan. 12, 1759.

121. Mary, b. Oct. 26, 1750; died Jan. 7, 1759.

122. David, b. Sep. 4, 1753; died Jan. 15, 1759.

123. Jonathan, b. Sep. 4, 1753; died Jan. 10, 1759.

124. Freedom, b. Aug. 3, 1755; no further record.

125. Marah, b. Aug. 24, 1757; no further record.

68. ZEBEDIAH ALLIS was born October 28, 1713, in Hatefild, Mass. When he was about three years old his parents moved to Sunderland, Mass., and in 1738 the family settled in Hunting Hills (now Montague), Mass. On Dec. 31, 1740, he married Mary, daughter of Samuel and Sarah (Lankton) Baker of Northampton, Mass., and they had eight children.

Zebediah Allis was a farmer in Hunting Hills, and at times taught school. He also served in the French and Indian War, 1746-1748.

126. Ruth, b. Nov. 3, 1742; died July 6, 1744.

127. Ruth, b. Dec. 4, 1744; no further record.

128. Mary, b. July 12, 1747; d. Feb. 12, 1756.

129. Mehitable, b. Sept. 16, 1749; no further record.

130. William, b. Feb. 6, 1752; *

131. Zebediah, b. July 2, 1754; *

132 Moses, b. Feb. 13, 1756; *

133. Mary, b. Aug. 25, 1759; no further record.

FIFTH GENERATION.

75. JULIUS ALLIS was born in Somers, Conn., September 18, 1732. On November 14, 1755, he married Hannah, daughter of Obadiah Dickinson of Hatfield, Mass., and settled in Deerfield, but his farm was afterwards set off to Conway on account of the distance from the town of Deerfield. Later he moved to Sullivan, N. Y., where he died August 16, 1817, his wife having died September 3, 1814.

Julius Allis was in the Revolutionary War, enlisting September 23, 1777, and served in the Northern Department. His nine children were :

134. Mary, b. Oct. 4, 1756; m. Abijah Brown on July 30, 1782, being his second wife, and had Alice, Polly, Betsey and Elisha.

135. Timothy, b. July 12, 1759; died Oct. 6, 1776. A Revolutionary soldier.

136. Lydia, b. Dec. 25, 1761; m. James Wing of Conway on September 20, 1781, and died October 7, 1840.

137. Hannah, b. Nov. 9, 1765; m. Jonathan Smith of Whately, November 6, 1784, and had six children:

Abigail,	b. May 15, 1795.	Hannah,	b. Feb. 18, 1803.
Eliakim,	b. Oct. 19, 1797.	Columbus,	b. Oct. 10, 1805.
Orson,	b. Aug. 20, 1800.	Alvil,	b. Sep. 7, 1807,

138. Sylvia, b. Nov. 3, 1767; m. Joseph Frost.

139. Joel, b. Feb. 12, 1769; *

140. Submit, b. Sep. 22, 1772; m. Eliphas Hickok.

141. Rachel, b. Oct. 11 1775; died April 23, 1813.

142. Martha, b. Apr. 30, 1777; died April 19, 1803.

76. JOHN ALLIS was born in Somers, Conn., on November 12, 1734, and died November 14, 1774. He married (first) on May 11, 1762, Sarah, daughter of Deacon Nathaniel and Sarah (Chapin) Burt, who was born on Nov. 15, 1739, and died at Longmeadow, Mass., July 9, 1768. He married (second) Esther, daughter of Seth and Joanna (Kellogg) Dwight of Somers, Conn., on December 27, 1770. She was born September 30, 1744, and married (second) on January 3, 1787, Deacon Aaron Horton of Somers.

John Allis was a farmer in Somers and a soldier in the French and Indian War. Children by first wife:

143. Sarah, b. June 1, 1765; died March 9, 1768.
144. Electa, b. Feb. 10, 1767; no further record.

78. SAMUEL ALLIS was born in Somers, Conn., in 1735. He married (first) Zerviah Stoughton, on February 8, 1758, who died December 3, 1758; he married (second) Lucy Morton, on May 11, 1762, who died on March 21, 1765; he married (third) Olive Meacham (or Makepeace, according to some authorities) on January 22, 1767. He lived in Somers and had the following children:

By first wife:

145. Girl, b. Nov. 26, 1758; died Nov. 26, 1758.
146. Girl, b. " "

By second wife:

147. Lucy, b. Oct. 19, 1764; married Dr. Daniel White of Whitestown, N. Y., and Hatfield, Mass., on March 8, 1796, and died Jan. 7, 1814. No children.

By third wife:

148. Oliver, b. April 18, 1768; no further record.

149. Zerviah, b. Jan. 29, 1769; no further record.

150. Lovice, b. Oct. 20, 1771; no further record.

151. Cynthia, b April 27, 1773; married on January 21, 1798, Samuel White of Thetford, Vermont, and died Aug. 27, 1849. Their four children were:

Backus, b. Dec. 17, 1798. Cynthia, b. July 25, 1803.
Marinda, b. Jan. 9, 1801. Austin, b. July 19, 1805.

152. Olive, b. Aug. 10, 1776; married David Chapin of Somers. No children.

153. Chloe, b. Aug. 20, 1778; died Aug. 23, 1832.

79. LUCIUS ALLIS was born May 9, 1737, in Somers, Conn., and lived there as a boy and young man. At the age of about 21 he left his home town for Whately, Mass., and while there was married on December 10, 1761, to Jemima, daughter of Ensign Abel and Jemima (Chapin) Bliss of Springfield, Mass. She was born October 12, 1740, and died June 9, 1764. Soon afterwards Lucius moved to Conway, Mass., being one of the first settlers of that town, and married (second) on August 14, 1766, Mary, daughter of Thomas Wells of Deerfield, Mass., who died on July 2, 1776. On June 16, 1777, he married (third) Mehitable, daughter of Nathaniel and Hannah (Smith) Graves of Athol, Mass. She was born October 21, 1732, and died July 31, 1800. He married (fourth) on Aug. 30, 1804, Lois, daughter of Eleazer, and Sarah (Belding) Graves of Athol, who was born February 2, 1755.

Lucius Allis became a wealthy farmer in Conway, was very prominent in town affairs, and after the death of Col. Pyncheon was the most important man in the western province of Massachusetts. He owned the only pair of high top boots in the district. He also owned a close carriage (only two were known in that section for many years) and a span of driving horses, and these, together with his boots and his hat, were always loaned for weddings and funerals. Over and above his boots and his carriage he had some public spirit. He is said to have bought and given to the town the common by the old church. At first he and his wife rode seven miles on Sundays to the Deerfield meeting horseback, with a child in the arms of each, as there was at that time no church in Conway.

Lucius Allis was for a time a soldier in the Continental Army. On September 23, 1777, he enlisted in Thomas French's company, Col. David Wells's regiment, and served in the Northern Department, taking part in the capture of General Burgoyne. He lived in Conway nearly 60 years, and died March 12, 1822, at the age of 85 years. He left to his son Samuel one farm in Conway, and some of his descendants are now living on the farm in Conway that he willed to his son Solomon. His ten children were:

By first wife:

154. Zelinda, b. Jan. 7, 1763; married Isaiah Wing on August 21, 1786, and died October 15, 1835.

155. Child, b. June 3, 1764; died same day.

By second wife:

156. Samuel, b. June 20, 1767; *

157. Lucius, b. June 19, 1768; married Jane Cottel and resided in Charlemont, Mass. He adopted Zerviah, daughter of Noah and Esther (Cottle) Look, who was born Nov. 19, 1795, and married Josiah Lyman on May 26, 1819.

158. Solomon, b. Oct. 26, 1769; *

159. Sarah, b. Apr. 15, 1771; married (first) Barnabas F. Howell, and (second) Graves Crafts on March 1, 1827, and died April 3, 1852.

160. Thos. Wells, b. Oct. 16, 1772; *

161. Elijah, b. Dec. 5, 1773; *

162 Child, b. Oct. 7, 1775; died same year.

By third wife:

163. John, b. August 3, 1778; died August 14, 1778.

82. ABEL ALLIS was born in Somers, Conn., on October 23, 1745. He married (first) on September 5, 1769, Hannah, daughter of James and Eunice Porter of Hatfield, Mass., and (second) Lydia ———, who died April 15, 1806.

Abel Allis lived in Hatfield, in 1768 in Deerfield, and afterwards in Ashfield and Conway, Mass., where he died February 3, 1804. His nine children were:

By first wife:

164. Gratia, b. 1770; married John Sherman.

By second wife:

165. Phebe; died young.

166. John B., b. July 8, 1772; *

167. Elijah, b. May 20, 1774; *

168. Silas, b. Apr. 7, 1776; *

169. Pliny, b. 1777; shot himself by accident.

170. Eunice, b. Apr. 3, 1778; married on November 29, 1798, Elisha DeWolf, and d. November 28, 1864. Lived in Ashfield. Mass., and had nine children:

Hannah, b. Nov. 2, 1799.		Minerva, b. Aug. 7, 1813.
Charles, b. Oct. 6, 1801.		Elisha, b. Mar. 12, 1816.
Seth, b. Jan. 9, 1804.		Sophia, b. July 27, 1818.
William, b. Mar. 22, 1807.		George, b. June 10, 1821.
Eunice, b. May 29, 1811.		

171. Henry; *

172. Lucinda, b. Mar. 27, 1780; married Reuben Waite.

83. LEMUEL ALLIS was born in Somers, Conn., June 22, 1749, and married about 1778 Rebecca Davis of that town. He moved to Massachusetts about the time of his marriage and lived in Plainville and Chester. He is said to have been a chaplain in the Revolutionary War, and it is reasonable to suppose that, like his father Samuel, he was a minister by vocation. His six children were:

173. John, b. May 19, 1779; *

174. Hannah; b. about 1781; married Mr. Robison.

175. Justin, b. about 1783; was a wealthy farmer. He married three times and died without issue; probably married (3) on October 20, 1848, Harriet. daughter of Captain Oliver and Lucy (Parker) Shattuck of Whately who was born May 13, 1786, and was the widow of Luther Longley and Alexander Ward.

176. Lemuel, b. July 9, 1784; *

177. Roxanna, b. Sep. 15, 1786; married Truman Leonard of Preston, Conn., on June 1, 1811, and died Sep. 12, 1846. Their children were:

Emeline,	b. Mar. 16, 1812.	Roxanna A.,	b. July 2, 1823
Ebenezer,	b. Sep. 7, 1813.	Franklin,	b. June 5, 1825
Ezra,	b. Feb. 28, 1815.	Harriet A.,	b. Feb. 7, 1827
Dorcas	b. Apr. 5, 1817.	Louisa P.,	b. Apr.27, 1830
Lavinia,	b. Jan. 22, 1819.	Sarah A.,	b. Jan. 6, 1833
Truman,	b. Sept. 7, 1720.		

178. Sally, b. about 1789; married Francis Holton on February 19, 1822, and died June 19, 1849.

84. ELISHA ALLIS was born in Hatfield, Mass., in 1747. He graduated from Yale University in the class of 1769, and a few years after leaving college he settled on a farm in Williamsburg, where he remained for about eight years. While there he married, January 27, 1774, Mary, daughter of Obadiah and Martha Dickinson of Hatfield and widow of Samuel Ingram. In February, 1791, he and his family moved to Brookfield, Vermont, having built a house and barn there during the previous summer.

Elisha Allis served as representative in the Legislature in 1793, 1795-8 and 1813, as judge of the County Court, and was otherwise much employed in public business, holding the entire confidence of the community as an honest, upright, Christian man. He was a deacon of the Congregational Church in Williamsburg, and held the same office in Brookfield for many years. He was a man of temperate habits and retained all his mental faculties until his death in Brookfield on April 3, 1835, nearly 88 years of age. His eight children were:

179. Electa, b. April 1, 1775; died August 16, 1775.

180. Electa, b. June 29, 1777; died Sept. 9, 1779.

181. Elisha, b. April 8, 1779; *

182. Polly, b. Nov. 10, 1781; married Elisha Pride.

183. Martha, b. Jan. 15, 1784; died July 10, 1809.

184. Harriet, b. June 1, 1786; no further record.

185. Obadiah, b. Jan. 26, 1789; died unmarried Sept. 6, 1813.

186. William, b. Feb. 6, 1793; *

87. JOSIAH ALLIS was born in Hatfield, Mass., in 1754, and died in Whately, Mass., on April 17, 1794. On March 1, 1774, he married Anna, daughter of Elisha and Lucy (Stearns) Hubbard of Hatfield, who was born December 26, 1755. She married (second) on November 27, 1799, Salmon White, Jr., of Whately, and died June 21, 1839.

Josiah Allis moved from Hatfield to Whately about the time of his marriage and became a wealthy farmer. He was very prominent in church and town affairs, at different times holding nearly all of the town offices, and was a representative to the General Court in 1787-8 and a delegate to the convention to revise the Federal Constitution in 1788. Also he was a colonel in the militia. His children were:

187. Elijah, b. Oct. 21, 1775; *

188. Electa, b. Feb. 16, 1777; married Elial Allen of Deerfield on December 16, 1802.

189. Josiah, b. Jan. 5. 1779; *

190. Anna, b. Dec. 3, 1780; married on March 1, 1811, Chester Sanderson of Ashfield, Mass , and had six children:

Sarah A.,	b. Nov. 11, 1811.	Elon,	b. June 29, 1818.
Elon,	b. Dec., 1814.	Thos. W.,	b. Sep. 22, 1819.
Almira,	b. Feb. 22, 1816.	Electa A.,	b. Jan. 30, 1822.

191. Lucy, b. Dec. 12, 1782; married Major Thos. Sanderson of Whately on Jan. 16, 1804, and died May 16, 1870.

192. Henry, b. July 29, 1784; *

193. Jere, b. July 25, 1786; *

194. Sally, b. April 22, 1788; married Eurotas Dickinson of Whately on January 12, 1812, and died July 28, 1886, age 98 years. Their ten children were:

Henry A.,	b. Oct. 27, 1812.	Salmon W.,	b. May 7, 1822.
John P.,	b. Jan. 17, 1815.	Mary A.,	b. Apr. 12, 1825.
Mary Ann,	b. Sep. 14, 1816.	Sarah Ann,	b. June 13, 1827.
Thos. S.,	b. July 24, 1818.	Geo. E.,	b. June 21, 1829.
Elial A.,	b. Feb. 5, 1820.	Mary A.,	b. Aug. 4, 1833.

195. Almira, b. Oct. 3, 1790; married Elam Bridges.

196. Stolham, b. May 1, 1792; *

197. Elisha, b. Jan. 4, 1794; *

88. JOHN ALLIS was born January 18, 1756, in Hatfield, Mass. On Sept. 30, 1779, he married Esther, daughter of Lieut. Samuel and Abigail (Dwight) Partridge of Hatfield, who was born March 26, 1761, and died on December 22, 1834.

John Allis was a wealthy farmer in Hatfield, and died there on March 1, 1829, age 73 years. His six children were:

198. Abigail, b. December 14, 1779; married Colonel Erastus Billings of Hatfield on July 9, 1798, and died October 17, 1829. Their children were:

Fanny, A.,	b. Dec. 3, 1798.	John Allis,	b. Feb. 23, 1806.
Silas,	b. Oct. 29, 1800.	Erastus,	b. May 11, 1809.

199. Fannie, b. Nov. 11, 1781; died Feb. 9, 1787.

200. Sophia, b. November 18, 1783; married Remembrance Bardwell of Hatfield on April 12, 1802, and died June 22, 1847. Their children were:

Eliza,	b. Oct. 22, 1803.	Dwight L.,	born in 1812.
Eliza A.,	b. Oct. 22, 1804.	Sophia A.,	b. Jan. 20, 1820.

201. John, b. Sept. 4, 1786; was killed Oct. 3, 1807, by falling from grist mill.

202. Josiah, b. May 2, 1794; *

203. Dwight Lathrop, b. Oct. 13, 1805; died July 6, 1809.

89. WILLIAM ALLIS was born in 1758 in Hatfield, Mass., and died in 1813 in Lowville, N. Y. On October 20, 1784, he married Sophia Smith, who was born in 1765 and died September 24, 1807. William lived in Hatfield, Mass., and Lowville, N. Y. He was a soldier in the War of 1812 and fought in the battle of Sackett's Harbor, receiving land script in payment. The city of Rochester, N. Y., stands on land that was once owned by him. His children were:

204. William, b. Dec. 13, 1785; *

205. Sarah, b March 13, 1787; married Quartus Hawkes of Hatfield on Aug. 4, 1808, and died Nov. 14, 1873.

206. Epaphroditus, b. May 8, 1789; *

207. Electa, b. July 15, 1792; married Jonathan Porter, Jr., of Hatfield on Dec 17, 1818, and died Oct. 1, 1855. Their five children were:

Moses C , b. Dec. 30, 1819.	Jonathan D., b. July 3, 1826.
Henry S., b. Dec. 24, 1821.	James, b. Nov. 30, 1828.
Sophia A., b. Apr. 18, 1824.	

208. Sophia, b. July 9, 1794; married Osee Smith of Whately on Nov. 25, 1812, and died April 25, 1861. Their seven children were:

Wm. Allis, b. Jan. 16, 1814.	Lavinia M. b. Sep. 20, 1824.
Harriet A., b. Nov. 7, 1816.	Erasta K., b. Dec. 10, 1827.
Laura A., b. Feb. 18, 1819.	Electa H., b. Mar. 15, 1830.
Wm. C. b. June 4, 1821.	

209. Dexter, b. Feb. 7, 1797; *

210. Mary, b. Oct. 15, 1799; married Elisha Wells on Nov. 8, 1820, and died Nov. 30, 1832.

211. Thos. Cutler, b. March 20, 1802; *

90. ABEL ALLIS was born in Hatfield, Mass., in 1760. He married (first) Miss Baker, and (second) on August 10, 1796, Lucretia, daughter of Richard and Anna (Hull) Mansfield, of Derby, Conn., who was born January 12, 1772, and died February 10, 1849.

Abel Allis was a farmer in Whately and Conway, Mass., and had six children by his second wife:

212. Mansfield, b. August 9, 1797; died August 18, 1797.

213. Richard Mansfield, b. September 10, 1799; died October 6, 1799.

214. Mansfield, b. November 9, 1800; died November 26, 1800.

215. William Mansfield, b. January 31, 1803; moved to Mississippi, married and died, leaving no children

216. Stephen Giles Mardenbrough, b. June 5, 1805; *

217. Caroline, b. September 15, 1809; married the Rev. Oliver Hopson, an Episcopal minister, September 9, 1833, and had eight children: Richard M., b December 22, 1834, William Allis, b. April 20, 1836, George B., b. January 18, 1838, Caroline S., b. January 26, 1840, Edward C , b. June 18, 1842, Elizabeth C., b. April 21, 1845, Mansfield C., b. March 23, 1848, and Mary C., b. March 3, 1850.

93. DANIEL ALLIS was born in 1763 in Hatfield, Mass., and died October 26, 1828. On March 2, 1782, he married Lydia, daughter of Peter Train of Whately, who was born in 1763 and died February 17, 1849. He lived in Whately, Mass., and had twelve children:

218. Moses, b. September 20, 1782; married and moved away from Whately.

219. Daniel, b. September 26, 1784; married on November 30, 1810, Fanny, daughter of Heman Swift of Whately, and died January 11, 1818, at West Whately.

220. Eleazer, b. July 17, 1786; died young.

221. Harris, b. February 13, 1788; no further record.

222. Osee, b. June 26, 1790; *

223. Eurotas, b. May 27, 1793; no further record.

224. Otus, b. May 27, 1793; no further record.

225. Austin, b. June 12, 1794; *

226. Martha, b. September 30, 1795; married Capt. Enos Waite of Whately and moved to Ohio.

227. Lydia, b. October 11, 1797; married on January 22, 1818, Justus Morton of Whately.

228. Sophia, b May 24, 1800; married in 1817 Henry Waite of Whately and had the following children, two of whom were born in Ohio: Fidelia, b. February 3, 1818, Sophia, b. December 12, 1820, Henry, b. September 16, 1822, Lucius, b. December 12, 1825, Dwight. b. June 18, 1828, Nancy, b. February 2, 1838, and Angelina, b. July 21, 1844.

229. Eleazer, b. September 23, 1803; *

94. ELEAZER ALLIS was born in Hatfield, Mass., about 1765. He married (first) on December 16, 1784, Mary, daughter of Samuel and Mary (Boltwood) Ingram of Amherst, Mass., and their seven children were:

230. Eleazer, b. December 20, 1785; died December 21, 1785.

231. Lucinda, b. February 7, 1787; married Joshua Horton of Sheshequin, Pa., in 1814, and died Apr. 20, 1864 Their children were Ithiel, Lucinda, Esther, Ulysses, Fanny, Eleazer, Lewis, Luman P and Nelson.

232. Lucretia, b. February 2, 1788; married William Warfield of Orwell, Pa., and had five children: Ellen, Liflette, Shepherd, Elmira and Laura

233. Eleazer, b. September 2, 1789; *

234. Ithiel, b. about 1791; *

235. Mary, b. about 1792; died about 1809.

236. Silas, b March 14, 1794 *

Eleazer Allis lived in Hatfield for a few years after his marriage and then moved with his wife and family to Vermont and settled on the Lamoille River. About 1795 his wife, Mary, died and he married (second) Miriam Pudmont (or Parmont) of Georgia, Vt., who bore him two children. Both children died in infancy and Miriam did not long survive them.

In 1800 or 1801 Eleazer Allis, with his children, left Vermont for Bradford County, Pa., and soon after arriving there he married Esther Rutty of Sugar Creek. They travelled up Wysox Creek and eventually settled in what is known as Allis Hollow. That section of the country was then wild and untravelled and Eleazer, with the help of the older children, made the first clearing there and built the first log house. By occupation he was a farmer, hunter and trapper, and lived in Allis Hollow until his death on November 28, 1837, and was buried in the Allis Hollow Cemetery. Esther, his wife, died on September 23, 1831. Their ten children were:

237. Aurilla, b August 7, 1802; married Rufus Foster in 1818 and died March 2, 1868. Their children were James, Charles, William Eufrasia, Julia, Phoebe, Sarah, Delphene and Mary.

238. Laura, b. April 29, 1804; married Abel Darling, January 12, 1826, and died on May 6, 1882. Their nine children were Ordelia, Lucretia, Theressa, Caroline, Eliza, Adelaide, Ann, Hollace and LeRoy.

239 Electa, b. August 6, 1806; married Harry C. Parks on March 5, 1826, and died October 21, 1887. Their children were Warren, Hollace, Charles, Minerva, Sarah, Chloe, Martha, Mary, Eliza and Lettie.

240. Orinda, b. July 11, 1809; married on February 24, 1840, James Cleveland and died on February 15, 1846. Their children were: Annis Orinda, b. January 1, 1842, Robert Oscar, b. Dec. 25, 1825, and Sarah Ellen, b. Aug. 22, 1843.

241. Ezra Rutty, b. October 16, 1810; *

242. Ellen, b. June 25, 1811; married Silas Mills and died on September 17, 1790. Their three children were Sophia, Violetta and Vespacion.

243. Eliza, b. about 1814; married Lewis Thayer and had two children, Oscar and Cordon.

244 Corrissa, b. December 1, 1818; married Henry D. Rockwell, February 23, 1848, and died April 26, 1891. Their children were Melvin, Lemuel, Catherine and Edward.

245. William Nelson, b. June 20, 1821; *

246. Esther, b. October 1, 1825; married Nathaniel N. Parks on February 24, 1848, and died April 17, 1888. Their children were: Mahlon W., b. May 10, 1849, Morris J., b. September 1, 1850, and died May 14, 1852, Newel J., b. February 11, 1852, and died February 15, 1853, Oscar N., b. September 12, 1853, Fayland H., b. February 11, 1855, and Ettie E., b. July 15, 1864.

97. ABEL ALLIS was born about 1755 in Kensington, Conn., and died there on July 3, 1816. About 1791 he married Thankful Dickinson, who was born in 1753 and died January 27, 1829. His name appears in some records as Abel Ellis, and his descendants used that surname.

Abel Allis was a farmer in the Great Swamp District, Kensington (Berlin), and probably lived on the farm which he inherited from his father, John Allis. His children were:

247 William, b. February 16, 1792; *

248. John, b. about 1793; *

98. NATHANIEL ALLIS was born February 23, 1742, in East Guilford (Madison), Conn., and died February 16, 1825. He married, October 2, 1766, Hannah, daughter of Reuben Norton of Guilford, Conn., who was born May 1, 1746, and died March 12, 1785. According to some records he was married a second time, on June 6, 1791, to Abigail Bushnell.

Further information in regard to Nathaniel Allis is very meagre. He lived in East Guilford, and his will, which was probated on February 22, 1825, shows that he owned considerable property. His children were:

By first wife:

249. Rachel, b. July 5, 1767; married William Allis (No. 130).

250. Hannah, b. Feb. 4, 1770; no further record.

251. Chloe, b. Feb. 9, 1773; no further record.

252. Sarah, b. March 24, 1778; married Jesse Murray August 9, 1797.

253. Rebecca, b. January 15, 1780; married Thomas Anderson in March, 1810.

254. Pierce, b. Nov. 3, 1783; drowned in Long Island Sound on March 20, 1803.

By second wife:

255. Bushnell, b. about 1792; died when a young man.

100. EBER ALLIS was born August 29, 1745, probably in East Guilford, Conn. He married (1st) Sarah Mann of Sunderland, Mass., who died in 1782, and (2nd) Sarah Cooley, on March 6, 1783.

Eber Allis, for a period of years, lived in Oblong, N. Y., Salisbury, Conn., and Hatfield and Deerfield, Mass., but eventually settled in South Deerfield, Mass., and was no doubt a farmer by occupation. He was a Revolutionary soldier also, enlisting at the first call for volunteers on April 26, 1775, under Capt. Jonas Locke. His eight children were:

By first wife:

256. Electa, b. March 21, 1770; married Reuben Jewett of Templeton and South Deerfield, Mass., in 1790, and died October 15, 1835. Their children were:

Phila,	b. Jan. 25, 1791.	Dan'l Allis,	b. July 14, 1804.
Sally,	b. Nov. 23, 1793.	James M.,	b. Jan. 22, 1806.
Anna,	b. Apr. 6, 1795.	Tryphena,	b. Apr. 28, 1808.
Reuben,	b. Apr. 3, 1797.	Dwight,	b. Dec. 17, 1812.
Electa,	b. Oct. 15, 1799.	Electa M.,	b. Mar. 15, 1815.
Tryphene,	b. Feb 10, 1802.		

257. Daniel, b. Dec. 27, 1772; died Oct. 22, 1773.

258. Sarah, b. February 28, 1775; married Caleb Stockbridge of Hatfield, Mass., on January 21, 1796.

259. Daniel, b. August 4, 1777; died August 31, 1778.

260. Lucy, b. August 9, 1779; died in 1790.

261. John, b. June 15, 1782; died December 22, 1782.

By second wife:

262. John B., b. June 12, 1784; died June 24, 1784.

263. Son, b. August 2, 1787; died the same day.

103. TIMOTHY ALLIS was born December 5, 1752, probably in East Guilford, Conn., and died August 28, 1801, in Huntington, Conn. On March 2, 1775, he married Elizabeth Clark, who died October 15, 1817.

Timothy Allis lived in Oblong, N. Y., Salisbury, Conn., and Hatfield, Mass., until he was about twelve years of age. His parents then moved from Hatfield to Deerfield, Mass., and he lived there until the time of his marriage, when he moved to Connecticut and settled on a farm in Huntington. His six children were:

264. Elisha, b. May 20, 1776; died September 14, 1779.

265. Parmela, b. April 14, 1779; married Enoch Lane and died December 22, 1865.

266. Elisha, b. November 7, 1780; *

267. Betsy, b. March 6, 1783; married Zina Chatfield.

268. Isaac, b. March 8, 1785; *

269. Polly, b. January 1, 1789; married Eben Fairchild of Old Farms, Conn.

104. JOHN ALLIS was born December 15, 1753, probably in East Guilford, Conn. His early years were spent in Oblong, N. Y., Salisbury, Conn., and Hatfield and Deerfield, Mass., but in 1768, after the death of his father, he went back to Hatfield and lived there until he was 21 years of age. He then went to Bolton, Conn., and married Dolly West of that town in 1775. A few years after his marriage he moved to Stafford, Conn., later to Monson, Mass., and in 1779 to Deerfield, where he died in August, 1790. On August 4, 1791, his widow married George Roberts of South Deerfield, and died October 23, 1828, in Great River, N. Y.

John Allis was a Revolutionary soldier. He enlisted in Capt. Turner's company, Lieut. Col. John Brooks' (7th) regiment, on April 3, 1781, and served through the war. He is described in the "Massachusetts Soldiers and Sailors of the Revolutionary War" as six feet one inch in height, complexion, light; hair, dark; occupation, farmer; and is reported to have been on command at Dobb's Ferry. The record of his five children, which is very incomplete, is as follows:

270. Lois, b. June 23, 1776; married (first) Jonathan Ellis in 1779, and (second), about 1812, Mr. Wells, and died in 1840 in Westfield, N. Y.

271. Daniel, b. about 1780; never married; lived in Conway, Mass., Semporius, N. Y., and Deerfield, Mass.

272. John, b. about 1782; no further record.

273. Lydia, b. about 1784; " " "

274. David, b. about 1786; " " "

106. RUSSELL ALLIS was born April 28, 1756, probably in East Guilford, Conn. He lived in Oblong, N. Y., Salisbury, Conn., and Hatfield, Mass., until nearly ten years of age, and from then until about the time of his marriage in Deerfield, Mass. In the year 1775 he married Sarah, daughter of Jonathan and Mehitable (Lilly) Edson of Whately, Mass., who was born in 1757 and died January 9, 1832.

Russell Allis settled in Whately and lived there until his death on March 6, 1835. He was a saddler and harness maker by trade, and a deacon of the Baptist church. He was also a soldier in the Revolutionary War, enlisting August 17, 1777, in Capt. Salmon White's company, Col. Woodbridge's regiment, and serving for a short time in the Northern Department. His six children were:

275. Roxa, b. February 24, 1776; married February 23, 1795, Lemuel Waite of Whately and died on October 21, 1843. Their children were:

Russell, b. July 29, 1796. Fidelia, b. May 10, 1807.
Dency, b. Dec. 21, 1798. Allen, b. Nov. 5, 1809.
Harris, b. Nov. 17, 1800. William, b. Mar 31, 1812.
Lemuel, b. Jan. 12, 1803. Electa, b. Aug. 1, 1814.
Roxana, b. Feb. 9, 1805. Eliza A., b. Dec. 22, 1816.

276. Sarah, b. February 19, 1778; married February 2, 1798, David Stockbridge, Jr., of Whately, and died on July 16, 1839. Their children were:

Annis, b. Dec. 17, 1798. Julia A., b. Aug. 1, 1806.
Chester, b. May 25, 1801. Chas. D. b. Oct. 2, 1816.
Emily W., b. Jan. 10, 1803. Amaret S., b. Dec. 8, 1819.
Hiram F., b. June 8, 1804.

277. Lura, b. February 19, 1780; married (first) Joseph Smith of Whately on July 17, 1800, and (second) Amasa Woodruff, and died November 4, 1857. Their children were:

Dexter, b. in 1801. Lewis, b. Sept., 1808.
Irene, b. Nov. 4, 1802. Elvira, b. about 1810.
Orrin, b. Sept. 24, 1804. Joseph L., b. May 17, 1812.
Porter, b. Sept. 21, 1806.

278. Demis, b. December 31, 1782; married January 13, 1803, Zebina Bartlett of Whately and died on March 19, 1863. Their children were:

Alvin, b. Oct. 1, 1803. Elizabeth S., b Jan. 11, 1817.
Sarah, b. Jan. 7, 1805. Zebina W., b. Mar. 18, 1819.
Tryphena, b. Nov. 10, 1806. Lovisa D., b. July 24, 1824.
Maria, b. Feb. 16, 1810.

279. Annis, b. February 18, 1784; married Thomas Marsh of Whately and died November 8, 1839. Their six children were Almira, Sophia, Jane, Norman, Margaret and Mary Ann.

280. Polly, b. April 6, 1786; married January 5, 1809, Chester Belden of Whately and had three children:

Champion, b. July 26, 1809. Zerviola, b Aug. 12, 1819.
Emeline, b. May 16, 1815.

117. EBENEZER ALLIS was born March 21, 1753, probably in Bolton, Conn. His parents soon moved to Stafford Springs, Conn., and a few years later they went to Conway, Mass., but eventually settled in Shelburne Falls, Mass. He lived in Shelburne Falls until his death, April 7, 1825, and is said to have been a Revolutionary soldier.

Ebenezer Allis married (first) Jemima (or Joanna), daughter of Eliakim and Jemima (Allis) Root of Coventry, Conn., who was born on June 3, 1746, and died in 1818. He married (second) Abigail Seekins, who was the widow of Joseph Clesson, of Deerfield, Mass., and died Sept. 22, 1838. He probably had several children, but on account of the loss by fire of some of the old records of Shelburne Falls it has only been possible to find the name of one son:

281. Isaac; *

118. STEPHEN ALLIS was born March 4, 1758, in Stafford, Conn., and died December 3, 1848, in Buckland, Mass. He married (first) Thankful Munn on March 10, 1785, who was born December 5, 1759, and died on March 2, 1796; (second) Mary Munn on December 14, 1797, who was born October 24, 1772, and died on July 18, 1801; (third) Sophia Cole, February 23, 1802, who was born October 3, 1772, and died January 24, 1811; (fourth) Thankful Comstock on December 31, 1811, who was born August 29, 1759, and died December 7, 1813; (fifth) Mrs. Rachel Trow on February 15, 1815, who was born in 1772 and died November 9, 1862.

Stephen Allis, as a boy, lived in Conway and Shelburne Falls, Mass., his parents having moved from Stafford, Conn., when he was but a few years old. Later on he lived in Ashfield and Buckland, Mass., and was a farmer by occupation and a prominent citizen. He was also a soldier in the Revolution, enlisting July 22, 1779, in Captain James Walsworth's company, Col. Elisha Porter's (Hampshire Co.) regiment, and serving at New London, Conn. His children were:

By first wife:

282. Naomi, b. December 12, 1785; married Lemuel Taylor of Buckland on March 30, 1820, and died September 28, 1825. They had one son, Stephen Allis Taylor.

283. Samuel, b. March 27, 1787; married on November 29, 1832, Abigail, daughter of Josiah Johnson of Buckland, who was born April 2, 1791, and died February 4, 1871. Samuel Allis died July 30, 1856, without issue.

284. Experience, b. Aug. 4, 1789; died unmarried Feb. 19, 1852.

285. Rodolphus, b. May 21, 1791; married (first) on November 26, 1818, Polly Boyden, who was born December 12, 1789, and died September 16, 1831; (second) on March 1, 1838, Elizabeth Brownson, who was born May 22, 1795. Rodolphus Allis died without issue.

By second wife:

286. Roswell, b. May 2, 1800; *

By third wife:

287. Sophia, b. April 2, 1803; died March 19, 1812.

288. Arilla, b. April 28, 1805; no further record.

130. WILLIAM ALLIS was born on February 6, 1752, in Montague, Mass., but moved to Vermont at an early age and lived there until his death in 1802. He was a farmer by occupation and also a soldier in the Revolution.

He was one of the company of men who responded to the alarm of April 19, 1775, in connection with the battle of Lexington, and was enrolled in Captain Thomas Grover's company, Col. Williams' regiment, but also served in other companies and regiments during the year 1775.

William Allis was twice married, although the name of his first wife is not known. His second wife was Rachel Allis (249), daughter of Nathaniel and Hannah (Norton) Allis. After the death of her husband she moved to Chautauqua, N. Y. Their children were:

289. Girl; died young.
290. William, b. October 25, 1796; *
291. Hannah, b. about 1798; no further record.
292. Nathaniel, b. July 29, 1801; *
293. Rachel; no further record.

131. ZEBEDIAH ALLIS was born July 2, 1754, in Montague, Mass. He married (first) Martha Brooks on February 6, 1776, and (second) Lucy Tuttle about 1793. He was a farmer and lived in Montague until soon after his first marriage, when he moved to Colchester, Vermont, and settled there.

Zebediah Allis was a soldier in the Revolution. He enlisted in Capt. Thos. Grover's company, Col. Williams' regiment, being one of the company of men who responded to the alarm of April 19, 1775, in connection with the battle of Lexington. He also served in Capt. Asahel Gunn's company, Col. David Wells' regiment, enlisting September 23, 1777.

It has not been possible to obtain much information in regard to Zebediah's children on account of meagre town records and the fact that little or no family record was kept. He is known to have had the following children:

By first wife:

294. Clarissa, b. about 1777; died young.
295. Randol, b. about 1778; married (first) Anna Verenne on February 18, 1804, and (second) Caroline Baulch, and is said to have had a son, Ransom.
296. Olive; married Michael Irish.
297. Orilla; married Thomas Parker.
298. Miranda; married Stephen Irish.
299. Winthrop, b. April 1, 1785; *
300. Clarissa; married Mr. Clark.

By second wife:

301. Orib, b. Nov. 1, 1794; *

132. MOSES ALLIS was born February 13, 1756, in Montague, Mass., and died in Laport, Lorain Co., Ohio, on March 30, 1842, age 86. He married on December 18, 1781, Anna, daughter of Solomon and Mary (Taylor) Newton of Montague and Deerfield, who was born about 1760 and died October 21, 1808.

Moses Allis lived in Montague for several years after his marriage, but in 1795 moved into New York State and settled three miles south of Coventry. He was a farmer by occupation and is also said to have been a shoemaker. About 1830 he moved again, this time to Laport, Ohio, with his son William, and spent the remainder of his life there.

Moses Allis was a soldier in the Revolution and served through the war, receiving a pension thereafter from the United States Government until his death. The following information about him appears in the "Massachusetts Soldiers and Sailors of the Revolutionary War":

"Private, Captain Israel Chapin's company, Col. John Fellows' regiment; muster roll dated Aug. 1, 1775; enlisted April 27, 1775; service three months, twelve days; also, company return dated Oct. 8, 1775; also, order for bounty coat or its equivalent in money, dated Dorchester, Dec. 18, 1775; also, return of men enlisted into Continental Army from Capt. Moses Harvey's (5th) company, 6th Hampshire Co. regiment, dated March 5, 1778; enlisted for town of Montague; joined Capt. Ephraim Cleveland's company, Col. Michael Jackson's regiment; enlistment, three years."

Moses Allis had five children, three of whom were born in Montague:

302. Leonard, b. January 24, 1786; *

303. Fanny, b. November 24, 1790; married Clark Provin on January 1, 1811. He was a school teacher in Clinton, Illinois, and died September 2, 1864. Their ten children were William, died in infancy; Daniel K., died in army in Civil War; William Henry, died in army in Civil War; Wesley, died in 1866; Leonard Allis, died at age of 35; Joel Henry; Dennis Todd; George Reed; Annie Relief, married Alex. Johnson; Cynthia Ann, married Elisha Johnson.

304. William, b. September 15, 1793; *

305. Calvin, b. April 3, 1797; died October 20, 1800.

306. Luther, b. September 5, 1799; died March 28, 1800.

SIXTH GENERATION.

139. JOEL ALLIS was born February 12, 1769, in Conway, Mass. His parents moved to Sullivan, Madison County, N. Y., when he was a boy, and on January 4, 1797, he married Sarah, daughter of Eber and Bethia (Jenkins) Lee of that town, who was born January 3, 1773, and died November 20 or 28, 1820. He is said to have married a second time a widow by the name of Lansing.

Joel Allis was a farmer in Sullivan, N. Y., for a number of years, but eventually settled in Orleans County, about 125 miles further west, and died September 17, 1851, age 82 years. His eleven children, all by his first wife, Sarah, were:

307. Electa, b. December 23, 1797; died on July 24, 1852. On October 27, 1817, she married Ancel Densmore and had one child, Welthy A., who was born February 22, 1819, married Daniel McDonald on January 6, 1841, and died May 28, 1842, leaving a daughter, Welthy A., born May 25, 1842. Ancel Densmore died on March 17, 1819, and Electa married (second) on August 10, 1820, Hollis Maynard and had the following children:

1. Sylvia, b. May 1, 1821; married Cyrus Yale Horton on June 23, 1842, and died December 27, 1900, leaving no children.
2. Mandana, b. October 7, 1823; died May 30, 1854.
3. Olive, b. August 28, 1825; married Hiram M. Blake on October 25, 1849, and died without issue.
4. Jane, b. August 10, 1827; married Chester Blake on March 30, 1850, and died July 8, 1854, leaving no children
5. Esther E , b. June 15, 1830; died November 27, 1878.

308. Polly, b. January 9, 1799; married Lucius Bond of Albany, N. Y., and died December 16, 1882.

309. Sarah, b. September 9, 1800; died October 8, 1840. On April 9, 1822, she married John Chapman and their four children were:

1. Sarah Jane, b. May 29, 1824; married on December 15, 1845, Hiram L. Stoddard and died September 2, 1857. They had five children: (1) Olive Emily, b. August 10, 1847; married Hulbert H. Warner, October 29, 1871, and died December 2, 1908, leaving no children. (2) Cyrus Chapman, b. May 11, 1849; married Mary V. Craig, November 15, 1871, and had two children: Hulbert Craig and Harvey LeRoy. (3) Chester Everett, b. April 19, 1850; married Ellen L. Barker, July 4, 1872, and had two children: Floyd Ivan and Charles W. (4) Sylvia A., b. Oct. 10, 1853; married Orlando L. Topping, December 6, 1876, and died April 22, 1889. Their children were Olive E., Smith Alexander and Gladys Edna. (5) Alice Artemisia, b. August 18, 1855; married John J. McCullough, May 17, 1881, and had two children: Warner Stoddard (b. February 11, 1882, and died June 5, 1907) and Alice Edwina (b. January 14, 1885, and died February 18, 1901.)

2. Joel Allis, b. February 4, 1826; died on July 5, 1879. On June 11, 1851, he married (1st) Loretta Burgess, who died on Nov. 16, 1862. Their four children were: Vinal John, b. November 16, 1852; Irving Eugene, b. January 25, 1855; Cora Almira, b. September 19, 1857; and Eva Loretta, b. March 20, 1860 On October 14, 1863, Joel A. Chapman married (2nd) Phylinda E. Parsons, and had four children: Milton Everett, b. March 19, 1865; Jennie Booth, b. August 27, 1867; Mary Louise, b. on June 23, 1869; Ernest Lorenzo, b. on February 2, 1872.

3. Milton John, b. December 25, 1827; married and had three children.

4. Margaret Almira, b. January 1, 1829; married William Winton and had a daughter, Sarah.

310. Milton, b. October 18, 1802; *

311. Asa, b. January 6, 1805; *

312. Sophia, b. November 25, 1806; married Thomas Chapman and had a daughter, Velura. Sophia died Feb. 5, 1837.

313. Emily, b. September 23, 1808; married William Jennings and died in 1878.

314. Bethiah, b. February 10, 1811; married Cyrus Yale Chapman and died March 16, 1841. They had two chilldren, one of whom was John Yale Chapman.

315. Eber, b. November 25, 1812; married, but had no children, and died May 1, 1887.

316 Russell, b. December 22, 1814; died December 25, 1865. He married, moved to Michigan, and is said to have had several children.

317. Vinal, b. April 16, 1817; *

156. SAMUEL ALLIS was born June 20, 1767, in Conway, Mass., and died March 15, 1845. On January 20, 1790, he married Hannah, daughter of Israel Dickinson, who was born July 13, 1772, and died August 11, 1830. He was a farmer in Conway, and his eight children were:

318. Mary W., b. April 22, 1791; died on December 24, 1857. On June 14, 1810, she married Elisha Clarke, who was born September 8, 1786, and died July 19, 1862. Their children were: Samuel A., born April 24, 1812, and died March 26, 1898; Elijah D., born December 22, 1815, and died on January 21, 1816; Lucius L., born November 29, 1816, and died December 15, 1884; Elisha Jr., born June 1, 1818, and died August 9, 1851; Thomas D., born September 18, 1819, and died on April 25, 1871; a son, born and died March 17, 1823; a daughter, born and died July 7, 1825; a son, born and died Feb. 16, 1827; Jonathan G., born March 22, 1829, and died November 8, 1860; Tyler Thatcher, born Nov. 13, 1834, and died May 16, 1850.

319. Israel Dickinson, b. July 23, 1793; *

320. Zelinda, b. March 20, 1797; died April 21, 1830.

321. Oliver Partridge, b. March 18, 1799; died, unmarried, on March 17, 1887.

322. Samuel, b. July 7, 1802; died November 19, 1802.

323. Samuel, b. September 28, 1805; *

324. Mercy D., b August 13, 1808; married Daniel Hall of Ashfield, Mass., on March 6, 1832, and died September 30, 1889. Their five children were:

1. Harriet, b. June 19. 1835; died October 11, 1850.

2. Samuel Allis, b. September 1, 1839; married Angelina M. Allis (daughter of Eliot Clark Allis) and died on November 12, 1910. Their children were Hattie Elvira, b. February 17, 1865; Alice Dickinson, b. February 19, 1868; and Leon D., b. March 6, 1871.

3. Charles Daniel, b. June 19, 1846; died Oct. 1, 1850.

4. Hannah, b. August 19, 1849; died October 1, 1849.

5. Clarence D., b. July 27, 1851; married on April 30, 1884, Mary B. Woodard. Their children were George C., b April 9, 1892; Luna E., b. October 10, 1895; Helen H., b. October 17, 1896; and Nina M., b. October 17, 1896.

325. William, b. August 31, 1812; *

158. SOLOMON ALLIS was born October 26, 1769, in Conway, Mass., and died November 1, 1823. On March 14, 1794, he married Anna P., daughter of Israel and Mercy (Partridge) Dickinson, who died November 4, 1864. He was a farmer in Conway and his ten children were:

326. Parthena, b. January 17, 1795; married Willard Crittenden on June 29, 1824, and died March 19, 1870. Their six children were:

1. Mary Ann Dickinson, b. October 19, 1825; married Theodore T. Field on November 19, 1844, and died April 23, 1880 Their children were Egbert, b. Oct. 4, 1847; Cecil, b. Jan. 12, 1850; Irwin, b. April 17, 1857; Cynthia Elizabeth, b. March 29, 1860; Mary C., b. Feb. 27, 1869.

2. Lyman E., b. February 28, 1829; died Mar. 4, 1830.

3. Edwin, b. January 15, 1831.

4. Chauncey Smith, b. December 26, 1834.

5. Solomon Allis, b February 6, 1837.

6. William Elliot, b. Dec. 28, 1840; died Apr. 14, 1858.

327. Lucius, b. September 2, 1796; *

328. Thomas Wells, b August 28, 1798; *

329. John Dickinson, b. June 22, 1801; *

330. Emily, b. October 1, 1803; married in 1826 Lyman Smith of Whately, and died on March 26, 1888. Their children were: Ada, b. Jan. 23, 1827; Sarah, b. March 17, 1830; a child, b. September 9, 1832; Dolphus B., b. April 17, 1834; and Lydia Allis, b. November 15, 1836.

331. Elijah, b. March 14, 1805; *

332. Lois, b. April 3, 1807; married Asabel Stone in 1829.

333. Mary Wells, b. July 3, 1809; married on May 6, 1840, Lot Hall of Ashfield, Mass., and died July 14, 1889. Their six children were:

1. Sarah A., b. July 14, 1841; married on August 19, 1858, Edward D. Stevens, but had no children.

2. Eliza D., b. December 25, 1842; married on May 18, 1865, John H. Gardner, and had four children: John Jr., b. March 9, 1868; May, b May 15, 1870; Grace, b. January 6, 1872; and Blanche, b. April 13, 1879.

3. Harmony C., b. August 26, 1844; married Charles F. Howes on December 29, 1864, and had five children: Amanda, b. February 5, 1866; Lucy Mary, b. October 9, 1868; Laura Ann, b. November 9, 1870; Grace Eliza, b. March 3, 1877; Esther Bryant, b. November 20, 1882.

4. Emily A., b. December 10, 1846; died Oct. 9, 1862.

5. Frank Lot, b. June 21, 1848.

6. Ashbel S., b. April 21, 1850; died June 25, 1854.

334. Eliot Clark, b. February 13, 1816; *

335. Edward Partridge, b. February 8, 1819; *

160. THOMAS WELLS ALLIS was born October 16, 1772, in Conway, Mass., and died in Skaneateles, N. Y., June 28, 1848. He studied law at Yale University, and was one of the first graduates (1798). He then

taught school for a year or two in New Milford, Conn., and after that settled in Rhinebeck, Duchess Co., N. Y., as a lawyer, but owing to an accident sustained soon after commencing the practice of law he was so seriously injured that he was never able to resume his profession. In 1818 he removed to Skaneateles, when a new and growing town, and opened a day and boarding school for boys and girls, and spent the remainder of his life there.

Thomas Wells Allis married on May 11, 1804, Sally Allen, who was born September 30, 1778, in Conway, and died September 12, 1850, in Skaneateles. Their two children were:

336. Caleb Wells, b. September 29, 1814; *

337 Mary Louisa, b. July 1, 1820; married David Hall in September, 1841, and died April 16, 1880. Their two children were:

1. John C., b. October 27, 1842.

2. Thomas Wells, b. April 27, 1845; married Ellen J. Graves on October 20, 1868, and died December 1, 1913. Their eight children were: Loring B., b. Aug. 17, 1870; Clara L., b. Sept. 7, 1872; Luciele W., June 15, 1874; Philip Wells, b. April 12, 1876; Nellie I., b. November 11, 1877; Bulah M., b. August 8, 1879; Thomas W., b. April 18, 1886; and Ellenor R., b. August 10, 1888.

161. ELIJAH ALLIS was born December 5, 1773, in Conway, Mass., and died in Gorham, N. Y., in 1805. He was a farmer by occupation, and probably moved from Conway to Gorham about the time of his marriage to Lydia Warren. After his death Lydia married (second) Daniel Bale and had a son, Daniel. Elijah's four children were:

338. Dimmis, b. October 20, 1796; married Enos Childs, May 11, 1815, and died March 22, 1860. Their children were:

1. Elijah Allis, b. September 24, 1816.
2. Electa J., b. August 10, 1818.
3. Austin, b. March 29, 1823; married and had three children: Sarah, Dimmis (married Dr. L. E. Rockwell) and Mary.
4. Wallace, b. July 15, 1835.
5. Eliza B., b. November 21, 1837.

339. Thomas Wells, b. November 1, 1798; *

340. Oliver Graves, b. March 15, 1800; *

341. Elijah, b. February 24, 1802; disappeared from Albany, N. Y., when twenty years of age; no further record.

166. JOHN BELDING ALLIS was born July 8, 1772, in Ashfield or Conway, Massachusetts. On January 1, 1800, he married Lucy, daughter of Elisha DeWolf, and died on February 2, 1861. He lived in Ashfield and Conway, and his four children were:

342. Harriet, b. about 1807; married William Johnson of Vernon, Vermont, about 1840.

343. John, b. about 1810; *

344. Mary, b. August 22, 1814; married Ralph Arms and died at Granby, Canada.

345. Jane, b. August 3, 1818; married James W. Sprague of Buckland, Mass.

167. ELIJAH ALLIS was born May 20, 1774, in Ashfield or Conway, Mass. On June 20, 1799, he married Dolly Brown, who was born August 6, 1779, and died October 27, 1846. Elijah Allis settled in Wilmington, Vermont, and died there on October 8, 1850. His eight children were:

346. Dolly, b. October 13, 1802; married Enos R. Knapp on March 9, 1825, and died May 22, 1886. Their two children were:
Augustus W., b. March 17, 1826; died July 18, 1894.
Lucy L., b. August 8, 1832; died May 27, 1849.

347. Pomeroy, b. July 1, 1804; died, unmarried, Dec. 1, 1874.

348. Clemina, b. December 20, 1806; died May 26, 1817.

349. Diana, b. November 12, 1809; died January 3, 1891. On September 28, 1831, she married William H. Jones of Wilmington, who was born in September, 1807, and died in May, 1873. Their children were:

1. Harriet A., b. about 1832; died June 20, 1852.
2. Anna L., who died February 11, 1851.
3. W. Frank, b. April 7, 1840; married Martha, daughter of Wells Porter Allis, on April 23, 1862.
4. Royal H., who died May 7, 1851.
5. Wells P., b. November 6, 1845.
6. Varillus O., b. in August, 1849.

350. Lucy R., b. June 15, 1811; married Franklin Barnard on January 8, 1839, and died September 6, 1879. Their two children were:
Lucy A., b. March 27, 1845.
Frank E., b. January 13, 1851.

351. Sylvia, b. March 7, 1815; married Fayette G. Knapp on December 31, 1836, and died March 15, 1880. Their two children were:
Emma A., died January 29, 1851.
Gilbert A., b. July 5, 1845; died October 23, 1881.

352. Wells P., b. April 5, 1817; *

353. Clemina, b. August 13, 1821; died, unmarried, on February 29, 1848.

168. SILAS ALLIS was born on April 7, 1776, He married on July 7, 1796, Charlotte Hawley of Amherst, Massachusetts, who was born April 30, 1775, and died about 1852, in Andover, N. Y.

Silas Allis lived in Heath, Mass., and all his children were born there, but he eventually moved into New York State and spent the remaining years of his life in Groton and Andover, where he died about 1852. His nine children were:

354. Clarissa, b. March 10, 1800; married Josiah Warfield of Heath on December 16, 1815, and died March 14, 1862. Their children were:
   1. George W., b. November 4, 1818; married Arabelle Houghton on May 18, 1851.
   2. Elizabeth, b. January 13, 1821; married Milo Sweet on May 1, 1841.
   3. Eber, b. June 8, 1823; married Cynthia Stephens on September 17, 1846.
   4. Dorothy, b. January 2, 1826; married Nat'l Sweet on September 17, 1846.
   5. Henry H., b. March 30, 1828; died October 2, 1847.
   6. Horace, b. September 6, 1831; married Samantha Wallace on July 4, 1854.
   7. Delia, b. July 23, 1833; died September 30, 1850.
   8. Palmer, b. March 29, 1836; married Almeda Wallace on March 15, 1855.
   9. Miriam, b. August 7, 1842; married Daniel Krusen.

355. Pliny, b. June 10, 1802; *

356. Miriam, b. October 24, 1804; married Nathaniel Newell of Heath, Mass.

357. Sally, b. October 3, 1806; married Elisha Eldridge.

358. Silas, Jr., b. July 23, 1808; *

359. Betsy, b. August 4, 1811; died at 18 years.

360. Lucy H., b. November 5, 1813; married Leroy C. Davis of Andover, N. Y., on November 5, 1835, and died July 31, 1901. Their children were:
   1. Uriah, b. November 30, 1837; died May 28, 1896.
   2. Charles F., b. October 18, 1839; living in Andover.
   3. Hannah, b. February 22, 1845; died in 1855.

361. Charlotte, b. July 7, 1817; married Robert Wilsey.

362. Augusta, b. August 16, 1820; married Albert Scribner of Andover, N. Y., July 21, 1837, and died in 1897. Their children were Lorenzo, Spencer, Loducy and Jay.

171. HENRY ALLIS was probably born in Conway, Mass. In 1807 he married Dolly Bacon, who died June 30, 1831, and, although he married a second time, the name of his wife and date of marriage are not known.

Henry Allis lived in Conway for several years, and his first four children were born there, but he then went West with his wife and family and settled in Beloit, Wisconsin, where he spent the remainder of his life. His children were:

By first wife:

363. Alvan Porter, b. February 27, 1808; died in 1827.

364. Lydia W., b. February 1, 1810; married Amaziah Howes and had three children, Clara, Emma and Henry.

365. Henry Dearborn, b. May 15, 1813; *

366. Ardelia, b. February 9, 1815; married Franklin Bond.

367. Dorothy, b. in 1817; married Israel Stebbins and had two children, Ettie and Hattie.

368. Eliza, b. in 1819; married W. D. Hillyer and had two children, Ella and Millie.

369. Franklin, b. about 1821; married a Miss Gordon.

370. William, b. about 1823; married Charlotte Jackson, but died without issue.

371. Charles, b. about 1826; died, unmarried, in 1849.

372. Adaline, b. about 1828; died, unmarried, in 1845

373. Alvan P., b. in June, 1831; no further record.

By second wife:

374. George B., b. about 1835; no further record.

375. Sophia A., b. about 1836; married Col. Cobb.

376. Marie, b. about 1837; married Ivan Heith.

173. JOHN ALLIS was born on May 19, 1779, probably in Plainfield, Mass. On November 27, 1805, he married Lois Weston, and was a carpenter in Pittsfield, Massachusetts. He is known to have had the following children:

377. Harriet, married Charles Merriman and had the following children:

1. Louisa, died young.
2. Rhoda, died young.
3. Charles, b. May 12, 1829; died in January, 1914.
4. Wells, b. June 27, 1832; died on July 19, 1913. He married (1) Elizabeth Augerson and had three children: Scott, Grove and Forrest. On September 27, 1870, he married (2) Elizabeth Marshall and had three children: Jesse, Harriet and Ruby.

378. Louisa, never married.

379. Samuel, b. in 1810; *

176. LEMUEL ALLIS was born on July 9, 1874, probably in Plainfield, Mass., and died October 20, 1855, in Chatham, Ohio. He married (first) Rhoda Burroughs on April 11, 1805, who died March 13, 1825, and (second) Lydia Beals on May 18, 1825, who died February 16, 1887.

Lemuel Allis was a farmer and lived in Plainfield until 1834, at which time he moved west to Ohio and settled in Chatham. His children were:

380. Lucius, b. August 29, 1817; *

381. Roxana, b. June 12, 1820; married Samuel Wetherby and died October 17, 1868. Their children were:

1. Dyer, died young.
2. Alice, married Hiram Allis (No. 393) and died without issue.

382. Rhoda, b. September 28, 1822; married George Weston on December 31, 1845, and died October 13, 1914, at the age of 92 years. Their children were:

1. Asa Lemuel, b. December 9, 1853; married Elmyra Nead, January 22, 1882, and had three children: George I., b. May 29, 1884, May E., b. April 12, 1888, and Edith, b. July 29, 1890 (died October 18, 1890). Elmyra Nead died October 29, 1890, and Asa married (2nd) Ida Fields, November 24, 1892. They had two children: Lulu E., b. September 29, 1893, and Herbert R., b. July 30, 1899.

2. Inizetta, b. May 28, 1858; died May 17, 1860.

3 Arthur E., b. January 8, 1862; married Clara Brown, April 26, 1888, and had Lucy E., b. June 14, 1889, Burton L., b. Feb. 23, 1891, and Charles M., b. April 24, 1896.

4. George A., b. October 18, 1863; died Sept. 4, 1864.

5. Frank A., b. August 31, 1867; married Ina Allis on April 16, 1890, and had two children: Ethel R., b. Dec. 26, 1898, and Wells A., b. June 8, 1901.

383. Rebecca, b. August 22, 1824; married Allymen Eddy in September, 1849, and died March 6, 1892.

384. Justin, b January 16, 1826; *

385. Sally, b. December 25, 1827; married John Murray and died February 11, 1894. They had two children, Justin and Ada.

386. Elisha, b. October 30, 1829; *

387. L. Caroline, b. October 3, 1831; married Matthias Kelly on December 5, 1850, and is living in California. Their children were Ida, Edward and Burt, and two who died in infancy.

388. Parthena, b. November 28, 1833; died, unmarried, September 23, 1876.

389. Laura Amanda, b. April 14, 1836; married in February, 1855, Charles Fowler, and died September 18, 1855.

390. Wells, b. September 15, 1838; married Clara Landon on November 4, 1863, and had one child who died in infancy. He is a farmer in Chatham, Ohio. His wife died January 13, 1916.

391. Marila, b. March 9, 1841; married Eli Grimm and died September 6, 1903. Their children were Bayard, Ernest, Glendora, and a son who died in infancy.

392. Alonzo, b. July 22, 1844; *

393. Hiram, b. January 2, 1847; married Alice Wetherby and died November 5, 1912, without issue. He was a farmer in Chatham.

181. ELISHA ALLIS was born April 8, 1779, in Williamsburg, Mass., and lived there until about 12 years of age, when his parents moved to Brookfield, Vermont. He was a farmer and teacher, and lived in Brookfield until his death on March 16, 1877. On October 16, 1811, he married Mary Steele, who died April 5, 1855. They had eleven children:

394. William Steele, b. October 13, 1812; died July 6, 1813.

395. William Steele, b. March 19, 1814; died, unmarried, on November 22, 1841.

396. Martha Hopkins, b. January 23, 1816; married Dudley S. Bagley on September 12, 1843, and died in Milwaukee, Wisconsin on August 28, 1867. They had two children who died in infancy and four others:

1. Harmon F., b. June 15, 1845.
2. Helen, b. February 8, 1849.
3. George Colt, b March 1, 1851; married Cornelia E. Mead, November 29, 1876. Their children were Dudley S., b. October 11, 1877, and Ralph Colt, b. Dec 9, 1881.
4. Alice, b. March 4, 1853.

397. Mary Dickinson, b. November 2, 1817; married Dr. S. H. Smith on January 2, 1844, and died March 12, 1900. Their two children were Watson, b. about 1844, and S. Horace, b. about 1846.

398. Elizabeth L., b. August 18, 1819; married, May 22, 1843, Frederick Wheatly and died March 5, 1852. They had one child who died at the age of five months.

399. Andrew S., b. September 1, 1821; *

400. Harriet, b July 15, 1823; married A. L. Follansbee, July 2, 1863, and died on October 26, 1889, leaving no children.

401. Obadiah D., b. July 27, 1825; *

402. Elisha, b. September 23, 1828; *

403. Ellen Maria, b. November 28, 1830; married on March 11, 1856, D. M Brown of Williamstown, Vermont, and is living in Northfield, Vermont. They had seven children:

1. Alice Maria, b. January 28, 1857; married Luther Waldo of Williamstown and died on November 14, 1892. Their children were Edith Maria, b. November 12, 1889, and Raymond Brown, b. November 3, 1902.

2. Joseph, b. May 1, 1858; died the same day.

3. Mary Adeline, b. September 29, 1861; married on April 28, 1886, Charles S. Adams of St. Johnsbury, Vermont, and their children were Ruth Brown, b. February 11, 1892, Russell Steele, b. January 22, 1894, and Dorothy Cornelia, b. November 6, 1897.

4. Fanny Allis, b. November 6, 1864; married Burt W. Clogston of Williamstown, Vermont, on November 30, 1892. Their five children were Robert Elwin, b. June 13, 1894 (married Lizzie May Martin in August, 1914), Arthur Burt, b. November 30, 1895; Perley Walter, b. October 31, 1899; Leonora Ellen, b. August 24, 1901, and died September 11, 1901; Nellie Elizabeth, b. August 18, 1903.

5. Edith May, b. January 7, 1866; died June 28, 1882.

6. Ellen Lucy, b. April 30, 1867.

7. Walter Egbert, b. March 26, 1872.

404. Egbert Henry, b. April 15, 1836; was commissioned a surgeon in the United States Navy during the Civil War and was lost on the "Bainbridge" off Cape Hatteras in 1863.

186. WILLIAM ALLIS was born February 6, 1793, in Brookfield, Vt., and died May 1, 1868, in Holley, N. Y., of pneumonia. He was twice married: (first) on February 1, 1818, to Julia Ingersoll of Ellington, Conn., who died August 22, 1822, and (second) on November 17, 1831, to Maria, daughter of Amasa Jones of Wilkes-barre, Pennsylvania.

William Allis was a farmer and lived in Brookfield, Vermont, until a short time after the death of his first wife, when he and his son, William Dickinson Allis, started for western New York, using the overland route. They started with a horse and vehicle for Norwich, Conn. After striking the backwoods, as it was then called, the vehicle had to be abandoned and father and son took turns in riding the horse. Their experiences on that trip are given in the words of the son:

"Bear and panther tracks were crossed repeatedly, and every night we were obliged to keep a huge bonfire to keep off the roving packs of timber wolves, which, rendered desperate by hunger, were ready to attack man or beast after darkness. The cold was intense and both father and myself were badly frostbitten by the time we reached Norwich. After resting a few days with an aunt in Norwich we continued our journey towards Orleans County, N. Y., which was our destination."

They arrived soon afterwards in Orleans County and took up their residence in Holley. Later William Allis was elected sheriff of Orleans County. His children were:

By first wife:

405. William Dickinson, b. November 30, 1818; *

406. George Ingersoll, b. August 10, 1820; died September 29, 1821.

407. Julia Taylor, b. August 13, 1822; died August 18, 1822.

By second wife:

408. Elisha, b. December 8, 1832; *

409. Samuel Jones, b. August 17, 1834; *

410. Oscar Huntington, b. September 9, 1836. *

411. Mary Elizabeth, b. February 4, 1839; died, unmarried, on August 3, 1877.

412. Charles Frederick, b. April 25, 1843; *

187. ELIJAH ALLIS was born October 21, 1775, in Whately, Mass., and lived there until his death on July 9, 1860, age 85 years. On November 27, 1800, he married Electa, daughter of Captain Salmon and Mary (Waite) White of Whately, who was born September 22, 1775, and died April 8, 1859, age 84 years. They lived together over fifty-eight years.

Elijah Allis was the oldest of eleven children, and because of the death of his father at an early age the care of the large family, the large farm of over 100 acres and other interests of the family estate, largely fell to him. He was, however, a large-minded man and early developed those business habits that marked him as a skillful manager. He was town clerk and assessor for several years and representative to the General Court, deputy sheriff and postmaster twelve years, and an equal number of years a hotel keeper, also in trade a few years. He was forward in improvements of all kinds, a gifted speaker and a genial, pleasing companion. His four children were:

413. Salmon White, b. November 27, 1801; *

414. Josiah, b. July 17, 1803; *

415. Lydia, b. Dec. 1, 1805; was a school teacher in Whately. On April 18, 1864, she married Dr. Myron Harwood, as his second wife, and died on October 12, 1894, almost 89 years of age.

416. Judith White, b. November 8, 1807; married on December 22, 1831, Dr. Myron Harwood of Whately, being his first wife, and died March 9, 1862. Their children were:

1. Maria Louisa, b January 2, 1833; married Ephraim Boyce of Mississippi and died January 30, 1866.
2. Ellen Electa, b. November 12, 1834; married Chester R. Chaffee on January 5, 1861.
3. Lydia Allis, b. December 26, 1837; married John R. Smith of Springfield, Mass., on October 18, 1866.
4. Henry White Allis, b. June 6, 1843; died February 3, 1864.
5. Francis Alonzo, b. September 2, 1845; died same month.
6. Mary Eliza, b. Feb. 2, 1847; died March 13, 1847.
7. Mary Eliza, b. March 14, 1848; never married.
8. Fannie Allis, b. February 14, 1851; died soon.

189. JOSIAH ALLIS was born January 5, 1779, in Whately, Mass. He married (first) Mary Bull and (second) Elizabeth, daughter of Ebenezer and Mary (White) Arms of Greenfield, Mass., and widow of James Gould, born December 8, 1787. He settled in Prattsburg, N. Y., in 1803 and lived there until his death on November 15, 1848. His ten children were:

417. Emily, b. Jan. 1, 1810; married William Van Valkenburg.

418. Jerry, b. September 27, 1811; *

419. Horace B., b. October 18, 1813; *

420. Josiah, Jr., b. August 29, 1815; died young.

421. Josiah, Jr., b. July 18, 1817; *

422. Asha, b. November 17, 1819; died young.

423. Lemira, b. January 25, 1822; married D. W Sutton, May 1, 1856, and died May 20, 1862. Their children were:

1. Mary E., b. March 24, 1857; died on November 20, 1857.

2. John A., b. May 29, 1859; died August 12, 1859.

3. William H., b. October 28, 1860; married Hattie A. Butler on June 26, 1890, and had a daughter, Mildred L., born July 22, 1891.

424. Mary E., b. March 2, 1824; died young.

425. Henry E., b. December 25, 1826; *

426. Asha, b. April 29, 1831; died young.

192. HENRY ALLIS was born July 29, 1784, in Whately, Mass. When a young man he left Whately for Prattsburg, N. Y., and there became a blacksmith. In 1815 he married Charlotte Phelps and had four children as below stated. He died on January 24, 1824, at the age of 40 years, and his widow, for many years thereafter, took as boarders the students of Franklin Academy and was much beloved.

427. Anna, b. June 22, 1816; died, unmarried, in Nov., 1906.

428. Mary P., b. May 15, 1818; married L. O. Dunning in 1848 and died in June, 1877. They had a daughter, Anna G., who is living in East Bloomfield, N. Y.

429. Elijah, b. June 19, 1820; *

430. John, b. April 7, 1823; *

HORACE BULL ALLIS

193. JERE ALLIS was born July 25, 1786, in Whately, Mass., and died in Franklin, N. Y., April 19, 1885. On October 1, 1814, hé married Mary, daughter of Deacon Salmon and Lydia (Amsden) White of Whately, who was born June 3, 1793, and died Feb. 2, 1877.

Jere Allis was a hatter and furrier by trade. He went from Whately to Prattsburg, N. Y., at an early date, thence to Cazenovia, N. Y. (where he acquired a considerable competence), and later to Milwaukee, Wis., but died in Franklin, N. Y., almost 99 years of age. His old age was remarkable in that his mind, including memory, remained clear and acute, and his temper exceedingly sweet and sunny. His five children were:

431. Edward Phelps, b. Dec. 31, 1815; died August 16, 1831.

432. Elisha, b. August 26, 1819; died August 25, 1831.

433. Mary Ann, b. August 4, 1821; married the Rev. Henry Callahan of Seattle, Washington, on May 9, 1843. Their children were:

1. Edward Gardiner, b. July 5, 1846.
2. Mary, b. November 19, 1849.
3. Daughter, b. in March, 1854; died in infancy.
4. Henry White, b. April 15, 1856.
5. Robert Carroll, b. September 26, 1857.
6. Gilbert Allis, b. July 2, 1862.

434. Edward Phelps, b. May 12, 1824; *

435. Lucy Jane, b. September 19, 1828; married J. T. Gilbert on June 30, 1852, and died on November 12, 1889. They had four children:

1. Child, b. in 1853; died in infancy.
2. Joseph T., Jr., b. June 14, 1855; living, unmarried, in Gilbertsville, N. Y.
3. Samuel C., b. October 8, 1857; died April 3, 1885.
4. Miriam A., b. October 8, 1857; died June 13, 1860.

196. STALHAM or STOLHAM ALLIS was born May 1, 1792, in Whately, Mass., and died there June 11, 1864, age 72 years. He was thrice married: first, on December 24, 1818, to Annis, daughter of David and Sarah (Allis) Stockbridge of Whately, who was born December 17, 1798, and died December 9, 1838; second, on September 11, 1839, to Eliza, daughter of Joseph Sanderson, who died on July 12, 1860; third, in 1862 to Mrs. Eliza Wood, daughter of Abner and Martha (Wells) Dickenson, formerly of Whately but then of Ohio.

Stalham Allis was only three years old when his father died, and two years afterward his mother married (second) Salmon White, Jr., and took Stalham with her. He lived with Mr. White until old enough to learn a trade, when he was apprenticed to Major Thomas Sanderson of Canterbury, in the eastern part of Whately, and learned the tanner's and shoemaker's trade. After the death of Major Sanderson he had charge of the business for his sister (the widow of Major Sanderson) until 1825, when he bought out Solomon Atkins & Sons and moved to the center of the town, continuing the same business and accumulating a good estate.

Stalham Allis was a broad-minded and valuable citizen, foremost in all improvements and very prominent in public affairs, at different times holding nearly all the town offices. He was stern and inflexible in purpose when satisfied that he was right. He had the following children, all by his first wife:

436. Hubbard S., b. October 4, 1819; *

437. Elisha Chapman, b. April 6, 1821; died, unmarried, on October 1, 1848.

438. Elam Bridges, b. July 10, 1823; *

439. Stalham White, b. July 12, 1826; died November 13, 1831.

440. Edward Phelps, b. May 28, 1828; died December 3, 1831.

441. Stalham Edward, b. May 29, 1833; died, unmarried, on March 29, 1896.

197. ELISHA ALLIS was born January 4, 1794, in Whately, Mass., and died in Cazenovia, N. Y., August 6, 1867. He was twice married: first, on November 6, 1821, to Nancy, daughter of Gamaliel and Nancy (Kellogg) Loomis of Prattsburg, N. Y., who was born October 19, 1799, and died November 2, 1828; second, in 1830, to Diantha, daughter of James and Diantha Stanley of Cazenovia, who died May 3, 1870.

Elisha Allis removed from Whately to Cazenovia in 1812 and there learned the blacksmith's trade. He became an expert in his line of business, and is said to have understood a horse's foot better than any other man in Madison County, N. Y. He afterwards carried on the business in connection with a foundry for many years. His eleven children were:

By first wife:

442. Infant, b. August 22, 1822; died the same day.

443. Nancy Elizabeth, b. August 2, 1823; died March 19, 1845.

444. Electa Anna, b. September 5, 1824; married Dr. Joseph W. T. Rice, September 5, 1844, and died April 20, 1900

445. Benjamin B., b. November 6, 1826; died August 6, 1828.

446. Sophronia Loomis, b. October 1, 1828; married, November 25, 1857, M. McNamara Walsh of Rochester, N. Y., and had a son, Shirley Allis, who was born October 10, 1858, and died May 12, 1877. Sophronia died in Cazenovia on July 16, 1913, almost 85 years of age.

By second wife:

447. Augustus Gridley S., b. January 5, 1831; *

448. Mary Diantha Sophia, b. April 9, 1837; died December 6, 1841.

449. Jesse Ashbel, b. September 13, 1840; *

450. Elisha Burrill, b. November 18, 1846; died Aug. 14, 1847.

451. Burritt Elihu, b. December 26, 1849; died Dec. 15, 1850.

452. Herbert Morrill, b. January 8, 1853; died Jan. 29, 1858.

202. JOSIAH ALLIS was born May 2, 1794, in Hatfield, Mass., and died November 13, 1866. He married (first) on May 17, 1821, Salome Osborne of Pittsfield, Mass., who was born June 26, 1801, and died October 29, 1833. On May 18, 1839, he married (second) Louisa M., daughter of Seth Bardwell, who was born May 3, 1807, and died May 29, 1865.

Josiah Allis was a farmer in Hatfield, and his three children were:

453. Son, b. January 17, 1822; died in infancy.

454. Harriet Atwood, b. January 17, 1823; married on May 24, 1842, James Morton of Hatfield and died June 4, 1862. Their children were Josiah Allis, b. June 5, 1847, James E., b. September 11, 1850, Eurotas M., b. in Mar., 1856, and Harriet Allis, b. November 13, 1861.

455. Augusta Salome, b. December 29, 1824; married John D. Brown of Hatfield, December 14, 1842, and died August 21, 1865. Their children were Alice L., b. April 29, 1848, Jane F., b. September 23, 1851, and Harriet A., b. November 2, 1857.

204. WILLIAM ALLIS was born December 13, 1785, in Hatfield, Mass., and died October 5, 1875. He married (first) on March 23, 1809, Betsey, daughter of Moses Barber, who died May 30, 1855, and in 1857 he married (second) Lucy Williston, who died in 1886.

William Allis removed from Massachusetts to New York State, first settling in Lowville and later moving to Philadelphia, Jefferson County. He was a farmer by occupation and was a soldier in the War of 1812, taking part in the battle of Sackett's Harbor, as did also his father. His eight children, all by his first wife, were:

456. Sophia, b. May 8, 1811; married William Bennett and died September 25, 1887. Their children were Emeline, Dexter and William.

457. William, b. November 22, 1812; died, unmarried, on May 17, 1843.

458 Charles, b. February 12, 1817; *

459. Fanny, b. October 3, 1819; married Truman Oatman and died May 11, 1900. Their children were Betsy, Sophia and Albert.

460. Betsy, b. March 24, 1822; married Abram Demarest and died October 23, 1895. They had a son, David, who was born in 1855.

461. Dexter, b. May 20, 1825; *

462. John, b. October 25, 1827; *

463. Mary, b. May 15, 1830; married Joshua Roberts and is living in Philadelphia, N. Y.

206. EPAPHRODITUS ALLIS was born May 8, 1789, in Hatfield, Mass., and died March 23, 1862. On March 25, 1813, he married Sarah, daughter of Levi and Sally (Richardson) Chapin of Chicopee, Mass., who

was born on September 12, 1792, and died in November, 1869. He lived in Chicopee and Springfield, Mass., and had three children:

464. William S., b. March 29, 1814; *

465. Sarah A., b. June 16, 1816; married Willard Nichols on December 16, 1835, and died February 7, 1909, age 93.

466. Martha A., b. April 9, 1818; married Timothy Hill, May 2, 1842.

209. DEXTER ALLIS was born February 7, 1797, in Hatfield, Mass., and died December 28, 1882, nearly 86 years of age. On November 18, 1824, he married Mary, daughter of Daniel Waite of Springfield, Mass., who was born May 27, 1806, and died July 19, 1886.

Dexter Allis lived in Hatfield for a while, and was a farmer by occupation, but later moved to Springfield, where he was engaged in the real estate business. He was active in church and town affairs and his children were:

467. Waitstill Hastings, b. October 11, 1825; died, unmarried, February 18, 1901. He was for many years in business in Springfield, Mass.

468. Daniel Waite, b. August 9, 1828; *

469. William Penn, b. April 9, 1830; *

470. Elizabeth Hastings, b. November 22, 1831; is living in Hatfield. On January 1, 1857, she married Samuel F. Billings, who was born January 18, 1828, and died May 5, 1896, and their children were:

1. Edward Holmes, b. April 29, 1858.
2. Silas Herbert, b. Oct. 22, 1859; died March 28, 1860
3. Louis Allis, b. November 28, 1861.
4. Elizabeth Hastings, b. October 11, 1864; married Charles I. Abbott on October 24, 1900. They had a son, Howard B., who was born November 17, 1902.

5. Samuel Fellows, b. August 21, 1866; married Sarah G. Langdon on October 29, 1902, and had a son, Gordon L., who was born May 25, 1904

6. Allis S., b. July 29, 1869; died October 24, 1870.

471. Mary Waite, b. October 9, 1833; living in Winona, Minn. On October 20, 1858, she married Dr. C. S. Hurlbut of Springfield, Mass., who was born on March 18, 1832, and died January 6, 1901, and their children were:

1. Mary Allis, b. April 26, 1860; married on November 27, 1901, Prof. J. S. Gaylord of Winona, Minn.

2. Dexter Allis, b. September 23, 1562; died December 22, 1863.

3. Martha Asenath, b. January 6, 1865.

4. Marion Elizabeth, b. December 10, 1866; died February 3, 1913.

5. Mabel Grace, b. February 22, 1869; died December 8, 1900.

6. Cornelius Searle, Jr., b. June 1, 1871; married on October 4, 1899, Marion C. Adams and had three children: Charlotte, b. July 12, 1904, Cornelius Searle, 3rd, b. June 30, 1906, and Eleanor, b. April 12, 1911.

211. THOMAS CUTLER ALLIS was born in Hatfield, Mass., on March 20, 1802, and died in Quebec on September 24, 1874. He married on July 27, 1837, Julia Ann, daughter of John and Julia (Noble) Mather, who was born April 2, 1810, and died October 12, 1877.

Thomas Cutler Allis lived with his oldest sister in Deerfield, Mass., until he was 16 years of age, when he decided to go to Stanstead, Quebec, Canada, and learn the blacksmith's trade from an old friend of the family, Deacon Arms, formerly of Conway, Mass. He walked all the way from his home to Stanstead, 300 miles. He remained with Mr. Arms until 21 years of age and afterwards lived in Danville,

Canada. He became an expert at his trade and people would go fifty miles to get one of "Deacon Allis's axes". He was very successful in his business and at one time owned a store, five farms, a saw mill and shop in Danville. He used to buy cattle and take them through the woods to the Quebec market via the old Craig Road, a road built by the soldiers under Sir Craig after suppressing the rebellion in Canada. His eight children were:

472. Solon Mather, b. June 29, 1838; *

473. John Mather, b. December 15, 1839; *

474. Thomas C., b. January 5, 1842; was a soldier in the Union Army in the Civil War and was captured by the Confederates and placed in Andersonville Prison, Savannah, Georgia, where he died from starvation October 16, 1864.

475. Dexter, b. June 1, 1843; died July 1, 1843.

476. William, b. December 1, 1844; died November 1, 1866, as the result of a boiler explosion.

477. Julia N., b. October 27, 1846; died in September, 1852.

478. James W., b. February 7, 1848; died in October, 1851, from smallpox.

479. Mary, b. in 1849; died in October, 1851, from smallpox.

216. STEPHEN G. M. ALLIS was born on June 5, 1805, and died in Waverly, Illinois, on July 9, 1887, at the age of 82 years. He married in 1836-7, Joanna, daughter of Frederic and Parmela (Wyman) Chapin, who was born October 28, 1805, and died January 11, 1886. He left Massachusetts about the time of his marriage and settled in Waverly, Illinois, and all of his six children were born there:

480. William, b. December 12, 1837; died March 12, 1838.

481. Frederic W., b. July 22, 1839; died August 1, 1839.

482. Caroline, b. March 16, 1840; died September 6, 1840.

483. R. Mansfield, b. in December, 1841; died on February 20, 1844.

484. Louise, b. June 23, 1843; died January 7, 1844.

485. Anne, b in September, 1845; died September 21, 1848.

222. OSEE ALLIS was born June 26, 1790, in Whately, Mass., and died March 6, 1819. On November 5, 1813, he married Ellise, daughter of William and Tirzah (Morton) Mather of Whately, who was born April 24, 1794, and died February 16, 1876. After the death of her husband she married (second) Horace Morton. Osee Allis was a farmer in Whately and had the following children:

486. Austin, b. in 1814; died July 15, 1820.

487. Harriet Mather, b. February 13, 1817; married Walter Brown on February 9, 1837, and died October 10, 1891.

488. Son, b about 1819; died in infancy.

225. AUSTIN ALLIS was born in Whately, Massachusetts, June 12, 1794, and died June 23, 1852. He married (first), October 24, 1825, Samantha, daughter of Elijah and Sally (Loomis) Sanderson of Whately, who was born November 26, 1805, and died December 26, 1836; (second) on February 21, 1839, Elvira, daughter of Jacob Warner of Williamsburg, Massachusetts. He was a wheelwright by occupation and had the following seven children:

By first wife:

489. Adaline S., b. in 1826; died January 5, 1849.

490. Sarah Frances, b. September 19, 1828; died May 22, 1832.

491. Luther Sanderson, b. August 22, 1830; *

492. Mary Louise, b. May 15, 1832; married Hiram W. Smith of Whately on April 24, 1850, and died on March 5, 1898. Their two children were:

1. Flora, b. November 7, 1851; died in 1863.

2. Elizabeth M., b. November 13, 1853; married Erastus C. Lyman in February, 1893, and had a daughter, Ethel Louise, who was born December 1, 1893.

493. Austin Judson, b. December 8, 1836; *

By second wife:

494. Isabel Josephine, b. April 13, 1840; married Charles F. Taynton of Florence, Mass., on February 21, 1866, and died August 31, 1868. They had a daughter, Caroline T., who was born May 20, 1867, and married, September 16, 1907, Ulric Newman of Columbus, Ohio.

495. Ernest Austin, b. June 30, 1842; *

229. ELEAZER ALLIS was born September 23, 1803, in Whately, Mass., and died in Paynes Point, Ogle County, Ill., on January 18, 1884, nearly 81 years of age. On September 20, 1829, he married Miranda, daughter of William Cook of Hatfield, Mass., who was born June 12, 1805, and died December 18, 1894, age 89 years.

Eleazer Allis lived in Whately until about the time of his marriage and then moved to Hatfield, but about 1842 he left Massachusetts for the West and settled in Paynes Point, Illinois. He had eight children, the first six of whom were born in Hatfield, and he and his three sons served in the Union Army during the Civil War (1861-5):

496. Ruth W., b May 21, 1830; married Milo Haselton, March 16, 1857.

497. Sarah, b. June 2, 1832; married E. C. Bragg of Williamsburg, Mass., on October 4, 1854.

498. Emeline C., b. April 30, 1834; married Lorenzo S. Bardwell of Hatfield, Mass., on January 1, 1857, and lived in Paynes Point, Illinois.

499. Alonzo, b. May 25, 1836; died, unmarried, in the Union Army on February 22, 1864.

500. Anna M., b. July 3, 1838; married George Ireland, March 10, 1859.

501. Eugene, b. September 27, 1841; married Kate Peterfield on January 18, 1859.

502. Eliza, b. August 17, 1844; no further record.

503. Taylor, b. April 21, 1847; married, June 16, 1888, Sophia Clapp of Paynes Point and died about 1908.

233. ELEAZER ALLIS was born September 2, 1789, probably in Hatfield, Mass. He lived in Hatfield and on the Lamoille River in Vermont until about 11 years of age, when his father moved to Bradford County, Pa., and settled in Allis Hollow. That part of the state was then a very wild and untraveled country, and Eleazer did his share of the work of making a clearing and building a log house.

Eleazer Allis was a farmer, and about the time of his marriage on May 25, 1820, to Diana Eastabrook he bought a farm on South Hill, Orwell, Bradford County, Pa., upon which he settled. He died on May 20, 1877, nearly 88 years of age, and his wife, Diana, died on May 30, 1870. His five children were:

504. Edwin Ingram, b. June 25, 1821; *

505. Larancy M., b. April 29, 1823; died July 16, 1823.

506. Miriam L., b. November 24, 1824; married Harry Stephens on April 16, 1846, and died June 27, 1890. Their three children were Ethalynda, Elhanan and Harry.

507. Hiram K., b. October 26, 1831; *

508. Ordensa H., b. March 25, 1838; married Thomas R. Pickering on November 24, 1857, and died October 8, 1883. Their children were Alpha, Gertrude and Lyni.

234. ITHIEL ALLIS was born about 1791, probably in Vermont. When he was about nine years of age his father moved to Bradford County, Pennsylvania, and settled in Allis Hollow, and Ithiel helped in the building of the first log house in that section. He was a farmer by occupation, and about 1824 married Harriet Barnes. His four children were:

509. Ithiel Judson, b. in 1825; *

510. Oscar F., b. in 1829; married Minseyette Bacon and died May 1, 1885. *

511. Joel M., b. in 1833; married Mary Nichols and died February 3, 1865. *

512. Eliza Harriet, b. April 10, 1838; married J. G. Spicer.

236. SILAS ALLIS was born March 14, 1794, probably in Vermont. When he was about six years old his father moved to Bradford County, Pennsylvania, and settled in Allis Hollow, and he helped in the making of a home there. On April 27, 1825, he married Margaret Lent of Rome, Pennsylvania, who was born on March 15, 1801, and died February 23, 1894, almost 93 years of age.

Silas Allis was a farmer and a carpenter in Allis Hollow, and lived there until his death on November 1, 1870. He also owned property in Orwell, Pa. His children were:

513. Henrietta Augusta, b. March 14, 1826; died on January 5, 1911, age 85 years. On Mar. 24, 1849, she married Harry Parks of Rome, Pa., who died February 21, 1892.
514. Henry S., b. February 4, 1829; *
515. Henderson Knapp, b. February 22, 1832; *
516. Halla Catherine, b. September 13, 1835; died, unmarried, on February 27, 1902.
517. Helen E., b. August 5, 1838; died October 10, 1840.
518. Hester Roena, b. December 15, 1841; is living at Evans Corners, Montana. On March 1, 1866, she married Carydon E. Thayer of New York.
519. Harrison Clay, b. March 24, 1845; *

241. EZRA RUTTY ALLIS was born October 16, 1810, in Allis Hollow, Pa., moved to Rome, Pa., but soon after his marriage settled in Orwell, Pa., where he died February 14, 1885. He married about 1834 Margaret, daughter of Jacob and Thankful Wickizer of Wysox, Pa., who was born August 7, 1811, and died March 6, 1881. Their children were:

520. William Wallis, b. February 7, 1835; *
521. Jacob Harrison, b. August 7, 1837; married Phebe A. Barber, Jan. 1, 1873, and died April 12, 1908, without issue.
522. Mariam, b. May 9, 1839; married Joseph H. Allen of Rome and died March 15, 1899. Their children were Stella, b. in October, 1860; George S., b. Dec. 9, 1862 (married Cora B. Towner), and Frank, b. in April, 1871.
523. George Rutty, b. March 20, 1842; *
524. Helen, b. November 10, 1846; married George L. Forbes of Rome, September 19,1867, and they have an adopted daughter, Ellie M.
525. Frank E., b. July 15, 1854; died April 12, 1856.

245. WILLIAM NELSON ALLIS was born June 20, 1821, in Allis Hollow, Pa., and died August 28, 1892. On April 13, 1848, he married Martha Young of Danville, Pa., and settled in Rome, Bradford County, Pa., where he followed the occupation of a wagon-maker. He had one son.

526. H. D., b. December 22, 1856; *

247. WILLIAM ELLIS (ALLIS) was born February 16, 1792, in Kensington (Berlin), Conn., and died in 1875, age 83. He married on September 16, 1815, Lydia, daughter of Amos A. and Mabel (Andrus) Webster of Berlin, who was born November 29, 1791, and died on August 6, 1876, age 85 years.

William Ellis moved from Berlin to New Britain, Conn., and was a successful farmer, owning one of the oldest and best farms in the place. His nine children were:

527. Sylvender, b. September 18, 1816; *

528. Charlotte, b. May 5, 1818; was educated in Troy, N. Y., and went to Camden, S C., as a teacher. On September 1, 1846, she married James J. Huddleston of Columbus, Miss., and lived in Liberty, Mo , Warsaw, Ill., and Iowa City, Iowa., where she died November 24, 1887. Their three children were:

1. Julia Ellis, b. June 25, 1847; died, unmarried

2. Thomas Garlick, b. February 1, 1850; died January 14, 1862.

3. Katie May, b. May 15, 1853; married William Nichol and is now living in Chicago, Ill. They had a daughter, Ellis Huddleston, b. in 1889.

529. William, Jr., b. February 4, 1821; *

530. Edwin C., b. December 5, 1823; *

531. Jerusha, b. June 1, 1826; married, March 9, 1857, Josiah E. Atwood of Newington, Conn., and died May 29, 1903. Their children were:

1. Kate May, b. September 10, 1860; married Arlan P. Francis of Newington and had a daughter, Helen, b. in December, 1889.

2. Isabelle Ellis; married Geo. C Atwell of New Britain and had Ralph, Edith, Elbert, Arthur and Marjorie.

3. Elbert Webster, b. Sept. 15, 1868; married Lillian Gilbert and had two children: Rachel and Charles.

532. Jane, b. July 2, 1828; died August 23, 1837.

533. Julia, b. August 22, 1830; married Hubert L. Judd of New Britain on August 14, 1851, and died in 1886. They had six children: Julia Ellis, b in 1852, Morton, b. in 1854, Florence Bremer, b. in 1857, Edward Henry, b. in 1859, Emma Julia, b in 1860, and Morton Ellis, b. in 1864.

534. Julius, b. August 22, 1830; died May 13, 1838.

535. Henry Julius, b. May 2, 1837; *

248. JOHN ELLIS (ALLIS) was born in Kensington (Berlin), Conn., in 1793, and died July 17, 1865, in New Britain, Conn. He married on December 5, 1819, Irene, daughter of Daniel and Hannah (Bartholomew) Judd of Farmington, Conn., who was born November 13, 1793.

John Ellis moved from Berlin to New Britain, and was a successful farmer, but previously was an extensive manufacturer, owning and operating a brass foundry. His four children were:

536. Abel, b. March 2, 1821; married Matilda Henshaw, November 7, 1847, and died in New Mexico without issue.

537. Daniel, b June 2, 1822; was a soldier in the Union Army in New Mexico in 1863 and never returned.

538. Martin, b. May 22, 1826; *

539. Gustavus, b. February 15, 1828; *

266. ELISHA ALLIS was born in Huntington, Conn., November 7, 1780, and died August 10, 1825. On October 21, 1807, he married Phebe Wells. He lived at "The Landing" (now Shelton) in Huntington, and was a farmer by occupation. His children were:

540. Harriet, b. December 15, 1808; married Mr. Lee.

541. Jeanette, b. October 27, 1811; married Nathaniel Bertram and died August 25, 1837.

542. Wells, b. September 5, 1813; *

268. ISAAC ALLIS was born March 8, 1785, in Huntington, Conn., and died July 19, 1858. He married (first) Zephy Curtis, who died April 1, 1827, and (second) on July 1, 1827, Sophia, daughter of John and Esther Beers of Ansonia, Conn. She was born in August, 1807, and died December 5, 1884—an energetic, Christian woman.

Isaac Allis owned a large farm in Huntington and was a saddler and harness-maker in connection with farming. During the War of 1812 he enlisted in the Connecticut militia under William Edwards and served in April, 1814, in Bridgeport, Conn. His four children were:

By first wife:

543. Agur; married in September, 1835, Esther M., daughter of Sherman and Polly (Candee) Buckingham, who was born May 21, 1817. He was a tailor in New Haven and died December 4, 1853, without issue.

544. Edward; died in infancy.

By second wife:

545. Sylvester Beers, b. October 10, 1828; *

546. Sarah Anagusta, b. Apr. 11, 1835; married (1) Miles Beardsley and (2) John A. King, and moved to Grand Rapids.

281. ISAAC ALLIS was born in Shelburne Falls, Mass., probably about 1775, and on March 24, 1796, he married Phebe Green of that town. The absence of town records, which were lost by fire many years ago, has made it difficult to learn anything about Isaac, but the records of the First Congregational Church would seem to indicate that he had at least two children:

547. Joel, b. about 1797; *

548. Phebe, b. about 1799; no further record.

286. ROSWELL ALLIS was born May 2, 1800, and died November 17, 1854. On December 20, 1821, he married Martha Smith, who was born August 5, 1802, and after her death he is said to have married a second time. He was a farmer in Putney, Vt., and Shelburne Falls, Mass., and had three children:

549. Mary Marie, b. January 10, 1823; married (first) on September 20, 1842, Zephaniah Richmond and (second) on May 18, 1852, Joel Rugg. She lived in Canandaigua, N. Y., and Buckland and Shelburne Falls, Mass., and had the following children by her first marriage:
   1. Martha Olivia, b. June 23, 1844.
   2. Virginia, b. April 24, 1846.
   3. Caroline S., b. April 24, 1846.
   4. Mary L. Orient, b. June 26, 1848.

550 Newton R., b April 5, 1828; *

551. Rachel P., b. September 19, 1831; married on January 10, 1849, John A Dodge and died May 20, 1912, almost 81 years of age. Their children were:
   1. Larue, b. March 17, 1850.
   2. Sarah M., b, September 18, 1852.
   3. Juliette, b. August 15, 1857.
   4. William S., b. October 16, 1859.

290. WILLIAM ALLIS was born on October 25, 1796, probably in or near the town of Addison, Vermont, and died April 12, 1860, in Bridgeport, Conn. He was twice married: first, in 1821, to Nancy Pierce, who died April 28, 1840, and, second, to Martha Plumb, who died about 1880.

William Allis moved from Vermont when a young man and settled in Bridgeport, Conn., where he was a truckman by occupation. His seven children were:

By first wife:

552. Lucius Pierce, b. September 5, 1822; *

553. Emily, b. March 11, 1825; died September 11, 1825.

554. Eliza Frances, b. May 22, 1828; married (first) on June 1, 1849, David Granger and had a daughter, Emma Allis, who was born September 2, 1851. On September 22, 1857, she married (second) Samuel Cole and died August 22, 1895.

555. Mary Jane, b. August 19, 1830; married George Bennett of New Haven on May 14, 1849, and died in April, 1915, nearly 85 years of age. Their children were:
    1. Ella A., b. March 3, 1850.
    2. Mary Allis, b. October 28, 1852.
    3. Georgia L., b. April 7, 1858.

556. George Cornelius, b. March 19, 1835; *

By second wife:

557. William Edmond, b. September 13, 1841; married Harriet A., daughter of William R. Kimball of Cornish, N H., who was born July 12, 1840-1, and died on December 10, 1882. He was engaged in the hotel business in New York City until 1889 and then moved to Wethersfield, Conn., where he died September 22, 1892, leaving no children

558. Alexander, b. February 19, 1843; died on November 1, 1849.

292. NATHANIEL ALLIS was born on July 29, 1801, probably in or near the town of Addison, Vermont, and died March 13, 1884, nearly 83 years of age. He married (first) on July 14, 1824, Eveline Searle, who died June 21, 1842; (second) Sally Hamilton, in December, 1842, who died September 16, 1868; (third) in March, 1869, Elizabeth Kingsland, who died in 1898.

Nathaniel Allis was a farmer in Addison and lived there all his life. He had six children, all by his first marriage:

559. Nathaniel Oscar, b. May 1, 1825; died November 24, 1826.

560. William G., b. March 31, 1827; *

561. Edwin E., b. May 21, 1832; died February 22, 1834.

562. Edgar Augustus, b. May 21, 1832; *

563. Newton, b. February 29, 1835; died March 1, 1838.

564. Sarah Maria, b. July 15, 1840; married Ira B. Strong on October 20, 1857, and died November 1, 1890. They had the following children:
   1. Flora Allis, b December 28, 1860.
   2. Elizabeth P., b. May 31, 1863.
   3. Arthur G., b. July 24, 1870.

299. WINTHROP ALLIS was born April 1, 1785, in Colchester, Vermont, and died in June, 1842. He was first married in 1808, but the name of his wife is unknown, and in 1821-2 he married (second) Fluvia Gates, who was born April 27, 1800.

Winthrop Allis was a cabinet-maker by occupation and lived in Cleveland and St. Marys, Ohio. His fourteen children were:

By first wife:

565. Myrana, b February 9, 1809; no further record.

566. Walter W., b. March 30, 1811; no further record.

567. Whiting, b, in January, 1813; married Ann Haddick; no further record.

568. Flora, b. January 19, 1815; married Henry Woods and had Alpheus, George, Anna and Alice.

569. Frilia, b. January 18, 1817; no further record.

By second wife:

570. Nelson, b December 22, 1822; *

571. Martha, b. November 22, 1824; married Albert Crowley and died on May 7, 1880. Their children were Nettie, Elizabeth, Dora Belle, William and Nina.

572. Maryan, b December 30, 1826; died May 27, 1827.

573. O'Havet, b. February 27, 1828; married Stephen Wirthlin and died in March, 1880. Their children were Frank, Benjamin, Mary, Stephen and Joseph.

574. Lewsina, b. April 1, 1830; married Charles Young and died in June, 1911, age 81 years. Their children were Olivia and Charles W.

575. Wilson, b. October 7, 1832; died August 3, 1834.

576. Edwin Z., b. October 12, 1835; *

577. Hannah, b. January 27, 1839; married James Applegate.

578. Fluvia, b. November 17, 1840; married WIlliam Mullen and had two children, Edward and Ola Belle.

301. ORIB ALLIS was born November 1, 1794, in Colchester, Vermont, and lived there until his death. On February 21, 1816, he married Lucinda, daughter of Amos Preston and had the following children:

579. Boy, died in infancy.

580. Girl, died in infancy

581. Henry, b in 1819; died in 1820.

582. George, b. in 1820; died in 1821.

583. Lorenzo, b. July 8, 1823; *

584. Caroline, b. about 1825; died in infancy.

585. Girl, b. about 1827; died in infancy.

586. Caroline, b. in 1828; died in infancy.

587. Cordelia Ann, b. in 1830; a teacher of fine penmanship.

588. Alphonzo, b. in 1832; died, unmarried, in New Orleans, Louisiana.

589. Mary Catherine, b. in 1835; married a Mr. Robinson.

590 Edgar Sylvanus, b. in 1837; no further record.

591. Girl, b. about 1839; died in infancy.

592. Julia Paulina, b. in 1842; married a Mr. Patton.

302. LEONARD ALLIS was born January 24, 1786, in Coventry, N. Y. He was twice married: first, in 1814, to Roxey Converse, who was born September 7, 1796, and died May 29, 1833; second, to Polly Risley, who was born February 15, 1798, and died January 14, 1887, age 88 years.

Leonard Allis was a farmer in Coventry for many years, and was also proprietor of a hotel in that town. Afterwards he moved to Ellisburg, Pennsylvania, where he died December 28, 1844. He had four children by his first wife:

593. Calvin Converse, b. February 20, 1815; *

594. Anna, b. March 26, 1817; married on November 24, 1842, Rev. Albert Guy of Coventry, N. Y., and died September 30, 1854. They had a daughter, Anna, who was born on August 16, 1843, and married Dr. Benjamin F. Beardsley of Hartford, Conn.

595 Frances M., b March 15, 1830; is unmarried and lives in Hartford, Conn., with her niece, Mrs. B. F. Beardsley.

596. Spencer Franklin, b. April 24, 1835; *

304. WILLIAM ALLIS was born September 15, 1793, in Coventry, New York. He was a farmer there for many years, but eventually moved to Ohio and settled near the town of Elyria, where he lived until his death on October 31, 1864. In 1817 he married Betsey Wilson and their five children were:

597. Edward, b. May 20, 1818; *

598. Ira, b. February 4, 1821; died, unmarried.

599. Leonard, b. April 27, 1823; *

600. Franklin, b July 8, 1830; married and had one child, but detail information is missing.

601. Angeline, b. January 21, 1836; married Elbert Haring of Elyria, Ohio, on October 7, 1868, and had two children, Carleton Angelo and Anna Elberta.

SEVENTH GENERATION

310. MILTON ALLIS was born October 18, 1802, and died January 1, 1879. He was twice married, (first) on February 22, 1837, to Mary Smith, who was born on July 22, 1816, and died August 31, 1871, and (second) in March, 1875, to Mrs. Esther Stone.

Milton Allis moved from Conway, Mass., to New York State when a young man. His younger days were spent on the Erie Canal, and after learning how to manage a boat he ran a packet for several years. Afterwards he worked at farming in Orleans County, New York, for a few years, and in 1852 settled on an eighty-acre farm in

Rome, New York, where he spent the remainder of his life. His seven children were:

602. Vinal, b. December 14, 1837; died March 27, 1850.

603. Lydia, b. May 25, 1840; married George McConnell on April 10, 1860, and had two children, Eli and Ida.

604. Joel Howland, b. January 12, 1843; married on May 14, 1885, Jennie E. Ousterhout. He is a farmer by occupation and both he and wife are living at this time (1916).

605. Hannah Cordelia, b. April 24, 1845; married Oscar Gilbert, February 25, 1868, and died March 18, 1910. They had two children:

1. Charles M., b. October 16, 1869; married Ida Conrad on November 18, 1891, and had Vera M., b. June 2, 1897, and Gladys M., b. November 12, 1901.

2. Bertha A., b. October 16, 1875; married Charles H. Getter on November 7, 1896, and had Gertrude, b. October 29, 1897, Arthur C., b. March 21, 1902, and Florence L., b. January 4, 1905.

606. Ansel, b. April 10, 1848; was a soldier in the Union army during the Civil War and died July 15, 1866, soon after returning home from the army.

607. Sarah Marie, b. April 27, 1850; married Stephen Pringle on August 16, 1881, and died December 21, 1897. Their two children were Clarence, b. April 2, 1885, and Don, b. July 17, 1891.

608. Lyman Newell, b. August 31, 1853; *

311. ASA ALLIS was born January 6, 1805, and died January 20, 1877. On September 15, 1831, he married Sally Amelia Hall, who was born June 18, 1814, and died July 25, 1892. He was a farmer in Chili Station, N. Y., and had five children:

609. Cornelia Emeline, b. June 30, 1832; married Barney D. Deuel on January 1, 1855, and died June 18, 1867. Their children were:

1. Clarence Allis, b. August 12, 1852; married Fannie Smith on March 6, 1878, and lives in Chili, N. Y. They had six children: (1) Clare Joseph, b. August 11, 1879; (2) John Yale, b. August 8, 1881; (3) Celia Cornelia, b. May 15, 1884; (4) Ray Hart, b Feb. 19, 1889; (5) Grace Phoebe, b. March 19, 1891; Eldon Barney, b. September 22, 1895.

2. Viola Amelia, b May 16, 1865; unmarried.

610. Melvin Hall, b July 12, 1834; married in 1866 Thankful H. McClure and died September 11, 1892, without issue.

611. Sarah Sophia, b October 9, 1837; died May 27, 1902. On February 4, 1874, he married Chauncey Smith and had a son, Percy Allis, who was born August 19, 1878. In September, 1902, Percy A Smith married Kathryn Roberts and their two children were Ernest, b. July 21, 1903, and Dorothy, b October 8, 1911.

612. Madison, b. about 1841; died April 16, 1841.

613. Melvira, b. about 1850; died January 14, 1850.

317. VINAL ALLIS was born on April 16, 1817, and died June 8, 1865. On May 20, 1847, he married Maryetta, daughter of Joseph and Mary (Crittenden) Lee, who was born January 30, 1815, and died May 19, 1875. He was a farmer by occupation, and had the following children:

614. Edward M., b. May 29, 1849; died September 4, 1849.

615. Joel, b. October 10, 1851; *

616. Josephine, b. October 10, 1851; married Edwin Farr on November 17, 1880, and is living in Canastota, N. Y.

617. Emma Jane, b. May 4, 1855; married Martin F. Fancher on March 17, 1875, and had two children:

1. Amy, b. May 29, 1876; married George Bloss and died March 22, 1913, leaving a daughter, Ruby, who was born in March, 1903.

2. Claude, b. about 1878; married Gladys Pierson.

319. ISRAEL DICKINSON ALLIS was born July 23, 1793, in Conway, Mass., and died October 18, 1869. In 1820 he married Patty Butler, who was born in 1797, and died March 24, 1876. He was a farmer in Conway and Hawley, Mass., and had four children:

618. Thomas L., b. December 3, 1821; *

619. Solomon D., b. January 24, 1825; *

620. Martha, b. in 1827; died, unmarried, in 1845.

621. Mary, b. February 28, 1835; married Samuel Wilder on March 3, 1853, and had three children:

1. Laura, b. September 5, 1855.

2. Charles, b February 18, 1860; married Adelia Hartwell, who was born August 28, 1861.

3. Henry, b. April 12, 1867; married Josie Farrington and had seven children: Samuel Alden, b. February 16, 1896, Charles Henry, b. February 14, 1897, Jessie F., b. March 8, 1898, William Dean, b. February 5, 1902, Mary D., b. June 4, 1906, Arthur F., b. June 21, 1908, and Lydia C., b. February 23, 1910.

323. SAMUEL ALLIS, born September 28, 1805, in Conway, Mass., was apprenticed to learn the trade of a saddle and harnessmaker when 17 years old and remained in Conway until he became of age. From Conway he went to Williamstown, Mass., and worked at his trade six months, and then went to Troy and Ithaca, N. Y. While in Ithaca, Samuel Allis became interested in Christian work in the Presbyterian Church, and when the church decided to establish a mission among the Indians in the West, under the patronage of the American Board of Commissioners of Foreign Missions, he determined to cast in his lot with Rev. John Dunbar and Rev. Samuel Parker.

The party left Ithaca in the spring of 1834, their destination being the Flat Head or Nez Perce Indians, west of the Rocky Mountains. They went by way of the Erie Canal and Lake Erie, and crossed Ohio by stage, eventually arriving at St. Louis, Missouri. There they found that the party of traders they were to accompany to the mountains had already gone, and learning of a mission among the Pawnee Indians nearby decided to go there for a time, but before joining the Pawnees they spent several months among the missions of the Kickapoos, Shawnees and Delawares at Fort Leavenworth, Kansas, learning the Indian characters, customs and manners.

The missionaries then went on to Bellevue, Nebraska, which was the government agency for the Omahas, Otoes and Pawnees. There they met the agent, in council with the Pawnees, and made known their object. The Indians were much pleased to learn that the missionaries were to come among them to teach them the truth about the "Great Spirit", and in accordance with the desire of the Pawnee chiefs it was deemed best to divide the missionaries among the different bands. The missionaries, therefore, separated and Samuel Allis went with the Loup or Wolf Pawnees.

During his trip with the Indians back to their village he had his first experience of sleeping upon the ground. The second morning after leaving Bellevue he was awakened at about three o'clock in the morning by the Indians hurrying to saddle up and leave camp, as the prairies were on fire. Quoting from his own words:

SAMUEL ALLIS

"This was the first sight of the kind I ever witnessed, and I could see by their movements that we were in danger. All were hurrying to pack their ponies, and the reader can readily imagine something of the fix I was in, for I had two horses, a saddle and a pack horse, and was as awkward in packing a horse as a monkey would be running a threshing machine, but I soon learned the art perfectly. My host was true to me in assisting me to get away and deputized two young Indians to assist me, and even held my stirrups as if I had been General Sherman or some other noted general. They have often talked and laughed at my first prairie experience, but I have since for six months at a time slept on the ground without seeing a white man's house. When I was once mounted I had to thank the good Lord for my deliverance. On that same trip another party was surrounded by the fire and four Indians and several horses burned to death. I have several times since then been exposed to prairie fires and sometimes had to fight to my utmost ability."

Upon arriving at the Indian village Samuel Allis was royally entertained by the chief and other prominent men of the tribe, and if he had understood the Pawnee language he would have enjoyed himself immensely. The following days were very busy ones for him, as well as the Indians, who were making preparations for their winter hunt, and he had many new experiences. During the winter he was engaged in learning the language, hunting buffaloes with the Indians, taking lessons in cooking, drying meat, dressing robes, and other employments, and attending powwow balls, concerts and medicine feasts.

During the year 1835 the Rev. Samuel Parker and his assistants established the mission among the Nez Perce Indians, Samuel Allis deciding to remain with the Pawnees.

In the spring of 1836 reinforcements arrived from the East for the Nez Perce and Pawnee missions, among whom was Miss Emeline Palmer, who became the wife of Samuel Allis a short time afterward. She was born May 19, 1808.

At that time the Indians were about to change their location, and until they had settled in their new home (which was about 100 miles west of Bellevue and was their reservation until transferred to the Indian Territory) Mr. and Mrs. Samuel Allis stopped at Bellevue. He procured four acres of land there and built a temporary house, and on account of the hostility of the Sioux they remained in Bellevue until the spring of 1842, farming and keeping stock, when they moved out on the reservation (now Geneva) and commenced operations. He built his own house, stables, sheds and fences, and raised his own crops, and was well provided for by the winter of 1844-5, even though the preceding winter was the coldest of his experience, during which a part of his livestock was frozen to death, as well as many of the Indians and their horses.

In the summer of 1845 Samuel Allis built a schoolhouse—did all the work himself—and the following spring commenced teaching school, the Indians sending their children to him except for a period during the winter hunt, when they would leave for a few weeks. A year or two afterwards he and his family moved back to Bellevue and worked among the Otoes and Omahas until 1851, when they settled on a farm in St. Marys, Mills County, Iowa. A few years later they moved on to another farm nearby and Samuel Allis lived there until his death on December 12, 1883, age 78.

Samuel Allis was the U. S. Interpreter for John Danver's treaty with the Pawnees in August, 1856, and held the position of Government Interpreter until about the beginning of the Civil War. He lived among the Indians on the eastern border of Nebraska for nearly forty years, and during that time was exposed to many hardships, frequently without the necessities of life, and in danger of life many times. He was invariably shown kindness by the Indians with whom he was associated, and became convinced that when they learned a person and proved him to be their friend they were kind and generous. He found them to be very intelligent in spite of their numerous superstitions, and knew them to be good orators, having heard them make many speeches to the government officials from the President down, some of which would not have disgraced the walls of Congress.

Samuel Allis had the following children:

622. Otis E., b. August 7, 1837, in Bellevue; died in infanncy.

623. Henry M., b. March 20, 1839, in Bellevue; married Gussie Turner on November 18, 1888, and died December 20, 1888, without issue.

624 Martha, b. November 15, 1841, in Bellevue; married on July 4, 1872, George W. Hollins and died in Kenosha, Wis., on May 4, 1913.

625. Otis E., b. December 4, 1843, in Genoa; *

626. Harriet E., b July 15, 1849, in Bellevue; married Dr. W. R. Wall on May 26, 1872, and died September 28, 1888.

325. WILLIAM ALLIS was born August 31, 1812, in Conway, Mass., and died January 13, 1886, in Kalamazoo, Mich. He lived in Conway until about 22 years of age, then going to Auburn, N. Y. While there he met Amy Jeffries and they were married October 19, 1835. She died in Rochester, N. Y., January 4, 1903.

William Allis was a builder by occupation, but was also a vocal teacher in his younger life and taught in the country singing schools. He lived in Auburn, N. Y., for a time, later moving to Port Byron, N. Y., and Kalamazoo, Michigan, where he died. He was a broad-minded and capable man, a deacon in the church, and always glad to lend a helping hand to any in need. His four children were:

627. Jane Zelinda, b. October 14, 1840; married on June 23, 1862, Columbus Coleman of Muskegon, Mich.

628. Gardner Samuel, b. January 31, 1844; *

629. Emma Zulette, b March 30, 1849; died, unmarried, September 3, 1869.

630. Mary Luella, b. May 17, 1853; died July 21, 1854.

327. LUCIUS ALLIS was born in Conway, Mass., September 2, 1796, and died December 30, 1875, in Barre, Orleans County, N. Y., over 79 years of age. On October 6, 1825, he married Fanny A. Griswold, who was born July 16, 1803, and died June 16, 1876.

Lucius Allis lived in Conway until about 25 years of age, and then purchased a farm, all heavily wooded, in Barre, N. Y., upon which he settled. His children were:

631. Myron G., b. June 18, 1826; *

632. Lucina A., b. January 19, 1830; married Reilly M. Tinkham on July 11, 1853, and died December 1, 1907, without issue

633. Willis G., b. November 1, 1841; married (first) Hattie Raymond on December 23, 1873, who was born May 6, 1842, and died February 27, 1885; (second) Annie Smith on October 20, 1887, who was born May 4, 1842, and died March 10, 1901, (third) Julia Timmerman on March 20, 1903, who was born July 16, 1842, and died November 8, 1908. He is living in Albion, N. Y.

634. Elliot E., b. February 21, 1845; *

328. THOMAS WELLS ALLIS was born in Conway, Mass., August 28, 1798. From 16 to 21 years of age he was apprenticed to learn the trade of a tanner, currier and shoemaker, and after serving his apprenticeship he followed the occupation of shoemaking in Conway for four years. He then moved to York, Livingston County, N. Y., where he worked at his trade five years, and then went to Riga, Monroe County, N. Y., and engaged in farming, which occupation he followed the remainder of his life. After living in Riga about eight years he moved to Alabama, Genesee County, N. Y., and several years later moved to Cambridge, Lenawee County, Mich., where he died March 18, 1867.

Thomas W. Allis was twice married: (first) on May 16, 1823, to Sarah Munson, daughter of Bezaliel and Levina (Munson) Smith, who was born February 3, 1801, and died July 10, 1829; (second) on February 10, 1830, to Pamelia, daughter of Roswell and Pamelia (Dickinson)

Root, who was born November 22, 1800, and died in Cambridge, Mich., August 25, 1873. His children were:

By first wife:

635. Solomon W., b. February 6, 1825. *

636. George R., b. April 26, 1829; *

By second wife:

637. Sarah M., b. March 24, 1831; died, unmarried, on April 1, 1862.

638. Mary Eveline, b. October 17, 1834; married Harry Gillette of Adrian, Mich., on January 22, 1878.

639. Edgar, b. February 20, 1838; died October 31, 1860.

329. JOHN DICKINSON ALLIS was born June 22, 1801, in Conway, Mass. He lived in that town all his life and was a farmer by occupation. He was a soldier in the Union Army during the Civil War, enlisting in June, 1861, and died in service on January 5, 1863.

John D. Allis was married (first), October 15, 1825, to Lydia, daughter of Bezaliel and Levina (Munson) Smith, who was born December 29, 1804, and died December 20, 1836; (second) on May 6, 1841, to Hannah Hall, who died in September, 1852; (third) on February 23, 1854, to Delia B. Taylor, who was born September 2, 1818, and died October 10, 1886. His children were:

By first wife:

640. Eliza J., b. May 1, 1827; married Solomon D. Allis (619).

641. Sally M., b. Apr. 7, 1829; married Solomon D. Allis (619).

642. Infant, b. July 3, 1831; died July 4, 1831.

643. Rufus W., b. June 21, 1834; *

644 John D., b. December 20, 1836; died in the Union Army in 1863.

By second wife:

645. Lois Stone, b. May 22, 1842; married Charles M. Smith on May 22, 1866, and died on August 26, 1874. Their children were Anna A., b. November 25, 1868, Lucelia H., b. December 6, 1872, and Belle L., b July 2, 1874.

646 Luna A., b. July 15, 1844; married E. Wellington Wood on May 22, 1866, and died on January 4, 1870.

647. Paulina A., b. November 24, 1848; married George E. Thayer in 1873 and died February 17, 1901. Their children were:

1. Luna A., b. October 9, 1874; married C. S. Tillson on September 8, 1897, and had a son, Charles Richard, b. April 22, 1899.

2. George Fred, b. July 19, 1878.

By third wife:

648. Infant, b. July 29, 1855; died in infancy.

649. Hattie A., b. September 27, 1856; died, unmarried, April 12, 1876.

650. Samuel Baxter, b. May 10, 1858; died, unmarried, November 16, 1879.

651. Mary Lincoln, b. July 1, 1861; *

331. ELIJAH ALLIS was born March 14, 1805, in Conway, Mass. He was twice married: (first) to Melissa Toby; (second) to Jane Randall, and died soon after his second marriage. He had a daughter by his first marriage, who lived only two years, and he and Melissa adopted Hettie Kellogg, who married John L. Hunt.

652. Cornelia, died at the age of two years.

334. ELIOT CLARK ALLIS was born February 13, 1816, in Conway, Mass., and died in Whately, Mass., March 10, 1874. When a young man he moved from

Conway to Whately and bought the farm originally owned by Elisha Allis, living there until his death.

Eliot C. Allis was twice married: (first) on April 7, 1841, to Alvira, daughter of Daniel and Polly (Scott) Dickinson of Whately, who was born August 28, 1821, and died August 25, 1861; (second) on June 25, 1863, to Cornelia A., daughter of Horace Johnson, who was born in 1829. His five children were:

653. Angelina, b. October 30, 1842; married Samuel A. Hall of Ashfield, Mass , on May 23, 1864, and had three children:

1. Hattie Elvira, b February 17, 1865; married Clayton C. Robbins on September 6, 1882, and had Earl Clayton, b. March 26, 1883, Alice Eleanor, b. August 1, 1885, and Ada H., b. January 13, 1895.

2. Alice D., b. February 19, 1869.

3. Leon, b. March 6, 1877.

654. Lucius, b. August 20, 1844; a soldier in the Civil War, enlisting in the 31st Regt. Mass. volunteers, and died June 23, 1865, at Mobile, Alabama.

655. Esther, b. July 27, 1846; died September 10, 1861.

656. Irving, b. January 28, 1849; *

657. Henry, b. November 4, 1855; died August 8, 1856.

335. EDWARD PARTRIDGE ALLIS was born February 8, 1819, in Conway, Mass., and died December 18, 1899, age 80 years. He lived in Conway until 1844 and then moved to Michigan, where he purchased a new farm and grew up with the country. He was a farmer all his life and was a charter member of the Madison Grange. On April 2, 1851, he married Isabel H. Jennings, who died February, 26, 1900. Their children were:

658. Elliot W., b. March 27, 1853; unmarried and is a horticulturist in Adrian, Michigan. He is also Secretary of the Lenawee County Horticultural Society and Deputy Inspector of Nurseries for the state.

659. Lucius F., b. July 11, 1857; *

660. Mary C., b. November 24, 1859; married Warren M Beal on December 15, 1897, and is living in Adrian, Mich.

336. CALEB WELLS ALLIS was born in Rhinebeck, N. Y., September 29, 1814, and died in Skaneateles, N. Y., May 25, 1897, age 83 years. He married on July 15, 1840, Latitia, daughter of Valentine and Jane Willets of Skaneateles, who was born November 25, 1818, and died January 31, 1884.

When he was four years of age his parents moved from Rhinebeck to Skaneateles and he was educated in his father's school there, after which he was clerk for a year or two in a store in Lyons, N. Y. At the age of 15 he entered the store of Richard Tallcot in Skaneateles as clerk, and held that position until taken in as partner, which event occurred before he was 21 years old. Although he lived in Syracuse for a year and in Brooklyn for about three years, he was continuously connected with mercantile life in his home town until the spring of 1885, a period of 56 years.

For over 60 years Caleb W. Allis was a representative man in his community, holding many official positions in village and town and being Supervisor during the Civil War, in 1862-3-4. He was one of the founders of the Bank of Skaneateles, organized in 1869, and acted as its cashier for some time, and he was made president in 1880. His judgment and advice were frequently sought and cheerfully given to his many friends during his life and he settled many estates. He was a member of the Orthodox Society of Friends, and in politics was first a Whig and afterwards a Republican. His three children were:

661. Emily, b. March 8, 1842; died March 21, 1843.

662. Thomas Valentine, b. May 15, 1844; *

663. Frances Julia, b. April 14, 1846; educated in the Packer Collegiate Institute, Brooklyn, N. Y She is very prominent in reform work and has been associated with Mrs. Frances E. Willard of the W. C. T. U. She has been Superintendent of the National W. C T. U. and World's Superintendent of the Y. W. C. T. U., and is at the present time honored secretary of the latter association. She has also been President of the Loyal Legion Temperance Society of New York, and is a member of other organizations of a similar nature.

On September 21, 1871, she married Willis A. Barnes, a lawyer of New York City, where they are living at this time.

339. THOMAS WELLS ALLIS was born November 1, 1798, in Hopewell, New York. On November 18, 1824, he married Elizabeth Clements of Queensbury, New York, who was born on January 18, 1805, and died February 9, 1888, in Medina, New York, age 83 years.

Thomas W. Allis settled on a farm in Murray, N. Y., about the time of his marriage, and all his children were born there, but eventually moved to Albion, N. Y., where he died November 18, 1875, age 77 years. His children were:

664. James Clements, b. August 23, 1825; *

665. Elijah Hedding, b. December 7, 1827; married (first) on March 10, 1853, Velina Chapman, who died September 15, 1889, and (second) on January 28, 1892, Sarah Jane Mosey, who is now living in Albion, N. Y.

Elijah H. Allis was a farmer in Albion for over forty years. He then engaged in the shoe business, and finally the grocery business, which he conducted for fourteen years until his death, April 23, 1904.

666. Nathan Bangs, b. January 9, 1831; *

340. OLIVER GRAVES ALLIS was born in Hopewell, N. Y., March 15, 1800, and died in Kendall, N. Y., December 23, 1848. On February 10, 1823, he married Mary Ann Beach, who was born October 12, 1803, and died September 6, 1880.

Oliver G. Allis went from Hopewell to Hartland, N. Y., when 15 years of age, and later settled upon a farm in Kendall, being one of the pioneers there. In addition to being a farmer he was a surveyor, and was a leading citizen of the town, holding all of the town offices at different times. He had a large family of children as follows:

667. Lydia Ann, b. July 8, 1824; died at the age of 18 months.

668. Martha, b. October 7, 1825; married James M. Chaplin on December 22, 1841, and died September 16, 1889. They had three children, Mary, Oliver and Orson.

669. Lydia, b. March 6, 1827; married Edwin Hoxie and had Marian, Ida and John. She died in 1908 in Pasadena.

670. Dimmis, b. April 5, 1829; died, unmarried, in 1856-7.

671. Hulda, b. May 4, 1830; died, unmarried.

672. Mary, b. January 12, 1832; married Myron Webster of Kendall Mills, N. Y., and had two children, Rome and Orson.

673. Orson, b. April 25, 1833; married Emaline A. Gould on May 1, 1870, and adopted a child, naming her Eva Allis, who is now living in Jamestown, N. Y. Orson Allis was a merchant in Corry, Pa., and died November 15, 1900, and Emaline died February 11, 1902.

674. Oliver, b. January 29, 1835; died, unmarried.

675. Olive, b. February 29, 1837; married Byron Aylsworth and had two daughters.

676. Elizabeth, b. October 1, 1838; married Emerson Rogers and had two children. She died July 21, 1865.

677. Sarah, b. June 27, 1841; is living in Tidioute, Pa. She married George Hastings on March 11, 1861, and had the following children:

1. Adelbert, b. September 23, 1863; is married and has one son.

2. Lucinda, b. October 25, 1866; married William Turner and has one daughter.

3. Mary A., b. May 5, 1870.

4. Edwin C., b. November 15, 1875.

5. George D., b. May 4, 1880; is married and has four children.

6 Sarah Allis, b. February 15, 1887.

343. JOHN ALLIS was born about 1810 in Wisdom, Mass. In 1840 he married Candace Wolcott and died on September 10, 1868, age 58 years. He lived in Deerfield, Mass., and was a farmer by occupation. His children were:

678. William H., b. July 5, 1841; died June 14, 1909.

679. Sarah A., b. August 27, 1844; died September 2, 1904.

680. Philip W., b July 21, 1848; died May 17, 1907.

352. WELLS PORTER ALLIS was born April 5, 1817, in Wilmington, Vt., and died February 14, 1886. On March 9, 1847, he married Mary A. Bowker, who

was born June 9, 1821, and died September 28, 1857. He was a cooper in Wilmington and had four children:

681. Charles F., b. February 29, 1848; *

682. Mary E., b. September 20, 1849; died August 7, 1864.

683. Martha A., b. August 20, 1851; married W. Frank Jones of West Dover, Vermont, December 14, 1886, and died December 29, 1893.

684. Henry W., b. August 10, 1857; died April 14, 1864.

355. PLINY ALLIS was born June 10, 1802, in Heath, Mass. He was twice married: (first) in 1822 to Sophronia, daughter of Miner Fink, who died March 31, 1870; (second) on August 10, 1872, to widow Mary Smith of New Haven, Conn.

Pliny Allis remained in Heath until about 1828, when he moved to Andover, N. Y., but eventually returned to Massachusetts, where he remained until his death. His children, all by his first marriage, were:

685. Albert, b September 14, 1823; died August 8, 1848.

686. Charles, b. February 16, 1825; *

687. Lucinda, b. May 10, 1827; married Simeon Peck and had a son, William.

688 Eliza, b. November 7, 1829; married Michael W. Taintor of Andover on January 21, 1851.

689. Martha, b. October 13, 1831; married Alonzo May.

358. SILAS ALLIS was born July 23, 1808, in Heath, Mass. He was a farmer by occupation, and moved from Heath to Almond, N. Y., but finally settled in Mansfield, Pa., where he died June 19, 1875. He was twice married: (first) about 1834 to Mary Ann Sweet,

who was born August 28, 1811, and died in March, 1851; (second) on June 24, 1853, to Sabra Richmond of Rutland Township, Pa., who died July 31, 1890. His four children were:

By first wife:

690. Marcelia A, b June 29, 1835; married Lorenzo D. Collins and died August 3, 1900.

691. Vienna Alice, b. August 16, 1838; died January 21, 1907. On December 31, 1854, she married Lorenzo W. Collins of Andover, New York, and had the following children: Freemont N., b. August 26, 1856; Horace C., b. January 9, 1858; Alice M., b. November 27, 1860; Converse, b. November 14, 1862; William, b. May 24, 1865; Mary Ann, b. May 30, 1870; Bessie May, b. August 22, 1882.

By second wife:

692. Mahalia, b. July 16, 1856; no further record.

693. George, b. May 14, 1858; *

365. HENRY DEARBORN ALLIS was born May 15, 1813, in Conway, Mass., and died April 9, 1893, in Evansville, Ind., age 80 years. He went West with a peddler's wagon when he was a young man and settled in Evansville in 1835, where he married, in May, 1841, Eliza Bingham of Baltimore, Md., who died in 1894. His children were:

694. Girl, b. about 1842; died the same year.

695. Henry G., b. about 1844; died in 1849.

696. Margarette, b. in September, 1846; married Mr. Jensen in October, 1869, and died in September, 1912. Their children were Dearborn, b. in July, 1871, and Adelaide, b. in October, 1877.

697. Adelaide, b. in February, 1849; is unmarried and lives in Evansviile, Indiana.

698. Charles C., b. in May, 1851; *

699. Byron B., b. in 1853; died in 1857.

700. Harrison F., b in September, 1855; unmarried and is living in Evansville.

701. John B., b. in September, 1857; unmarried and is living in Evansville.

702. Mary C., b in 1860; died in 1861.

379. SAMUEL ALLIS was born August 7, 1810, in Pittsfield, Mass. In 1841 he married Elizabeth, daughter of Russell and Jerusha (Curtis) Smith, who was born about 1819 and died January 24, 1907. He was a farmer by occupation and about the time of his marriage moved from Pittsfield and settled in Canaan, Columbia County, N. Y., where he died October 1, 1894, age 84 years. His children were:

703. Harriet Elizabeth, b. April 10, 1842; is living in Springfield, Mass. On February 13, 1861, she married Francis A. Russell of Canaan, N. Y., and had a daughter, Amelia Elizabeth, who married Frank Ellsworth and is living in Springfield.

704. Smith, b. about 1844; was a Union soldier in the Civil War and died in service.

705. Esther, b. about 1846; married John H. New of Ghent, N. Y., and died about 1875. They had one daughter, Kathryne, who married Smith D. Niver and had Alicia and John D , and is now living in Cohoes, N. Y.

706. Lucy, b March 16, 1848; married Amos G. Myers, May 23, 1867, and had four children:

1. Leon Justin, b. March 18, 1869.
2. Esther Cordelia, b. April 18, 1875.
3. Chester Goodwin, b. April 18, 1875; died July, 1875.
4. Ruby May, b. May 4, 1889.

707. Justin R., b. October 12, 1852; *

380. LUCIUS ALLIS was born August 29, 1817, in Plainfield, Mass. When he was 17 years of age his parents moved from Plainfield to Chatham, Ohio, and in 1837 he married Eliza Sutliff, who died April 11, 1911, age 92 years. He was a farmer in Chatham for several years and then moved to Michigan and settled in Hillsdale, where he died May 6, 1873. His children were:

708. L. A., b. May 27, 1844; *

709. William J., b. January 6, 1850; is a doctor in Hillsdale, Mich., and is unmarried.

384. JUSTIN ALLIS was born January 16, 1826, in Plainfield, Mass., and lived there until eight years of age. His parents then moved to Chatham, Ohio, and he lived there until about the time of his marriage to Janet Blake, when he settled on a farm in Garnett, Kansas. He died in March, 1903, leaving one son:

710. Burton, b. in August, 1854; is unmarried and lives on the farm in Garnett

386. ELISHA ALLIS was born October 30, 1829, in Plainfield, Mass., and lived there until five years of age, at which time his parents moved to Chatham, Ohio. On September 10, 1851, he married Amanda Palmer and was a farmer in Chatham until his death, July 29, 1902. His children were:

711. Lee, b. April 30, 1856; married (first) Cora Rogers and (second) in January, 1882, Alice Brainard, and died September 7, 1907, without issue.

712. Mary, b. in 1860; married a Mr. Kinney and died soon afterward.

713 Dora, b May 18, 1864; married Joseph Seabold of Akron, Ohio, on December 26, 1890, and died January 26, 1915, without issue.

714. George, b. May 30, 1871; married (first) Jessie Blanchard on March 22, 1895, and (second) Julia Horton on January 1, 1899, and is living in Lodi, Ohio.

715. Verne, b. March 27, 1878; *

392. ALONZO ALLIS was born July 22, 1844, in Chatham, Ohio. On January 16, 1867, he married Cynthia Packard and is a farmer in Chatham. His seven children were:

716. Luella Orpha, b. March 29, 1868; living, unmarried, in Chatham, Ohio.

717. Minnie Emilia, b. November 23, 1869; living in Chatham. On November 29, 1899, she married Rudolph R. Hartman and had a son, Clayton Allis, who was born on December 28, 1903.

718. Roy Wesley, b. July 20, 1872; *

719. Charles Leslie, b. October 29, 1873. *

720 Edith Alice, b. May 22, 1875; married on May 3, 1905, Thomas W. Brinker and is living in Spencer, Ohio.

721. Frank Winslow, b. January 22, 1877; married Effa E. Frank on November 23, 1910, and is now living in Medina, Ohio.

722. Clara Belle, b. November 2, 1882; is living, unmarried, in Chatham.

399. ANDREW S. ALLIS was born September 1, 1821, in Brookfield, Vt. On July 19, 1854, he married Laura M. Walbridge, who was born January 20, 1834, and moved on to his grandfather's farm near Brookfield, where he remained until his death on July 26, 1894.

Mrs. Allis is still living on the farm with her son, Egbert Horace Allis, and is active and in good health at the age of 82 years.

Andrew S. Allis was an extensive farmer and raiser of high grade stock. He was a man of strict integrity, devoted to what he considered right, and was a leader in the town and church, holding nearly every office in both. He was kind and generous, of an even temper, and his judgment was excellent. His three children were:

723. Gertrude Maria, b. March 21, 1857; married on January 15, 1885, Prof. Audubon L Hardy of St. Johnsbury, Vt., and Amherst, Mass., and is living in Amherst. Their four children were:

1. Robert Allis, b. May 19, 1888; a graduate of Amherst College (1910), University of New York, and School of Commerce & Finance (1916).

2. Milton Audubon, b August 21, 1890; Amherst College (1913).

3. Paul Wallace, b. April 8, 1892; Amherst (1914).

4. Donald Egbert, b. Dec. 4, 1893; Amherst (1916).

724. Wallace Steele, b August 7, 1859; *

725. Egbert Horace, b. August 23, 1868; *

401. OBADIAH DICKINSON ALLIS was born July 27, 1825, in Brookfield, Vt. He attended Andover Theological Seminary, and after graduation married on December 8, 1853, Ann Eliza, daughter of Daniel and Aurelia (Skinner) Colt of Brookfield.

For three years after his marriage he taught school, first in Chelsea, Vt., and afterwards in Topsfield, Mass. He next accepted the pastorate of a church in Randolph, Vt., for a year, and then went to West Randolph (now Randolph) as pastor of the First Congregational Church, which position he held until within a short time of his death on June 26, 1866, at Dansville, N. Y., where he had gone for his health. His widow died March 21, 1869. Their children were:

726. Fortes Henry, b. December 8, 1854; married Anna Morton Yale on January 23, 1883. He was for many years a merchant in New Britain, Conn., but is now engaged in business in Haverhill, Mass.

727. Watson Colt, b. June 15, 1857; married Mary E. Trofton in 1883, who died in 1885. He is a teacher in San Francisco, Cal., at this writing.

728. Terence Skinner, b May 28, 1860; *

729. May Eliza, b. August 10, 1861; died June 3, 1879.

402. ELISHA ALLIS was born in Brookfield, Vt., September 23, 1828, and died January 20, 1881. He married (first) Harriet Murphy, April 5, 1853, who died in July, 1863, and (second) Fannie Matthews, May 10, 1859. He was a farmer and teacher in Brookfield and his children were:

By first marriage:

730. Watson Smith, b. about 1854; died in infancy.

By second marriage:

731. Girl, b. about 1860; died in intancy.

732. Leon Elisha, b. June 11, 1863; *

405. WILLIAM DICKINSON ALLIS was born November 30, 1818, in Brookfield, Vt. He lived there until soon after his mother's death, when he and his father left Vermont for western New York, taking the overland journey by way of Norwich, Conn., and eventually arrived in Holley, N. Y., after a trip filled with many experiences.

Mr. Allis was educated in the schools of Holley, Clarkson, Gaines and Brockport, N. Y., with a four-year course at Williams College, fitting himself to become a teacher. He left Holley for Rochester, N. Y., and was a teacher there for many years. He was the first principal of old school No. 6 and the last principal of old school No. 1 (replaced by the high school). For over 30 years he was connected with the Rochester Paper Company and was a member of the Veteran Grays. He died on July 23, 1904, age 86 years.

On July 7, 1847, he married Aurelia R., daughter of James and Mary Jones, who was born January 29, 1827, and died April 28, 1905. Their children were:

733. Chester Dewey, b September 30, 1848; *

734. James William, b. February 9, 1853; *

735. Edward Irving, b. February 9, 1857; died Feb. 28, 1887.

736. Irving Jones, b. August 20, 1859; died March 10, 1870.

737. Lena Elizabeth, b December 18, 1861; married Revere H. Herrold on August 10, 1887, and lives in Chicago, Ill.

408. ELISHA ALLIS was born in Holley, N. Y., December 8, 1832, and died in Easton, Pa., November 30, 1893. He studied law at Lafayette College, Easton, graduating in June, 1855, was admitted to the bar in 1857, and took up the practice of his profession in Easton. On December 13, 1860, he married Sarah B., daughter of George Packer of Harrisburg, Pa. (then governor of the state), who was born December 18, 1836, and now lives in Easton.

Mr. Allis was engaged in the practice of law in Easton for 36 years and also held the position of Assistant Supreme Court Reporter of Pennsylvania. The following is quoted

ELISHA ALLIS

from the resolutions adopted by the bar after his death:

"Resolved, that during his long career as an attorney he was a most patient and laborious student of the law; that his services were highly valued and sought as a master in chancery, as a counselor and an advocate; that he was pleasing and agreeable in his intercourse with his brother members of the bar; courteous and gentlemanly, punctual in his appointments, and a warm and constant friend; that in his relations with his clients his advice was safe and his judgment excellent; that in his relations with the court he was urbane and faithful; and as an advocate he was persuasive and forceful."

Elisha Allis had the following children:

738. Mary Packer, b. December 29, 1862; died Sept. 4, 1864.

739. Fanny Jones, b. November 6, 1865; died Feb. 22, 1899.

740. Eleanor Packer, b. April 17, 1869; is living in Easton.

741. Elizabeth Huntington, b. November 24, 1872; married on June 26, 1895, Orrin Serfrass of Easton and they had four children, William Allis, Sarah Packer, Elizabeth Huntington and Margaret, of whom the first two are living.

742. William F. Packer, b. January 26, 1875; *

409. SAMUEL JONES ALLIS was born August 17, 1834, in Holley, N. Y., and died January 20, 1915, in Erie, Pa. He went to Westfield, N. Y., with his parents when eight years of age and was educated in the Westfield Academy, after which he taught school in nearby towns for three successive winters. For a number of years he was engaged in the manufacture of agricultural implements in Westfield and was later engaged in the mercantile trade. In the early days of the grape industry he went to Harbour Creek, Erie County, Pa., where he remained for a few years, but in 1872 he moved to East Mill Creek (near Erie), and pur-

chased a part of the Scouller farm, upon which he spent his remaining years. He was much interested in public affairs and was a member of the Park Presbyterian Church.

On March 25, 1875, he married Frances O. Morton, who is now living in Erie. Their children were:

743. Harriet Elizabeth, b. February 17, 1876; is unmarried and lives in Erie, Pa.

744. William Alfred, b. September 22, 1877; is unmarried and Assistant Cashier of the Second National Bank of Erie.

745. Mary Belle, b. November 19, 1879; married on June 10, 1903, Wesley B Branfield of Erie.

410. OSCAR HUNTINGTON ALLIS was born September 9, 1836, in Holley, N. Y. On October 24, 1877, he married Julia, daughter of Judge Oswald and Cornelia (Hart) Thompson, who died April 15, 1912.

Mr. Allis studied at Lafayette College, Easton, Pa., and took his A. B. in regular course in June, 1864. In 1866 he received the degree of M. D. from the Jefferson Medical College and settled in Philadelphia as a physician and surgeon. He served as clinical aid to Professor Gross in surgical clinic, and was afterward surgeon to the Jefferson College Hospital and lecturer on orthopedic surgery; also surgeon in the Howard Hospital and Presbyterian Hospital. The Gross prize of $1,000, which was for the best article upon any surgical topic by any surgeon in the United States, was awarded to him for an essay on the hip. He was twice Mutter lecturer at the College of Physicians, and in 1913 delivered the Lane Lectures at the Cooper Medical College (now Medical Department of Leland Stanford, Jr., Univer-

OSCAR HUNTINGTON ALLIS

sity) of San Francisco, Cal. He is now living in Philadelphia and has two children:

746. Mary Elizabeth, b. August 20, 1878; is a graduate of Bryn Mawr College and lives, unmarried, in Philadelphia.

747. Oswald Thompson, b. September 9, 1880; is instuctor in Semitic Philology in Princeton Theological Seminary. He received the degree of B A from the University of Pennsylvania in 1901; B. D., Princeton Theological Seminary, 1905; M. A., Princeton University, 1905; Ph. D., University of Berlin, 1913; and was ordained into the Philadelphia Presbytery in May, 1914.

412. CHARLES FREDERICK ALLIS was born April 25, 1843, in Westfield, N. Y. His business career began in 1863, when he engaged in the banking business in his home town. The winter of 1864-65 was spent in Hartford, Conn., as chief clerk in a mustering and disbursing office of the United States government, and the following April he went to Northeast, Pa., and entered the First National Bank.

On February 1, 1866, Charles F. Allis left Northeast and accepted the tellership of the Second National Bank of Erie, Pa. He has since then been continuously connected with the Second National Bank of Erie, a period of over fifty years, during which time he has risen from the position of teller to that of vice-president. On May 6, 1868, he married Mary L. Scouller of Northeast, and both he and his wife are living in Erie, their address being 247 West 9th Street. Their children were:

748. Frederick Scouller, b April 18, 1871; *

749. Charles Edward, b. January 3, 1877; died Dec. 19, 1877.

413. SALMON WHITE ALLIS was born November 27, 1801, in Whately, Mass., and died September 18, 1868. On May 24, 1824, he married Emily W., daughter of David and Sarah (Allis) Stockbridge of Whately, who was born January 10, 1803. After his death she married (second) Hon. E. T. Foote in 1869, and (third) on January 30, 1879, Gen. Joseph Colton, and died December 10, 1887, age 84 years.

Salmon W. Allis was for a time in trade in Whately, but later he kept for a number of years the Tontine Hotel in New Haven, Conn. His three children were:

750. Henry White, b. in 1825; died on March 1, 1842, while a student at Yale University.

751. Frances E., b. in 1831; died February 7, 1849.

752. Gertrude, b. in 1835; married William A. Browning and died March 1, 1858.

414. JOSIAH ALLIS was born July 17, 1803, in Whately, Mass., and died May 23, 1866. On April 13, 1826, he married Eliza, daughter of Ebenezer White of Hatfield, Mass., who was born in 1801 and died August 9, 1866.

Josiah Allis lived with his parents on their large farm consisting of over 100 acres of fine meadow land, and was one of the best equipped business men in Whately. He entered into several different manufacturing operations, was a director of the Conway and Hampshire County Banks, also in an insurance company, and died just at the time when his plans were maturing. In politics he was a democrat, but fought shy of town offices, although he was a delegate to revise the constitution of Massachusetts. He left a large estate. His children were:

753. Justin Wright Clark, b. March 31, 1827; died, unmarried, January 31, 1882.

754. Silas Dickinson White, b. December 11, 1828; died, unmarried, July 30-1, 1902. He was a farmer in Whately for many years and was prominent in town affairs, holding different public offices, and served in the Legislature in 1883. He also lived in New York City for a time.

755. Mary Eliza White, b. September 29, 1830; died, unmarried, November 11, 1887.

756. Lewis Edward Sikes, b. July 14, 1832; died April 7, 1860.

757. Edmond Bridges, b. July 31, 1834; died February 17, 1835.

758 Edmond Bridges, b. December 11, 1835; graduated from Yale University in 1859 but died, unmarried, on October 12, 1861.

418. JERRY ALLIS was born in Prattsburg, N. Y., September 27, 1811, and died there December 23, 1888. He was twice married: (first) to Christina Quackenbush on September 3, 1834, who died December 25, 1854, and (second) to Ann Eliza Smith on September 3, 1855, who died March 25, 1869. He was a farmer by occupation and had the following children:

759. Horace H., b. October 6, 1840; died February 18, 1842.

760. Abram Q., b. November 4, 1843; *

761 Mary Alida, b. August 10, 1848; married J. E. Kilpatrick on November 25, 1879, and is living in Prattsburg, N. Y.

419. HORACE BULL ALLIS was born October 18, 1813, in Prattsburg, N. Y. When he was about 18 years of age he went to Arkansas, where he was for several

years a civil engineer in the employ of the U. S. government, making surveys for the Land Department and establishing the county and township lines. While engaged in this work he met Martha Cartwright Atkins, youngest daughter of George W. Atkins, and after a short courtship they were married December 18, 1839. She was born August 1, 1822, in Stewart County, Tenn., and died October 27, 1891, in Little Rock, Ark.

After several years as a government surveyor Mr. Allis engaged in the lumber and milling industries, and was a prominent citizen. In politics he was a Whig, and was a member of the Arkansas Legislature and Speaker of the House of Representatives. He was a Union man during the Civil War and was a delegate to the Baltimore Convention that nominated Lincoln for the second term, casting the vote of Arkansas for Lincoln. He died October 2, 1868, at Pine Bluff, Ark. His children were:

762 Emily Dianthe, b. January 28, 1841; married Dr. David S. Mills on June 30, 1863, and died July 5, 1875, leaving no children.

763. Josiah Pinckney, b. February 17, 1843; died Dec. 28, 1862.

764 George Bascom, b. November 9, 1845; *

765. Martha Lemira, b. February 10, 1850; died May 27, 1851.

766. Horace Green, b. February 3, 1855; *

421. JOSIAH ALLIS was born in Prattsburg, N. Y., on July 18, 1817, but eventually moved to Louisville, Ky., where he died. On June 17, 1843, he married N. J. Cookingham and had one daughter:

767 Mary E., b. July 10, 1844; died November 17, 1864.

425. HENRY E. ALLIS was born December 25, 1826, in Prattsburg, N, Y., and died there May 13, 1913, age 86 years. On January 26, 1860, he married Charlotte Jane Holcomb, and was a farmer in Prattsburg. His children were:

768. Addie L., b. March 4, 1861; married (first) Charles S. Burns on January 23, 1883, and (second) George M. Wilhelm, and is living in Prattsburg.

769. Louis P., b. August 6, 1865; married Caddie B. Terry on January 23, 1888, and is a farmer in Prattsburg.

770. Frank Holcomb, b. August 8, 1867; *

429. ELIJAH ALLIS was born June 19, 1820, in Prattsburg, N. Y., and died April 27, 1901, in Ames, Iowa, age 81 years. On June 4, 1861, he married Emily O., daughter of Simeon and Eliza Hayes, who was born in Prattsburg on June 11, 1832, and died in Ames, Iowa, on October 19, 1901.

Elijah Allis lived on the old home site in Prattsburg and was for several years postmaster of that town. His children were:

771. Lizzie May, b. May 28, 1863; *

772. Charles Henry Hayes, b. May 23, 1865; married Libbie M. Hagaman on July 23, 1889, and died November 14, 1889, in Corning, N. Y., without issue.

773. Florence Fay, b. May 28, 1868; died December 2, 1873.

430. JOHN ALLIS was born April 7, 1823, in Prattsburg, N. Y. On May 22, 1853, he married Mary Deming and settled in Chicago, Ill., where he was a railroad agent for many years, traveling extensively in the

West. On April 20, 1860, his wife, Mary, died and he married (second) on October 7, 1862, Ann Eliza Rosenkranz. They lived in Chicago until 1890, at which time they moved to Sonora, N. Y., and John Allis died there on November 30, 1895. He had three children by his first wife as follows:

774. Gertrude, b. October 7, 1856; married J. Barnes on October 16, 1880, and had a daughter, Gertrude A., who was born November 3, 1899. On November 13, 1909, she married (second) George Rosenkranz and is living in Hammondsport, N. Y.

775. Frank D., b. about 1858; died in infancy.

776. Lottie, b. about 1860; died in infancy.

434. EDWARD PHELPS ALLIS was born May 12, 1824, in Cazenovia, N. Y. He graduated from Union College, Schenectady, N. Y., in 1845, his education having been with a view to the practice of law, but he decided in favor of an active business life and in 1846 went West, locating in Milwaukee, Wis., where he opened a leather store in connection with William Allen, under the firm name of Allis & Allen. He remained in that business until 1854 and was very successful, building in the meantime some large tanneries at Two Rivers, Wis., of which he was the active managing director.

Edward P. Allis next engaged in the banking and real estate business with John P. McGregor. In 1861 he, with Mr. McGregor and C. D. Nash, purchased the iron foundry of Decker & Seville of Milwaukee and formed the Reliance Iron Works, being made manager. Within two

EDWARD PHELPS ALLIS

years he acquired the interests of the other two gentlemen and, retiring from the banking business, gave his full time to the new venture. From that time until his death on April 2, 1889, he was sole proprietor of the E. P. Allis Company, which became one of the largest manufacturing plants of its kind in the world.

From a moderate beginning Mr. Allis enlarged and extended the original Reliance Works until the buildings covered three city blocks, and he was the life and moving spirit of the immense industrial establishment he created. Starting with a business of $32,000 a year, with twenty employes and a payroll of $13,000, the enterprise broadened under his management into a business of $3,000,000 a year, with between 1200 and 1500 employes and a payroll of over $700,000. Those iron works were the first in the country to make roller mills for the making of flour by the roller process, and were also prominent in the manufacture of steam engines, saw mill machinery, mining machinery and heavy pumping machinery. Their products were sent to all parts of the world, including Cuba, Mexico, South America, Europe, Japan, Australia, and Sandwich Islands.

The turning point in the life of the old Reliance Works came in 1869, when the city of Milwaukee voted to erect and install its own waterworks and advertised for piping and machinery. Bids came in for piping from all over the country and nobody dreamed of Mr. Allis bidding on the work as his foundry was not equipped for the making of pipe, but when the bids were opened it was found that he had secured the contract. Of course the first thing to be done was to build a pipe shop, and in four months from the date of signing the contract the shop was completed and the first casting made, and from that time on the goods were made and delivered as fast as human skill could turn them out. He also secured the contract for the pumps and engines, and the machinery which he made and installed for the city of Milwaukee is an everlasting monument to his memory. That work brought an immense amount of engine work to the company, causing extended enlargements and improvements in the property, and the business was given such an impetus that very soon the Reliance Works of E. P. Allis became the largest machine shop in the West.

For nearly thirty years he gave to the great work of his life all that could be given by tireless industry, unflagging energy and persevering determination. Besides the Reliance Works he owned and operated the large Bay State Works in Milwaukee, a foundry on Bay Street, and rented and operated another foundry in the same city.

Mr. Allis became a fellow of the American Society of Civil Engineers in July, 1883, and always manifested an active interest in its affairs. In politics he was at first a Republican, but was later an advocate of the Greenback Party and accepted its nomination for Governor of Wisconsin.

The main cause of his phenomenal success was his unimpeachable reliability, whose word was as good if not better than his note. He was quick to decide, relied upon his own judgment, had executive ability of a high order, and attended strictly to his business. He was quiet in manner, simple in his tastes and inclined to be reticent. He was a fine scholar and always kept fully posted on all scientific, mechanical and political matters.

On September 12, 1848, he married Margaret Marie, daughter of William W. Watson of Geneva, N. Y., who was born September 28, 1828, and died December 20, 1909, at the age of eighty-one years. Their twelve children were:

777. William Watson, b. November 14, 1849; married Mary S. Phillips on November 14, 1877, and they have an adopted daughter, Elizabeth. He was for many years connected with the E. P. Allis Company, and after the death of his father carried on the business with his brothers, Charles and Louis, and his mother until they merged with the Frazer & Chalmers Company in 1902, under the name of the Allis-Chalmers Company. He is still connected with the Allis-Chalmers Company and lives in Milwaukee.

778. Edward Phelps, b. September 14, 1851; *

779 Charles, b. May 4, 1853; *

780. Jere, b. March 4, 1855; married Gladys Anne Butler of Chicago, Illinois, on April 18, 1890. He was for several years a ranch owner in Isinours, Minn., and afterward owned and operated a flour mill near Pittsburg, Penn. Later he lived in Philadelphia, Penn., and Chicago, Ill., but is now a farmer in Pecatonica, Ill.

781. Maud, b July 3, 1856; married Eustace Conway, a lawyer in New York City, and is living there at this time.

782. Ernest, b. July 11, 1858; *

783. Mary White, b. June 26, 1860; married John H. Keeling of London, England, on December 30, 1884, and has had four children:

1. Edward Allis, b. October 31, 1885; graduated from Eaton College and Christ Church College, Oxford University, and then entered the Foreign Office. After passing his examinations there he went to Constantinople as Secretary to the Embassy, and was later transferred as Secretary to Lord Kitchener at Cairo, Egypt. At the beginning of the war he was attached to Sir Ian Hamilton's staff, serving six months at the Dardanelles, Turkey, and was then transferred to Nish, Serbia, where he remained until the evacuation of the city. He is now Secretary to the English Embassy in Rome.

2. Mary Allis, b. September 18, 1891; married in 1915 Mr. Barnby, an officer in the English Aviation Corps.

3. John H., Jr., b. August 18, 1895; graduated from Eaton College and passed his examinations for Trinity College, Oxford University, but upon the breaking out of the war he applied for and obtained a commission in the Royal West Surrey (the Queen's regiment), was gazetted a 2nd Lieutenant and promoted to 1st Lieutenant the following April. In July, 1915, he left for the Dardanelles and landed at Sulva Bay on August 8th, taking part in the 28 days fight which followed, after which he was invalided for a short time and promoted to a Captaincy. He was then appointed Assistant Military Landing Officer at Salonica, Turkey, with the rank and pay of Staff Lieutenant, and holds this position at the present time.

784. Frank Watson, b. July 10, 1865; was a farmer and raiser of high grade stock in Madison, Wis., for over 20 years, owning one of the most up-to-date farms in that section. On January 18, 1890, he married Lillian Paige and died October 25, 1915, without issue. His widow is still living in Madison.

785. Louis, b December 30, 1866; *

786. Margy, b. August 12, 1868; died in infancy.

787. Margaret Watson, b October 26, 1869; married Richard H. Norris of Milwaukee on November 8, 1893, and has had the following children:

WORKS OF
THE EDWARD P. ALLIS COMPANY.
MILWAUKEE, WIS. U.S.A.

1 Richard H., Jr., b. November 7, 1894; attended Milton School and Harvard University, and is at present engaged in business with his father.

2. William Allis, b December 11, 1896; attended Milton School and is now a student at Harvard University.

3. Margaret Allis, b. May 2, 1898; will graduate from Dana Hall this year.

4 Thomas Wyatt, b. March 13, 1902; at Milton School.

5. Frank Watson, b. August 21, 1905.

788 Gilbert, b. January 4, 1871; *

436. HUBBARD S. ALLIS was born October 4, 1819, in Whately, Mass., and died there August 30, 1906, age 87 years. He was twice married, (first) on January 1, 1844, to Sibyl D., daughter of Dr. Chester and Mary (Hastings) Bardwell of Whately, who was born September 4, 1820, and died May 26, 1885, and (second) on November 27, 1888, to Mrs. Mary Bristol Colton, daughter of Augustus and Laura (Gannis) Bristol, who died December 27, 1900.

Hubbard S. Allis was educated in the town schools and the academy at Deerfield, Mass. He then went to Rochester, N. Y., and found employment as a clerk in the post office, eventually rising to the position of Deputy Postmaster, which he held for eight years, and was finally appointed Postmaster, which office he held for five years under Presidents Pierce and Buchanan. He was a member of the Board of Education and chairman of the Library Committee, and was prominent in politics, being chairman of the Democratic County Committee for a period of years, and was the party candidate for various city offices.

For seven years he was engaged in the banking business, prominent in the city railroad, and its treasurer seven years, and later engaged in the brokerage business until he returned to Whately to take charge of the family estate. He was a 32nd degree Mason and an Odd Fellow, and was half owner of the Daily Rochester Advertiser for four years. He had one daughter:

789. Gertrude A., b. December 16, 1844; married Major Joseph Billings of Hatfield, Mass., October 18, 1871, and lived at first in Hatfield, later in St Louis, Mo., and finally in Whately, Mass, where she died January 13, 1915. They had a daughter, Edith E., b. March 20, 1873, who married Paul H. Hesser in February, 1894, and had three children: Harvey Billings, b. August 19, 1895, Walter Joseph, b. April 25, 1897, and John Thornton, b. January 21, 1900.

438. ELAM BRIDGES ALLIS was born July 10, 1823, in Whately, Mass. On September 4, 1850, he married Clarissa S., daughter of Dr. Chester and Mary (Hastings) Bardwell of Whately, who was born September 20, 1823, and died April 27, 1858.

He was a tailor by trade and moved from Whately to Geneva, N. Y., and later went to Rochester, N. Y., where he was in the clothing business for a long term of years, but died in Geneva on September 4, 1893. He was a man of fine physical appearance, being six feet one inch in height and well proportioned, and his social qualities won for him a large circle of friends wherever he lived. His children were:

790. Edward B., b. July 26, 1854; married in November, 1882, Mary Tyler, daughter of Daniel Kingsley of Northampton, Mass., who was born November 6, 1882. He at first lived in Rochester, N. Y , but is at this writing in Benton Harbor, Mich.

791. Mary Hastings, b. March 28, 1857; married Charles H. Palmer of Rochester on March 14, 1883, and has had two children.

447. AUGUSTUS GRIDLEY S. ALLIS was born January 4, 1831, in Cazenovia, N. Y., and died May 23, 1901, in Syracuse, N. Y. He was educated in the Cazenovia Seminary and the Albany Normal School, from which he graduated in 1851. He then taught school in Brockport, N. Y., and Joliet, Ill., after which he attended Union College for a time, and in 1857 was admitted to the bar in Rochester, N. Y. Not long afterward he took up the practice of his profession in Syracuse and was a successful lawyer there for 40 years. He was also prominent in local affairs and was a member of the Assembly in 1868.

Augustus G. S. Allis was twice married: (first) on November 4, 1855, to Caroline P. Barnett, who died July 1, 1857, and (second) on October 1, 1861, to Harriet N. Little, who is at this writing living in Syracuse. His nine children were:

By first marriage:

792. Carrie Barnett, b. June 25, 1857; died September 17, 1857.

By second marriage:

793. Carrie L., b. August 6, 1863; is unmarried and lives in Syracuse.

794. Mary D., b. October 4, 1866; is a teacher in Syracuse.

795. Edward Stanley, b. November 11, 1868; married Mary L. Smith of Cleveland, Ohio, on June 13, 1908, and lives in Asheville, N. C.

796. Katherine B., b. October 8, 1871; is a stenographer in Syracuse.

797. Luella V., b. May 23, 1875; a teacher in Columbus, Ohio.

798 Anna Rice, b. May 5, 1878; died May 13, 1892.

799. Helen Elizabeth, b. May 29, 1882; married Rev. George K. Warren on September 6, 1905, and died July 15, 1909, leaving two children, Robert K., b. February 11, 1907, and William E., b. June 13, 1909.

800. William E., b. October 6, 1884; *

449. JAMES ASHBEL ALLIS (not Jesse) was born September 13, 1840, in Cazenovia, N. Y., and is now living in Syracuse, N. Y. On August 2, 1861, he enlisted in the Union Army, and on August 29, 1861, was mustered into service as a private in Company I, Third New York Volunteer Cavalry. He was promoted to 2nd Lieutenant on December 3, 1861, 1st Lieutenant in November, 1863, and Captain of Company C on July 24, 1864, and was mustered out at City Point, Va., November 29, 1865. He served in the Army of the Potomac and the Army of the James, and was commissioned brevet Major. At this writing he is superintendent of the Veteran Relief Fund.

After the war James Ashbel Allis studied law, was admitted to the bar and followed his profession for several years, but on account of failing health he was finally obliged to discontinue the practice of law and take up other work. He was justice of the peace for 13 years, and for a term of years has been connected with the city, at present being in its Public Works Department.

On October 1, 1873, he married Ellen E. Moore, who was born July 2, 1852, in Becket, Mass., and their children were:

801. William Moore, b. October 24, 1874; died May 1, 1875.

802. Olive Diantha, b. March 8, 1875; a teacher in Syracuse.

803. Mabel Moore, b. April 7, 1879; a teacher in Rochester, N. Y

804. Ida Louise, b. February 16, 1885; a teacher in Glen Ridge, N. J.

458. CHARLES ALLIS was born February 12, 1817, and died March 16, 1908, almost 91 years of age. He was twice married: (first) in 1851 to Miss White, who died in February, 1853, and (second) to Caroline Waite, who died in March, 1885. By occupation he was a farmer in Lowville and Philadelphia, N. Y., and had a daughter by his second marriage:

805. Hattie, b. in 1852; married Joseph McCartney and had a daughter, Josephine, who married Chauncey Welch and is living in Philadelphia, N. Y.

461. DEXTER ALLIS was born May 20, 1825, and died February 2, 1907, nearly 82 years of age. He married (first) Eunice Brown, who died about 1853, and (second) on September 18, 1855, Catharine E. Stickles, who was born November 28, 1835, and is living in Philadelphia, N. Y., as this book goes to press.

Dexter Allis was a farmer in Philadelphia, and had five children:

By first marriage:

806. William H., b. May 20, 1850; *

By second marriage:

807. Minnie Elizabeth, b. November 17, 1857; is a teacher in Kalamazoo, Mich. On May 20, 1880, she married Archibald Wheaton, who died December 13, 1902. They had a daughter, Ruth, b. April 15, 1884, who married Bernard L. Johnson on June 20, 1908, and had a son, Dexter W., b. November 23, 1911.

808. Herbert, b. in May, 1861; died in infancy.

809. Adelbert, b. in May, 1861; died in infancy.

810. John Warren, b. May 13, 1865; *

462. JOHN ALLIS was born October 25, 1827, and died January 11, 1909, over 81 years of age. He lived in Lowville, N. Y., was agent for the Rome, Watertown & Ogdensburg R. R. at Philadelphia, N. Y., and held the same position for the Utica & Black Mountain R. R. On November 7, 1858, he married Laura A., daughter of Thomas Wood of Philadelphia, N. Y., and had a daughter:

811. Nettie M., b. March 21, 1855; is living in Watertown, N. Y., at this writing. On June 23, 1886, she married Julius H. Patrick and has had the following children:

1. Laura, b. June 3, 1887.
2. Clarence, b. July 29, 1888; married Julia Paddock on January 15, 1912.
3. Marjorie, b. May 31, 1894.

464. WILLIAM S. ALLIS was born March 29, 1814, in Chicopee, Mass., and died April 25, 1871. On December 17, 1835, he married Caroline Washburn, and had two children:

812. Mary E., b. November 18, 1836; married John Coburn on November 15, 1859, and died February 2, 1910. Their children were: William A., b. November 5, 1860, Martha A., b. October 6, 1864, Caroline W., b. March 7, 1869, and John E., b. July 16, 1872.

813. Martha M., b. March 3, 1839; married Charles Banks on August 22, 1860.

468. DANIEL WAIT ALLIS was born August 9, 1828, in Hatfield, Mass., and died December 28, 1873. On December 7, 1854, he married Sarah Jane, daughter of Asaph Hurlbut of Springfield, Mass., who was born November 22, 1834, and died January 18, 1899.

Daniel W. Allis was a farmer in Hatfield and lived on Main Street, opposite the Howell Academy, his home now being occupied as a hotel. His five children were:

814. Josephine S., b. Jan. 30, 1858; died November 22, 1873.

815 Jairus Hurlbut, b July 9, 1862; died July 9, 1863.

816. Mary Wait, b. May 5, 1865; m. Edward H. Wilkinson of Springfield on June 22, 1904, and has a son, Edward Holman, who was born April 11, 1906.

817. Dexter Hurlbut, b. August 10, 1867; *

818. Edward Milton, b. December 9, 1870; *

469. WILLIAM PENN ALLIS was born April 9, 1830, in Hatfield, Mass., and was educated in the local schools. About three years after his marriage he moved to Wilbraham, Mass., but returned to Hatfield in a few years and remained there until 1886. He then moved to Williamstown, Mass., and later to Andover, Mass., but died in Wrentham, Mass., on December 31, 1908, at the age of 78 years.

William P. Allis was a farmer for many years and was afterward engaged in the real estate business for a time. On February 22, 1860, he married Amelia R. Baker, who died in Wilbraham in January, 1915. Their four children were:

819. Charles Dexter, b. March 18, 1862; died June 23, 1863.

820. Fanny Augusta, b. July 26, 1863; graduated from Smith College in 1884, and lives in Wilbraham, Mass., part of the year and in New York City the balance of the year.

821. Anna Amelia, b. July 26, 1863; graduated in 1884 from Smith College and was a teacher previous to her marriage on August 17, 1897, to Henry Mace Payne of Southold, L. I. They have a daughter, Helen Mace, who was born August 16, 1901.

822 William Baker, b. June 7, 1866; *

472. SOLON MATHER ALLIS was born June 29, 1838, in Danville, Quebec, Canada, lived there as a boy and was educated in the local schools. About 1860 he went to Springfield, Mass., and in August, 1862, enlisted in Company K, 27th Mass. Volunteers (Col. Horace C. Lee), and during the Civil War was in the battles of Gum Swamp, Kinston, White Hall and Goldsboro, N. C. In 1863, by order of Gen'l John G. Fortis, he was placed on detached service in the Engineering Department until October, 1864, when he was mustered out with his regiment at Norfolk, Va.

For the next two and a half years he was employed by the United States Government on the fortifications of Boston Harbor under Col. C. E. Blunt, U. S. Engr., after which he was employed on the preliminary survey of the Portland & Ogdensburg Railroad.

SOLON MATHER ALLIS

In 1879 he went to Arizona, where he was United States Deputy Mineral Surveyor for six years, and during that period laid out the town of Tombstone. For a year he was Superintendent of Mines in Mexico, after which (in 1886) he returned East and was elected Superintendent of Water Works in Malden, Mass., which position he held for six years, building the high service system during that time. Afterward he accepted a situation with H. McKay Twombly of Madison, N. J., and had charge of engineering construction, draining of land, etc., on his estate for four years.

Upon his return to Malden he was employed in landscape engineering in different parts of the United States, also spending a year in Nova Scotia in making surveys and plans for an electric power plant on the Port Medway River. He then worked a year for the Boston Elevated R. R. Company and later was inspector for Essex County on the construction of the new county bridge at Haverhill, Mass. At that time on account of failing eyesight he gave up engineering, and for several years acted as general agent for the Fraternity Publishing Company, visiting many parts of the United States. He is at this writing a farmer in Whitman, Mass.

On December 31, 1863, he married Victoria M. Higgins of Worthington, Mass., and has had two children:

823. James Cutler, b. July 21, 1866; *

824. William Dexter, b. June 3, 1881; is an inventor and expert machinist in Boston, Mass., and lives in Malden, Mass.

473. JOHN MATHER ALLIS was born December 15, 1839, in Danville, Quebec, Canada, and died July 16, 1899, in Valparaiso, Chile. At the age of 14 years he left Danville for Troy, N. Y., to make his own way in the world. His ambition was to obtain a good education, and to that end he attended school in the winters and worked during the summers to pay expenses. During that time he was engaged in different lines of work, and at the time of the breaking out of the Civil War was employed in the manufacture of rifle balls for the Federal army. He worked his way through Princeton University, graduating in 1866, and three years later entered the Union Theological Seminary of New York.

On June 14, 1870, he married Helen Caroline Arnold of Troy, who was born December 22, 1845. His first pastorate was in Albany, N. Y., and his second in Lansing, Mich., but he was obliged to go to California on account of his wife's health and she died there on September 18, 1875.

For the next six years he was a pastor in San Francisco, Cal., and at the same time labored extensively on the columns of the "Occident," a Presbyterian religious weekly. He then received a call to Lafayette, Ind., which he accepted, and there married Laura Livingston on June 2, 1883, who was born May 13, 1842.

While in Lafayette he was offered the opportunity to go to Chile, South America, and found a college for the instruction of young men who desired to prepare for the ministry, which he accepted, and in 1883 went to Valparaiso, Chile. He was not, however, limited to the teaching of theology. Besides preaching to the English congregation in Santiago (the capital of Chile and near Valparaiso, where he was finally stationed) he devoted much of his time to evangelization. He was commissioned to the United States to raise funds for the Instituto Ingles, a college that is known throughout all of South America, and he not only successfully accomplished that work but supervised the building, etc., of that handsome college upon his return to Chile. It was while in the United States on his commission that Princeton University, his Alma Mater, conferred on him the honorary degree of Doctor of Divinity in consideration of the valuable work he was doing in connection with the Church in Chile.

Very soon after his return to Chile Dr. Allis was made President of the Mission, which was legally incorporated in 1888, an office which he discharged with skill and honor until his death. He was a favorite speaker on occasions of special gatherings of the Anglo-American community and was asked to preach in 1887 on the occasion of the fifth jubilee of the reign of Queen Victoria of England. He was an eloquent speaker and full of energy and enthusiasm, devoted to his life work, sympathetic and true. He was beloved by poor and honored by men of high degree, and was known from Lima, Peru, to La Piz, Bolivia, and from one end of Chile to the other. He had the following children:

By first marriage:

825. Nora Caroline, b. June 16, 1872; is living in Cincinnati, Ohio, at this writing. On December 28, 1897, she married Rev. William L. Schmalhorst and has had the following children: John Bollinger, b. November 22, 1898, Helen Mildred, b. September 2, 1900, Dorothy Allis, b. January 26, 1903, Randolph, b. April 13, 1904, and Florence Martha, b. September 18, 1910.

By second marriage:

826. Clarence Livingston, b. November 29, 1883; *

827. Helen May, b. March 12, 1885; is living in Swathmore, Pa., at this writing. On December 20, 1911, she married Andrew F. Jackson and has two children, John Mather, b. October 3, 1913, and Helen Frances, b. October 21, 1915.

493. AUSTIN JUDSON ALLIS was born December 8, 1837, in Whately, Mass., and died April 28, 1914, in Florence, Mass. On January 29, 1859, he married Emma Josephine, daughter of William and Therza (Waite) Taynton, who was born June 9, 1839, in Bath, England, and died April 15, 1907, in Florence, Mass.

Austin J. Allis lived in Whately and Florence, Mass., and was a veteran of the Civil War. He enlisted in the 37th Massachusetts Volunteers on August 30, 1862, and served continuously until June 21, 1865, taking part in 21 engagements. After the war he was connected with the Florence Sewing Machine Company of Florence for about five years, and then bought a farm in North Farms, Mass., where he lived until 1887. He then sold the farm, retired from active business, and moved back to Florence, where he spent the remaining years of his life. His children were:

REV. JOHN MATHER ALLIS

828. Charles Ernest, b. July 4, 1859; *

829. Luther Austin, b. December 13, 1860; is unmarried and is a shipping clerk in Florence, Mass., at this writing.

830. William Clinton, b. November 30, 1866; *

831. Josephine Sanderson, b. August 30, 1870; is living, unmarried, in Florence.

832. George Lincoln, b. August 16, 1873; *

833. Robert Taynton, b. October 19, 1875; *

834. John Lester, b. May 13, 1877; served in the Second Regiment during the Spanish-American War. He was a locomotive engineer on the New York, New Haven & Hartford Railroad, living in New York City, and on July 31, 1907, married Alice M. Henchey. On September 23, 1907, his engine was sideswiped and he died from the effects of being scalded by live steam.

495. ERNEST AUSTIN ALLIS was born June 30, 1842, in Whately, Mass., and died March 16, 1897. He was thrice married: (first) to Florence A., daughter of Thomas C. Cutler of Hatfield, Mass., on May 4, 1869; (second) to Lucinda A., daughter of Henry and Minerva (Sheldon) Donaldson of Greenfield, Mass., and widow of Mr. Dickens, March 26, 1890, who died March 5, 1892; (third) to Emeline Thompson of Palmer, N. Y., on September 20, 1892, who is living in Saratoga Springs, N. Y., at this writing.

Ernest A. Allis was a mechanic in Whately. During the Civil War he served in the 37th Mass. Volunteers and afterward received a pension until his death. He had one son by his first marriage:

835. Frederick, b. June 12, 1870; died, unmarried, June 24, 1893, in California.

504. EDWIN INGRAM ALLIS was born June 25, 1821, at South Hill, Orwell, Bradford County, Pa., and died March 24, 1902, at the age of 81 years. On October 24, 1849, he married Lovina Hill, and was a farmer by occupation. Their children were:

836. Irving Melvin Allis, b. October 9, 1850; *

837. Ned Hunter, b April 6, 1854; *

838. Mary E., b Mar. 4, 1859; married Benjamin F. Richards on January 21, 1878 Their children were:

1. Floyd Edwin, b. December 19, 1879.

2. Guy F., b. April 11, 1881; married Purl Sexton on November 28, 1902.

3 Hugh L., b. March 21, 1884; married Lela Huff on September 8, 1912. and has two children, Allen McLellan, b. May 9, 1913, and Earl Benjamin, b Sept. 15, 1915.

4 Ray A , b May 10, 1886; married Lorena Wickham on March 28, 1905, and has had three children, Kathryn, b. Jan. 24, 1906, Nathaniel, b. May 10, 1909, and Mary E., b December 18, 1912, and died December 10, 1915.

5. Bernice Lovina, b. September 4, 1894; married on July 14, 1913, Ernest Jakeway and had a daughter, Anita May, who was born November 10, 1914, and died June 8, 1915.

839. Frank Roy; *

840. May; married Mr. Browning and had three children, Montague, Elizabeth and Emily.

841. Grant G.; *

507. HIRAM K. ALLIS was born October 26, 1831, in the old homestead at South Hill, Orwell, Bradford County, Pa., and died July 24, 1862. On November 24, 1853, he married Lucretia P. Darling, who was born March 14, 1830. On October 8, 1865, she married (second) Luke M. Stevens, who died February 5, 1878,

and at this writing is living in Smith Center, Kansas, with her son, Schuyler C. Stevens.

Hiram K. Allis was a farmer in South Hill all his life and had three children:

842. Ada Adel, b. August 26, 1854; died October 27, 1861.

843. William W., b. October 9, 1855; married and is engaged in the mercantile trade in West Warren, Bradford County, Pa., at this writing.

844. Leslie L., b. April 5, 1859; *

Stevens children, by second marriage:

1. Schuyler C., b. April 23, 1868; married Mary E. Elwell on March 23, 1892, and is residing in Smith Center, Kan. They have had three children: Nancy E, b November 23, 1894, Francis L., b. May 14, 1904, and Evelyn A., b. April 17, 1910.
2. Charles A., b January 9, 1870; married Emma S. Pauline and after her death he married a second time. At this writing he is living in Spokane, Wash.

509. ITHIEL JUDSON ALLIS was born in 1825 in Orwell, Bradford County, Pa. On February 12, 1857, he married Louise Lucretia, daughter of Enos A. and Temperance (Stone) Norton, who was born January 5, 1826, and died March 24, 1881, in Pike, Bradford County, Pa.

Ithiel J. Allis was a farmer in Orwell and also owned a saw mill. Soon after the breaking out of the Civil War he enlisted in the Union army and was a member of Company D, 17th Regiment, Pennsylvania Cavalry. He died in service July 10, 1863, in Washington, D. C., leaving two children:

845. Newton Emery, b May 28, 1859; unmarried and a farmer in LeRaysville, Pa.

846. Dora Isabelle, b. September 4, 1861; married on September 16, 1881, William Vought, a farmer, and is living in Windham, Pa., at this writing. Their four children were Grace Louisa, b. June 18, 1882, and died August 31, 1893, Leonard, b. May 4, 1885, Leon, b October 4, 1888, and Carrie May, b. July 19, 1893.

510. OSCAR F. ALLIS was born in 1829 in Orwell, Bradford County, Pa. He married Minseyette Bacon and eventually moved to Ohio, where he died May 1, 1885. He was a carpenter by occupation and his four children were:

847. Arthur; no further record.

848. Metta; no further record.

849. Ithiel, no further record.

850. William, no further record.

511. JOEL M. ALLIS was born about 1833 in Orwell, Pa., and died February 3, 1865. On January 31, 1858, he married Mary, daughter of George and Eliza Nichols of Standing Stone, Pa., who was born March 2, 1840. She married (second) Frank Holmes on July 11, 1866, and is at this writing living in King City, Mo.

Joel M. Allis was a farmer in Orwell and was a soldier in the Union army during the Civil War. He enlisted in 1862 in Company D, 141st Pennsylvania Volunteer Infantry and served up to within a week of his death, a period of nearly three years. He had one son:

851. Murton E., b. May 1, 1861; *

514. HENRY SHERBURN ALLIS was born February 4, 1829, in Allis Hollow, Bradford County, Pa., and died in July, 1915, at the age of 86 years. On January 1, 1852, he married Mary E., daughter of Benjamin P. Dresser of Wysox, Pa., who died March 3, 1886, and he married (second) Helen G. Vought, who died August 27, 1894. He was a farmer and had four children by his first marriage:

852. John A., b. April 25, 1854; died March 12, 1855.

853. Elizabeth, b. December 14, 1855; married on January 1, 1877, Frank D. Wood and had one daughter.

854. Charles Henry, b January 19, 1858; *

855. Margaret I., b June 20, 1860; married (first) George S. Allen of Rome, Pa., on September 6, 1882, and (second) F. D. Winwood.

515. HENDERSON KNAPP ALLIS was born February 22, 1832, in Allis Hollow, Orwell Township, Pa., and is living in Geneva, Minn., as this book goes to press. On February 18, 1855, he married Sophronia, daughter of Daniel and Lucy (Howe) Robinson of Orwell, Pa. He was a farmer by occupation and his six children were:

856. Miles Earl, b May 18, 1856; *

857. Jesse Benton, b. October 19, 1857; *

858. Eva Viola, b. July 6, 1858.

859. Flora Versula, b. June 16, 1860; married and is living in Bradford County, Pa.

860. George Henry, b. June 27, 1871.

861. Cora Belle, b. December 7, 1872.

519. HARRISON CLAY ALLIS was born March 24, 1845, in Allis Hollow, Pa. On March 24, 1868, he married Pluma, daughter of Daniel and Lucy (Howe) Robinson of Orwell, Pa., who was born September 17, 1846, and died March 18, 1916.

Harrison C. Allis is a farmer in Wysox, Bradford County, Pa., at this writing, and has had the following children:

862. Child, b. May 20, 1869; died in infancy.

863. Norman Lead, b. April 20, 1870; *

864. Cora Augusta, b. September 10, 1872; married Alfred H. Dougherty, a farmer of Orwell, on September 20, 1893. Their two children were Mary Lanett, b. January 13, 1896, and Milton Earl, b. February 12, 1900.

865. Clara Lanett, b. Oct. 18, 1874; married on July 4, 1892, Ernest C Brown, a farmer of Orwell. Their four children were Clarence Norman, b. April 18, 1893, Vivian Augusta, b May 15, 1897, Marcus Clay, b. December 24, 1903, and Lucy Leola, b January 14, 1906.

866. Lewis Eugene, b July 30, 1876; *

867. Leman I., b. December 24, 1879; died March 6, 1882.

868. Bert Silas, b November 29, 1887; *

520. WILLIAM WALLIS ALLIS was born February 7, 1835, in Rome, Pa., and died August 7, 1890, in Kansas. On June 14, 1857, he married Ellen E. Allen of Wysox, Pa., who was born July 21, 1830, and died December 20, 1881.

William W. Allis was a farmer in Rome and Orwell, Pa., but eventually went West with his wife and family and lived in Nebraska and Kansas. His children were:

869. Ida O., b. April 18, 1858; married (first) Edward Barker on December 25, 1878, at Bell Creek, Neb., and (second) Louis F. Ninneman in 1888 at Stockton, Kan. She had a daughter by her first marriage, Emma Josephine, b. on January 20, 1880, who married John W. Buss on July 14, 1895, and had the following children: Jesse E , b. June 19, 1896, Gertrude F., b. January 10, 1899, Gladys M., b. February 2, 1901, Derwin E., b. February 17, 1905, Hazel M., b September 2, 1907, and Alpha J., b May 29, 1910.

870. Ettie Victora, b. June 10, 1860,; married Harvey Watson Masters on March 4, 1878, at Arlington, Neb., and had four children:

1. Edna Earl, b. May 16, 1880; married Eugene Coleman on August 15, 1899, and they have a son, Henry E , b. March 9, 1901.

2. George Winfield, b. October 9, 1881; married Ruth Thompson on March 4, 1911, and they have one son.

3. Jesse Clayton, b. March 26, 1882; married Theresa Newn on December 9, 1912, and their two children are Margaret D., b. January 3, 1913, and Etta M., b. June 16, 1915.

4. Hazel Maud, b. October 16, 1889; married Alton C. Orr, September 4, 1907, and they have a daughter, Allis Virginia, b. June 23, 1908.

871. Willis Eugene, b. May 28, 1868; *

523. GEORGE RUTTY ALLIS was born March 20, 1842, in Orwell, Pa. He was 19 years of age when the Civil War broke out, and about two years later enlisted in the 37th Pennsylvania Militia and served for three months. In March, 1864, he enlisted in Company D, 17th Pennsylvania Volunteer Cavalry, and from then until his discharge on August 7, 1865, he was engaged in much hard service in the Union Army.

He was with Sheridan's cavalry corps all through the Wilderness Campaign, and was at Cold Harbor, Petersburg and Richmond. In August, 1864, Sheridan was sent with his cavalry and two corps of infantry to the Shenandoah Valley, and George R. Allis tells the following about the battle which took place there:

"The cavalry was kept busy scouting around Early's army until the 19th day of September. Sheridan was in line of battle with his whole army before daylight. The battle raged all day and just before dark the enemy broke and went through Winchester flying. Our regiment made three mounted charges and in the last one my horse was shot from under me. That closed my work for that day."

On November 29, 1870, George R. Allis married Nora Arlett Lyons of Orwell, who was born July 15, 1848, and died December 24, 1885. For about forty years he carried on the wagon making business in connection with his brother, Jacob H. Allis, in Allis Hollow, Orwell Township. Retiring from active business he bought a home in Rome, not far from Orwell, and is living there at this writing. His children were:

872. Neva A., b. January 17, 1876; married Lemuel Maynard of Rome on December 29, 1897, and their three children are Gerald Leigh, b. November 5, 1898, Sarah Angenova, b. August 24, 1900, and Mildred Elizabeth, b. June 23, 1904.

873. Nina Margaret, b September 29, 1882; married William Rice, Jr., of Rome on October 18, 1911, and they have a son, William Lyons, b. September 1, 1912.

874. George Percy, b. September 1, 1885; died February 16, 1901.

526. HALLIDAY D. ALLIS was born December 22, 1856, in Rome, Pa., and at this writing is a mail carrier in Towanda, Pa. On June 6, 1877, he married Emma S. Taylor, who died October 1, 1907. Their seven children were:

875. Robert A., b. May 28, 1878; *

876. William P., b February 24, 1881; *

877. Elizabeth M., b. May 24, 1883; married Wesley Robinson on May 6, 1903, and they have two children, Elsie A , b. June 12, 1905, and Hazel E., b. September 10, 1909.

878. Fred L., b. March 4, 1885; is living, unmarried, in Towanda, Pa.

879. Roger J., b. July 29, 1887; is living, unmarried, in East Towanda, Pa.

880. Gail S., b. July 2, 1889; married Irene Conrad on March 5, 1910, and is at this writing a yard conductor for the Pennsylvania Railroad in Rochester, Pa.

881. Murray G., b. July 28, 1891; *

527. SYLVENDER ELLIS was born September 18, 1816, in New Britain, Conn., and died April 6, 1886. On April 27, 1842, he married Lovisa, daughter of Seth and Peony (Bement) Alden, who was born June 9, 1816, in Enfield, Conn., and died January 29, 1904.

He was a successful building contractor and a skilled architect. In 1842 he moved from New Britain to Somers, Conn., and lived there for about ten years. He then went back to New Britain, built a residence on Chestnut Street, and spent the remaining years of his life there. His children were:

882. William Henry, b November 10, 1843; married Mary Cole and is living in New Britain, Conn., as this book goes to press.

883. Marion Roselle, b August 1, 1848; is living, unmarried, in New Britain at this writing.

529. WILLIAM ELLIS was born February 4, 1821, in New Britain, Conn., and died January 23, 1905, in Willapa, Pacific County, Wash., nearly 84 years of age. On February 29, 1852, he married P. Jane, daughter of Adam and Mary (Weaver) Boyce of Canton, N. Y., who died March 6, 1913.

William Ellis received a high school education and afterwards entered Yale University, from which he graduated at the head of his class in 1844. Two years later he graduated from a New York medical college, and for the next three years held the position of principal in a private school. In 1849 he went to Wisconsin and engaged in the practice of his profession in Washington Harbor, meeting with marked success during the eighteen years he was there and becoming well known throughout the state. He then invested in farming lands in Kansas and moved there with his family. In 1875 he decided to go further West and lived in Oregon for a year, but eventually settled upon a farm in Willapa, where he died.

William Ellis lived a long and useful life and gained for himself an enviable reputation. He was a man of principal, of high ideals and excellent judgment, and was esteemed by all who knew him. His seven children were:

884. Henry Eugene, b. March 15, 1853; *

885. William Marion, b. September 16, 1855; *

886. May Webster, b May 22, 1859; married George Whitcomb on December 25, 1881, and had seven children: John, b. October 12, 1882, Lucy, b. July 30, 1884, Albert, b. September 14, 1886, Leonard, b. Dec. 30, 1888, Charles, b. August 20, 1890, Evie, b. November 19 1892, and Markhannah, b September 8, 1897.

887. Julia Boyce b. October 24, 1862; married J. W. Goodell on December 25, 1881, and their children were Grace Bell, b. March 22, 1883, Mabel Pearl, b. April 29, 1887, Lester, b August 9, 1891, Loren, b. September 6, 1896, and Merle, b. March 28, 1902.

888. Lillian, b. November 28, 1865; married Charles J. Herman on July 2, 1887, and their children were William E., b. May 5, 1888, and Charles M., b. April 11, 1890.

889. Hubert Judd, b, May 12, 1868; *

890. Mary Katherine, b. July 14, 1871; married Percy P. Soule on December 24, 1894, and their children were Mabel E., b September 28, 1895, Mary Marjorie, b. Mar. 10, 1900, Harold Page, b July 28, 1902, and Samuel P., b. June 28, 1908

891. Grace Eve, b August 5, 1875; died December 10, 1876.

530. EDWIN C. ELLIS was born December 5, 1823, in New Britain, Conn., and died January 4, 1904, nearly 82 years of age. On September 21, 1853, he married Minerva, daughter of Sylvester and Hancy (Humphrey) Tuller of Simsbury, Conn., who was born May 1, 1825, and died March 5, 1904. He was a farmer and lived on the farm owned by his father. His children were:

892. Grace M., b. June 21, 1858; married Charles F. Smith of New Britain on November 19, 1884.

893. Anna, b. July 12, 1862; living, unmarried, in New Britain at this writing.

535. HENRY JULIUS ELLIS was born May 2, 1837, in New Britain, Conn. He has been a successful merchant in Amityville, L. I., and New Britain, Conn. He was a member of the firm of Brown & Ellis of New Britain and for a number of years conducted the "South Store" on South Main Street.

On December 6, 1865, he married Amelia, daughter of John and Phebe (Chichester) Terry, who was born May 20, 1845, and both are living in New Britain as this book goes to press. Their children were:

894. Carrie Amelia, b. September 14, 1868.

895. Lillian Jane, b. November 24, 1872; married (first) Herman W. Ritz of New Britain on June 5, 1895, who died on April 16, 1902, and (second) William E. Schulze of Hartford, Conn., on September 18, 1907, and is living in New Britain at this writing.

896. Bertha May, b. February 8, 1875; died August 3, 1887.

897. Hubert Henry, b. September 24, 1876; died August 15, 1887.

538. MARTIN ELLIS was born May 22, 1826, in New Britain, Conn., and died on May 23, 1887. On October 16, 1848, he married Lydia, daughter of Amon Richards, who was born February 27, 1828, and died on December 30, 1904. He was a successful farmer and real estate owner in New Britain and had the following children:

898. Charles D., b. August 1, 1849; *

899. Emma J., b. July 22, 1853; died December 18, 1863.

900. Jennie L., b. September 6, 1863; married Walter L. Carpenter of New Britain on October 15, 1884, and had two children:

1. Mabel E., b. July 2, 1888; married Arthur N. Rutherford on May 31, 1910, and they have a son, Irving W., b. February 26, 1914.

2. Ernest M., b. September 29, 1895; died August 7, 1901.

539. GUSTAVUS ELLIS was born February 15, 1828, in New Britain, Conn., and died April 21, 1877. He married, May 21, 1857, Julia C., daughter of Eliphalet and Julia Ann (Tuttle) Cooper of North Haven, Conn., who was born July 31, 1840, and died October 29, 1909. He was a clerk in the post office in New Britain and his children were:

901. Burton Judd, b. December 9, 1878; married May Belle Spencer on March 23, 1901, and is at this writing living in Meriden, Conn.

902. Louis Perrin, b. September 17, 1870; *

542. WELLS ALLIS was born in Huntington, Conn., September 5, 1813, and died there June 5, 1897, nearly 84 years of age. In September, 1835, he married Harriet Bell, who was born in Stamford, Conn., July 12, 1814, and died May 14, 1900, age 86 years.

Wells Allis moved from Huntington to Columbus, Ohio, about the time of his marriage and was engaged in the grocery business in that city until 1856, when he went back to his boyhood home and bought a farm, spending the remaining years of his life there. His children were:

903. Phebe Ann, b. June 19, 1836; married John H. Olstot of Columbus, Ohio, in May, 1856, and died November 11, 1892, in Fairfield, Conn. They had a daughter, Eva W., who was born April 19, 1857, and is at this writing the owner of a private day school in Columbus.

904. Elisha Wells, b. December 29, 1837; *

905. William Franklin, b. March 25, 1840; died in infancy.

906. Franklin Lee, b. October 8, 1843; married Susan Forbes, April 3, 1884, who died October 29, 1910. He has been a successful reporter for R. G. Dun & Company in Philadelphia, Pa., for over 30 years.

907. Harriet Elizabeth, b. April 23, 1849; married Charles F. Buckley of Southport, Conn., and is living there at this writing.

545. SYLVESTER BEERS ALLIS was born October 10, 1828, in Huntington, Conn., and died in Cold Spring, N. Y., January 24, 1891. He married (first) on October 9, 1847, Eliza Maria, daughter of Zerah P. and Maria (Todd) Tuttle of North Haven, Conn., who was born March 21, 1829, and died April 18, 1852; (second) on April 4, 1853, Frances J. Hill of Milford, Conn., at Rye, N. Y., who died February 9, 1863; (third) on December 22, 1866, Sarah Eliza Houghton of Putney, Vt., who died February 12, 1889.

The boyhood of Sylvester B. Allis was a repetition of thousands of other country youths. He was ambitious for greater knowledge than the limited opportunities of his native town afforded, and by becoming proficient in Latin and other studies from text books when he was not engaged in farm duties he was able to secure a certificate as a public school teacher.

SYLVESTER BEERS ALLIS

After the manner of those days he was early apprenticed to a tailor, but followed that trade only to secure a livelihood and to aid his ambition in the matter of education, until early in the 50's he drifted over into New York State and was appointed principal of the Nelsonville School in Cold Spring. He was subsequently promoted to principal of the Rock Street School, a position that he filled most successfully.

In 1862 he secured the appointment of postmaster of Cold Spring, which he held for nearly twenty years. A few years after assuming the duties of postmaster he started writing for the village newspaper under the nom de plume "Uncle John's Journal," and in 1870 formed a stock company to rescue the Cold Spring Recorder from failure. Thus the postmaster also became village editor, and gradually acquired the other interests until he became sole proprietor. In 1882 he gave his entire time to the paper and mastered the mechanical details of the printing business, but soon began to feel the effects of many years of arduous labor and gradually settled down to the routine where death found and summoned him.

From his obituary notice the following is quoted: "He was a loyal son to the town and country. He labored tirelessly and enthusiastically for the material and moral advancement of the community wherein he cast his lot; never avowedly discouraged but hopeful for the future and cheering the despondent, he laid down his last long sleep, well deserving the reward 'well done, good and faithful servant'."

Mr. Allis was a resident of Cold Spring for forty years and was closely identified with the interests of the town, holding many local offices, and was also interested in in the local Y. M. C. A. and chairman of the Republican Town Committee. He was a member of the Episcopal Church and the Hudson River Lodge of Masons of Newburgh, N. Y. His eight children were:

By second marriage:

908. Sylvester Hill, b. March 24, 1854; *

909. Stella Hill, b June 2, 1855; married Frank Adams of Bellows Falls, Vermont, on June 5, 1889, and their children are Walter Frank, b. February 1, 1890, Eugene Gerald, b. July 20, 1894, and Doris Christine, b. June 14, 1899.

910. Eugene G., b. August 6, 1856; *

911. Carrie; died in infancy.

912. Lorenzo; died in infancy.

913. Ferdinand Warren, b. November 17, 1860; *

By third marriage:

914. William Pelton, b. January 11, 1871; *

915. Ara Eliza, b. September 3, 1873; died September 6, 1873.

547. JOEL ALLIS was born about 1797 in Shelburne Falls, Mass. On account of the loss by fire of the early town records it has not been possible to learn anything about him, but it is recorded that he married Myranda Severence, who was born January 28, 1793. Their four children were:

916. Amanda M., b. July 17, 1819. ·

917. Hannah G., b January 20, 1823.

918. Diana S., b. March 25, 1825.

919. Ellen Root, b. May 5, 1827.

550. NEWTON ROSWELL ALLIS was born April 5, 1828, in Shelburne Falls, Mass., and died in February, 1893. He was twice married: (first) on January 10, 1844, to Laura Farley and (second) to Katherine Sullivan, who is living in Shelburne Falls at this writing. He was an all-round man and lived in Buckland and Shelburne Falls. His four children were:

920. Hurlbut Stephen, b. April 30, 1851; died in 1870.

921. William Elton, b. June 12, 1853; *

922. Adelbert N., b. October 8, 1861; married Ellen Walsh at Fort Dodge, Iowa, on December 9, 1885, who died March 15, 1905 He is at this writing the proprietor of the Fern Bank Creamery in Los Angeles, Cal.

923. Eliza Jane, b. August 12, 1862; married Joseph P. Kron on July 11, 1881, and is now living in Hartford, Conn. Their children are Earl Newton, b. June 7, 1882, Elizabeth Rosalie, b. October 17, 1884, Philip Henry, b. March 20, 1887, Bessie May, b. February 28, 1889, Edward Alfred, b. April 9, 1892, and Joseph Adelbert, b. July 8, 1903.

552. LUCIUS PIERCE ALLIS was born September 5, 1822, in Bridgeport, Conn. Information regarding his marriage is missing, but he moved from Bridgeport to Derby, Conn., when a young man and was engaged in the woodturning business for several years, after which he was the proprietor of two hotels. Later he moved to New Haven and was the proprietor of a hotel in that city. His children were:

924. Columbia Monterey, b. about 1848; married Mr. O'Brien and moved to Buffalo, N. Y.

925. Americus Montcalm, b. about 1850; died in infancy.

556. GEORGE CORNELIUS ALLIS was born March 19, 1835, in Bridgeport, Conn. Early in life he started out to make his own way, and as a boy worked on a farm, in a factory and in a newspaper office, also as compositor on several New York City newspapers, including the New York Tribune. When 17 years of age he started a retail business in periodicals, books and confectionery in Derby, Conn., and set type during his spare time for the local paper, keeping a few cases of type in his store for that purpose. From a small beginning his business gradually increased and in course of time he moved into larger quarters. He also originated a circulating library, which grew into large proportions. He has been in business in Derby continuously for over sixty years, and at this writing is a bookseller, stationer and jeweler in that town.

On January 26, 1860, he married Mary Morgan, daughter of William Church and Julia S. (Blackman) Warriner of Ansonia, Conn., and their children were:

926. Hattie Pierce, b. May 14, 1861; is living in Derby, Conn., as this book goes to press.

927. Georgia Genevieve, b. March 15, 1864; died, unmarried, on February 9, 1914.

928. George Cornelius, b. Mar. 17, 1871; died October 1, 1871.

560. WILLIAM G. ALLIS was born March 31, 1827, in Addison, Vt., and died December 10, 1889. In December, 1848, he married Paulina Cook, who died October 7, 1862. He was a farmer in West Addison, Vt., and his three children were:

929. Elizabeth, b. February 12, 1850; married Henry Harris in 1870 and their children were Fred, Gertrude, Edwin, Ward and Belle.

930. Eugene William, b. August 3, 1854; *

931. Eva Maria, b. September 16, 1858; married John Benson on March 5, 1874, and their three children were Herbert J., b. September 10, 1876, Carl L., b. October 15, 1878, and William, b. April 2, 1881.

562. EDGAR AUGUSTUS ALLIS was born May 21, 1832, in Addison, Vt., and died February 3, 1913, over 80 years of age. On February 26, 1854, he married Amelia Bowers, who is living in Bridport, Vt., at this writing. He was a farmer by occupation and his children were:

932. Minnie Amelia, b. October 27, 1862; married on December 29, 1882, Allison Davis, and they have one son, Roy Hammond, b. March 18, 1884.

933. Edgar Nathaniel, b. July 6, 1866; *

570. NELSON ALLIS was born December 22, 1822, in Canada. He was a carpenter by occupation and lived in Ohio for many years, but eventually moved to Enid, Okla., where he died May 23, 1900. He was a man of exemplary, Christian character and because of his many acts of kindness was known as Father Allis.

Nelson Allis was twice married, first to Sarah Benidum, and his children were:

By first marriage:

934. George W., b. July 6, 1844; *

935. Harriet; is married and lives in Chillicothe, Ohio.

By second marriage:

936. Child; died in infancy.

576. EDWIN Z. ALLIS was born October 12, 1835, in Cleveland, Ohio, and is living in East Toledo, Ohio, as this book goes to press. On April 27, 1855, he married Minerva Fowler, and their two children were:

937. Fluvia, b. March 16, 1856; married Alonzo Moore and they had a daughter, Nellie, b. in 1883.

938. Albert G, b. November 12, 1883; unmarried as this book goes to press.

583. LORENZO ALLIS was born July 8, 1823, in Colchester, Vt. In 1845 he graduated with honors from the University of Vermont, being valedictorian of his class, and soon after went to New Orleans, La., where he become associate editor of the New Orleans Picayune and also principal of the leading public school. While pursuing the double duties of editor and teacher he took up the study of law in the University of Louisiana, from which he graduated in 1849, and was admitted to practice in the federal and state courts. He remained in the South until 1856, when, on account of failing health, he moved to St. Paul, Minn., with his family, where he became a very prominent lawyer and was in some of the biggest cases on record in those days. He lived in St. Paul until his death on March 26, 1883—"one of the brightest ornaments of the Bar of Minnesota, a man of indomitable will and upright character."

On January 29, 1846, Lorenzo Allis married Mary P. Castle, who was born in Jericho, Vt., in 1823 and died February 25, 1913, age 90 years, in Grimes, California.

Mary P. Castle was a graduate of the Albany Academy in 1845, and was a teacher in New Orleans, La., previous to her marriage. Their children were:

939. Preston, b. in 1846; died in 1848.

940. Frederick, b. September 1, 1848; *

941. Mary Castle, b. July 2, 1850; married Franklin DeCou on April 19, 1870, and is at this writing living in Newport, Minn. Their children were:

1. Franklin Allis, b. in 1872; died young.

2. Lida Ashton, b. August 13, 1876; married Mott H. Kent on February 7, 1896, and their children were Doris May, b. January 19, 1899, Phillips Franklin, b. December 19, 1900, and Marjorie Eloise, b. July 27, 1902.

3. Lorenzo Allis, b. May 9, 1879; married Mary Belle Moody on September 10, 1901, and they have one son, Lorenzo Allis, b. February 19, 1907.

4. Mary Allis, b. January 18, 1881; married Philip M. von Nesselhaus, July 17, 1907, and they have an adopted daughter, Marguerite.

5. Sara Satterthwaite, b. April 17, 1883; married R. S. Galusha on November 26, 1904, who died in February, 1914. They had a daughter, Geraldine Eloise, b. on July 30, 1909.

6. Harold Allis, b. February 3, 1886; married (first) Elsie W. Hendrickson, June 30, 1908, and (second) Helen Wright in November, 1914, and has a son, Robert, by his second marriage.

7. Lily Deborah, b. Nov. 24, 1888; married George E. Tingle in November, 1914.

942. Aurelia Castle, b. in 1854; died in infancy.

943. Edmund Castle, b. November 29, 1856; married Louise Stevens in 1890. He is at this writing in business in San Francisco, Cal., being Secretary of the Congo Lumber Company.

944. Harold Lorenzo, b. May 21, 1860; married Mary Wheeler of Rockford, Ill., in 1885 and died July 17, 1905, in San Francisco, without issue.

593. CALVIN CONVERSE ALLIS was born February 20, 1815, in Coventry, N. Y. He assisted in the management of his father's hotel there until he was 30 years of age, and on June 29, 1845, married Matilda Church (who was born December 23, 1818, in Coventry), at which time he engaged in farming. On December 23, 1855, his wife died and he married (second) on September 24, 1856, Maria A. Horton, who was born in Oxford, N. Y., on July 16, 1837, and died in Ellisburg, Pa., on February 19, 1909.

Soon after his second marriage Calvin C. Allis moved to Candor, N. Y., and engaged in the foundry business. In the spring of 1860 he moved with his family to Ellisburg, Potter County, Pa., where he bought a farm and timber lands and lived there until his death on May 26, 1891, age 76 years. He was a very active man and well liked by all. He was trustworthy and at different times in his life held nearly all of the town offices. His ten children were:

By first marriage:

945. George Henry, b. June 10, 1848; *

946. Mary Elizabeth, b. August 8, 1851; died March 9, 1848.

947. Albert Calvin, b. October 1, 1854; *

By second marriage:

948. William Leonard, b. November 5, 1857; died, unmarried, November 27, 1886. He was engaged in lumbering and farming in Ellisburg, Pa.

949. Frank Marian, b. August 26, 1860; *

950. Robert Timothy, b. June 10, 1863; died on November 7, 1879.

GEORGE HENRY ALLIS

951. Mary Elizabeth, b. January 9, 1866; married Adelbert Pye on March 30, 1884, and is living in Ellisburg, Pa., at this writing. Their children were:

1. Isabelle M., b. December 31, 1884; married Hugh S. Beebe of West Bingham, Pa., on June 4, 1904, and their children are Cleone J., b. January 23, 1905, and died February 6, 1907, Beatrice Mae, b. May 25, 1907, Bernice Elisabeth, b. Apr. 6, 1910, and Kenneth Adelbert, b. September 20, 1913.

2. Matilda A., b. October 2, 1887; married Claude Swift of Coneville, Pa., on March 7, 1905, and their children are Alfred Adelbert, b. Dec. 8, 1905, and Lillian Mae, b. August 2, 1910.

3. Earl F., b. November 26, 1895.

4. Julian C., b. May 29, 1898.

952. Ella Maria, b. Mar. 23, 1868; married Roswell S. Carpenter on June 15, 1889, and at this writing is living in Ellisburg. They have one son, Calvin Clyde, b. on July 24, 1895.

953. Ira B., b. June 15, 1872; died July 22, 1875.

954. Anna, b. July 11, 1877; married Fred Gibson on December 28, 1898, and their children are Donald Cleone, b. December 18, 1899, James Calvin, b. February 28, 1903, and John Leon, b. August 10, 1910.

596. SPENCER FRANKLIN ALLIS was born April 24, 1835, in Coventry, N. Y., and died February 5, 1888, in Elyria, Ohio. He moved from Coventry to Elyria when a young man and was a farmer by occupation. On October 22, 1861, he married Elizabeth Kales, who is living in Seattle, Wash., as this book goes to press. Their four children were:

955. William Spencer, b. June 20, 1863; *

956. Leonard Guy, b. November 12, 1864; *

957. Vernette Elizabeth, b. July 6, 1867; married Maxine L. Longuet on June 23, 1892, and had a son, Louis Leonard. Her address at this writing is Winlock, Wash.

958. Anna Frances, b. December 20, 1871; is not married and lives in Seattle, Wash., at this writing.

597. EDWARD ALLIS was born May 20, 1818. He married Hannah Richards about 1846 and they had three children, but further information is missing:

959. Angeline, b about 1847; no further record.

960. William Leonard, b. in April, 1848; no further record.

961. Wilbur Daton, b. January 11, 1850; no further record.

599. LEONARD ALLIS was born April 27, 1823, in Charlotte, Mich., and died September 1, 1910, age 87 years. He was a cabinetmaker in Charlotte, and on January 14, 1858, married Elizabeth Leschy, who died in 1906. Their children were:

962. Clarence Morton, b in October, 1858; *

963. Ira W., b. June 13, 1860; *

964. Jesse F., b April 14, 1869; *

EIGHTH GENERATION

608. LYMAN NEWELL ALLIS was born August 31, 1853, in Rome, N. Y., and lived on his father's farm until he was able to purchase one for himself. About the time of his marriage he bought a forty-acre farm in Fayette, Hillsboro County, Mich., where he has since lived. He is an up-to-date, progressive farmer, raising

grain principally, and under his capable management his original farm has been more than doubled in size. On March 14, 1883, he married Loretta B. Davison, and their children were:

965. Edward Young, b. April 24, 1884; *

966. Eber Milton, b. March 19, 1890; at this writing is unmarried and engaged in special work for the State of Michigan near Grand Rapids.

615. JOEL ALLIS was born October 10, 1851, and is at this writing a farmer in Canastota, N. Y. On May 20, 1879, he married Cornelia Harp, who was born June 2, 1856, and they have had one son:

967. Floyd V., b. April 13, 1880; *

618. THOMAS L. ALLIS was born December 3, 1821, in Hawley, Mass., but settled in Conway, Mass., when a young man and was a farmer there until his death on January 1, 1878. He was twice married: (first) on March 29, 1845, to Esther Dickinson, who died in 1846, and (second) on April 4, 1847, to Julia Ann Hollis Johnson, who was born July 1, 1819, and died December 18, 1900. Their children were:

By first marriage:

968. William D., b. June 6, 1846; enlisted in the Union army in 1862 and died August 17, 1863.

By second marriage:

969. Martha, b. January 8, 1849; married Orrin D. Remington on June 20, 1867, and their children were Frederick C., b. Jan. 26, 1869, William E., b. July 18, 1871, and Cora E., b. June 9, 1881.

970. Darwin F., b. November 28, 1855; *

619. SOLOMON D. ALLIS was born January 24, 1825, in Hawley, Mass., and died in Conway, Mass., on December 27, 1906, age 81 years. He was twice married: (first) to Eliza Allis (640) on November 25, 1847, who died October 7, 1851, and (second) to Sally M. Allis (641) on March 4, 1852, who died July 23, 1909. He was a farmer in Conway and his children were:

By first marriage:

971. Sarah Elizabeth, b. March 7, 1849; married Roswell G. Rice on May 18, 1870.

972. Charles F., b. August 4, 1851; *

By second marriage:

973. Eliza J., b. December 3, 1852; died February 25, 1861.

974 William Dickinson, b. August 9, 1865; *

625. OTIS E. ALLIS was born on December 4, 1843, in Genoa, Neb., but eventually settled on a farm 12 miles south of Council Bluffs, Iowa. He has been a farmer all his life, but recently retired from active business and is at this writing living in Council Bluffs. On May 21, 1871, he married Ella Edwards, who was born in Lincoln, Neb., May 7, 1853, and their children were:

975. Sadie Agnes, b. November 30, 1872; married G. C Plumer on April 10, 1895, and their children are Irene, b. February 21, 1897, Adele, b. March 18, 1900, and Helen, b. October 15, 1910.

976. Oliver E , b. November 11, 1874; *

977. William R., b. October 15, 1876; *

978. Samuel, b. December 18, 1879; *

979. Emeline, b. March 8, 1883; not married at this writing.

980. Harriet E., b. March 15, 1885; married B. F. Anderson on January 25, 1906, and their children are Leonard, b. March 28, 1908, Allis, b. April 6, 1911, and Harriet, b. February 17, 1913.

981. Otis E., b. December 27, 1888.

628. GARDNER SAMUEL ALLIS was born January 31, 1844, in Port Byron, N. Y. He married (first) Sarah E. Hopkins of Albion, N. Y., in 1867, who died October 8, 1869; (second) Helen M. Bacon of Clinton, Conn., in 1873, who died in Rochester, N. Y., on August 13, 1903; (third) Mary L. Dransfield on December 31, 1904, who is living in Rochester at this writing.

In 1870 Mr. Allis began canvassing for Mr. C. C. Drew, a directory publisher of Rochester. In a very short time his interest in the work and ability as a salesman led to his being given charge of the advertising end of the business, and he ultimately became vice-president of the Drew-Allis Company. For over forty years he held the confidence and friendship of every business man in the cities covered by the Drew-Allis directories. He had hosts of friends and never made an enemy. Many of the features now used by all directory publishers were thought of and worked out by Mr. Allis and Mr. Drew in the 70's. He died in Newton, Mass., on February 11, 1913, while engaged in work on the directory of that city.

631. MYRON G. ALLIS was born June 18, 1826. He was a farmer in Albion, N. Y., and died February 13, 1894. On July 11, 1853, he married

Rachel Van Buren, who was born October 5, 1832, and is at this writing living in Albion. Their children were:

982. Viola J., b. January 16, 1858; married Marvin J. Grinnell on March 6, 1878, and their children were Allis, b. November 19, 1879, Myron H., b. July 27, 1885, Leon C., b. September 7, 1888, Edna V., b. October 31, 1895, and Olin M., b. October 8, 1898.

983. Euretus Lucius, b. November 28, 1862; married Anna Atwell on January 28, 1886, who was born on November 3, 1863.

634. ELLIOT EDWARD ALLIS was born February 21, 1845, in Barre, N. Y. He married (first) Clara Adelaide Poland on January 25, 1872, who was born August 1, 1846, in Bethel, Vt., and died April 30, 1889, and (second) Flora Best on January 3, 1896, who died March 22, 1901. He is a farmer in Oakfield, N. Y., and his children, all by his first marriage, were:

984. Mabel Mary, b. May 27, 1873; died May 19, 1874.

985. Bertha Adelaide, b. May 2, 1875; married Albert R. Avery of Oakfield, N. Y., on June 5, 1900, and they have had three children: Eunice Hortense, b. May 1, 1905, Ralph Elliot, b. July 28, 1911 (died in infancy), and Albert E., b. January 17, 1913.

986. Frances Poland, b. March 22, 1886; married on September 14, 1910, Glenn A. Anthony.

635. SOLOMON W. ALLIS was born February 6, 1825, in York, N. Y. He was twice married: (first) to Maryette Corbett, who died in 1869, and (second) to Elizabeth Blackman, who died in 1897. At first he was a farmer in Cambridge, Mich., but later moved West

to Iowa and settled on a farm on the prairie at Colo, where he lived until failing health caused him to sell his farm and retire from an active business life. He died on January 15, 1895, in Fremont, Ind., and his only child, by first marriage, was:

987. Lucy, b. in December, 1867; died in 1868.

636. GEORGE R. ALLIS was born April 26, 1829, in Riga, N. Y. His boyhood was spent in Riga, after which he lived in LeRoy, N. Y., and Romeo, Mich., for five years. For the next eight years he was employed as bookkeeper in the hardware store of Geo. L. Bidwell in Adrian, Mich., followed by twelve years as a farmer in Cambridge, Mich. He was for four years treasurer of Lenawee County, Mich., thirteen years secretary of the Farmers' Mutual Fire Insurance Company of Lenawee County, and until his sudden death on June 23, 1892, was actively engaged not only in the real estate and insurance business but in the management of his Lenawee County farms and his lumbering interests in the northern part of the state.

On April 11, 1859, he married Susan F., daughter of David B. and Sarah J. (Davis) Treat, who died December 21, 1908, in Flint, Mich. Their children were:

988. George Lee, b. Sept. 13, 1862; died in November, 1881.

989. Sarah Pamelia, b. January 17, 1877; graduated from Kalamazoo College, Kalamazoo, Mich., in 1900 and Chicago University in 1902, and on June 21, 1905, married Enos A. DeWaters of Flint, Mich., where she is living at this writing.

643. RUFUS W. ALLIS was born June 21, 1834, in Conway, Mass., and died April 7, 1907. On October 22, 1874, he married Hattie Ann, daughter of Leonard and Gratia Ballou of Whitingham, Vt. He was a farmer in Conway and his children were:

990. John B., b. August 8, 1875; died August 26, 1876.

991. Rufus Dickinson, b. September 16, 1876; *

992. Edna Lillian, b. July 19, 1881; died August 3, 1881.

993. Sarah Paulina, b. January 14, 1884; married Joseph J. Cummins on October 17, 1906, and they have two children, Ruth P., b. October 19, 1908, and Joseph J., Jr., b. January 29, 1910.

994. George Edwin Eber, b. April 28, 1888; died September 22, 1888.

995. Nicena Pearl, b. November 22, 1893; died Nov. 25, 1893.

651. MARY LINCOLN ALLIS was born July 1, 1861, in Conway, Mass. She is a graduate of Columbia University of New York City and has received degrees from that college. She has taught in Throope University of Pasadena, Cal., and in the Raymond Coaching School, San Francisco, Cal., and has also taught Art and Craft in London, Eng. Her ability, however, has not been confined to teaching. As an artist she has been very successful, having made many portraits in crayon and color.

Miss Allis has had many interesting and exciting experiences abroad, having travelled around the world, and during the course of her travels has been received by royalty and has looked into the lives of the poor classes as well. She has been engaged in a wide field of employment and is especially interested in anything that is for the betterment of humanity. At this writing she is a press reporter and writer of short stories, residing in Amherst, Mass., and also has several books in progress.

656. IRVING ALLIS was born January 28, 1849, in Whately, Mass., and is living there at this writing. On July 14, 1876, he married Augusta M., daughter of Jonathan and Betsey S. (Williams) Howes of Ashfield, Mass. He resides on the farm that was originally owned by Elisha Allis and is also a civil engineer. His six children were:

996. Sarah B., b. Dec. 13, 1877; married William H. Phinney of Holyoke, Mass., on November 23, 1904, and their children are William R., b. January 13, 1906, Wallace S., b. May 4, 1907, Ida Allis, b. April 10, 1911, and Charlotte H., b. November 26, 1912.

997. Clarence I., b. May 27, 1879; *

998. Lucius H., b. March 9, 1886; *

999. George Willis, b. November 10, 1889; unmarried and is living in Whately at this writing.

1000. Edward Elliott, b. June 3, 1893; unmarried and living in Whately.

1001. Isabelle Ruth, b. May 5, 1897; unmarried and living in Whately.

659. LUCIUS F. ALLIS was born July 11, 1857. On February 4, 1880, he married Samantha Gander, who was born April 26, 1859, and died June 18, 1895. He is at this writing a farmer in Adrian, Mich., raising pure bred Shetland ponies. His children were:

1002. Edward D., b. April 6, 1881; *

1003. Arthur L., b December 1, 1885; married Olga Schlieman, December 25, 1908, and is a farmer near Adrian, Mich., at this writing.

1004. Irwin Zera, b. May 31, 1889; died August 10, 1889.

662. THOMAS VALENTINE ALLIS was born May 15, 1844, in Skaneateles, N. Y. His early education was obtained in his home town at St. James Institute, and later he attended the Mt. Oakwood Seminary of Union Springs, N. Y.

He is a very successful inventor. For a time he was with the Bessemer steel works of Troy, N. Y., and has invented furnaces and mills for rolling steel plates that are now considered the best and most economical in this country and abroad. He has built furnaces in and around Cleveland, Ohio, Pittsburgh, Pa., and Baltimore, Md., as well as other manufacturing centers, and divides his time between these different locations.

On June 9, 1877, he married Charlotte E. Cushman and has one daughter:

1005. Henrietta Latitia, b. November 16, 1878; married Albert Kelsey of Philadelphia, Pa., January 18, 1899, and they have three children, Albert Washburn, b. Jan. 9, 1900, Charlotte Elizabeth, b. July 8, 1901, and Charles Cushman, b. November 23, 1907.

664. JAMES CLEMENTS ALLIS was born August 23, 1825, in Kendall, Orleans County, N. Y., and died May 4, 1888, in Clarendon, Orleans County, N. Y. He was a farmer all his life and moved from Kendall to Clarendon in 1857.

On January. 6, 1847, he married Sarah Elizabeth, daughter of Alonzo and Mary (Smith) Wheeler, who was born March 20, 1829, and died June 28, 1907. Their children were:

1006. Thomas Wells, b. October 14, 1849; *

1007. Ruth Elizabeth, b. February 28, 1852; married Herbert A. French of Medina, N. Y., October 3, 1883, and their children were: Clark R., b. July 12, 1885 (married Mrs. A. E. White on December 29, 1914), Girl, b. May 5, 1887 (died in infancy), Allis Elizabeth, b. June 19, 1888, and Girl, b. November 1, 1891 (died in infancy).

1008. Girl, b. in 1854; died in infancy.

1009. Oliver James, b October 20, 1855; *

1010. Jay Elijah, b. June 3, 1858; *

1011. Seth Alonzo, b September 19, 1861; *

1012. Clark, b. August 15, 1865; *

666. NATHAN BANGS ALLIS was born January 9, 1831, in Kendall, N. Y., and died there on October 31, 1858. On April 18, 1855, he married Helen Bement, who is living in Albion, N. Y. He was a farmer in Kendall and had one son:

1013. George B., b. September 23, 1856; died March 30, 1877.

681. CHARLES F. ALLIS was born February 29, 1848, in Wilmington, Vt., and at this writing is living in Readsboro, Vt. On May 27, 1879, he married Dora E. Davis and their children were:

1014. Edward L., b. February 9, 1880; *

1015. Ethel D., b. August 12, 1883; married Frank W. Johnson on June 29, 1907.

1016. Bertha M., b. November 24, 1886.

686. CHARLES ALLIS was born February 16, 1825, in Heath, Mass. He was a farmer in Heath, and on November 19, 1855, married Melissa E., daughter of George Harris. They are known to have had several children, but a complete record is missing:

1017. Charles, b. about 1856; no further record.

693. GEORGE ALLIS was born May 14, 1858. On December 23, 1876, he married Perlina Cruttenden and is at this writing a farmer three miles north of Mansfield, Pa. Their children were:

1018. Albert, b. August 3, 1878; died February 6, 1881.

1019 Adelbert, b. May 18, 1881; *

698. CHARLES C. ALLIS was born May 31, 1851. On September 18, 1873, he married Eliza Heilman and is at this writing a traveling salesman, residing in Evansville, Ind. Their children were:

1020. Willard C., b. June 10, 1874; *

1021. Marian, b. January 13, 1876.

1022. Maud, b. January 7, 1878; unmarried and lives in Evansville at this writing.

1023. Gordon Byron, b September 15, 1881; *

707. JUSTIN R. ALLIS was born October 12, 1852, in Canaan, N. Y. He was at first a photographer in Cohoes, N. Y., and later in Newark, N. J., and at this writing is engaged in the same line of business in Warrenton, Va. In 1873 he married Mary Helen Gates, who is now living in Warrenton, and their children were:

1024. Elizabeth May, b. December 17, 1875; married Franklin A. Shook on June 5, 1895, and is living in Washington, D. C., at this writing. Their children are Helen Edith, b. February 20, 1896, Kathryn Mildred, b. September 6, 1899, and Justin Allis, b. April 18, 1906.

1025. Son; died in infancy.

708. L. A. ALLIS was born May 27, 1844. On December 30, 1869, he married Elizabeth Howe, and is at this writing a farmer in Hillsdale, Mich. Their children were:

1026. Ina, b. February 8, 1871; married Frank A. Weston on April 16, 1890, and they have two children, Ethel R., b. December 26, 1898, and Wells A., b. June 8, 1901.

1027. Dilla, b. May 2, 1875.

1028. Luie G., b. August 27, 1882.

715. VERNE L. ALLIS was born in Chatham, Ohio, on March 27, 1878, and at this writing is a traveling salesman for the Vermont Farm Machine Company of Bellows Falls, Vt., living in Findlay, Ohio. On August 6, 1902, he married Viola Pearl Cassidy and their children are:

1029. Mary Loleta, b. May 2, 1908.

1030. Florence Eugenia, b. February 22, 1911.

718. ROY WESLEY ALLIS was born July 20, 1872, in Chatham, Ohio, and is living in Lodi, Ohio, at this writing. On December 24, 1901, he married Lydia G. Prouty and their children were:

1031. Warren R., b. July 29, 1904; died in infancy.

1032. Dorothy June, b. July 26, 1906.

1033. Maynard T., b. September 20, 1911.

719. CHARLES LESLIE ALLIS was born in Chatham, Ohio, on October 29, 1873, and is living there as this book goes to press. On March 20, 1897, he married Vesta E. Markley and their children are:

1034. Hubert Joseph, b. December 10, 1898.

1035. Eva Leona, b. August 23, 1900.

724. WALLACE STEELE ALLIS was born August 7, 1859, in Brookfield, Vt. He received his early education in the local schools and in 1877 entered the Norwich Free Academy of Norwich, Conn., from which he graduated with honors. He then entered Yale University, from which he graduated with honors in 1884, being one of the five Townshend prize speakers and being chosen a Commencement speaker.

Following his graduation from Yale he was for five years a member of the faculty of the Norwich Free Academy. During one year of that period, in addition to his academy work, he studied law in the office of the late Hon. Jeremiah Halsey. He was also for a time in the office of Wait & Greene and was admitted to the Bar in New London County on June 22, 1888. Two years afterward he began the practice of his profession in Norwich and soon won the confidence of the community.

Mr. Allis is a prominent citizen of Norwich and a very successful lawyer and was for two years City Attorney. In the fall of 1900 he was elected to the State Senate and in the session following, January, 1901, was a

WALLACE STEELE ALLIS

member and chairman of the important committees on banks and revision of the statutes. In 1915 he was again placed upon the committee for revision of the statutes, and in January, 1917, was appointed a member of the state tuberculosis commission by Gov. Marcus H. Holcomb. He was vice-president of the Uncas National Bank of Norwich for several years until 1903, when he was elected president. He is also a corporator of the Norwich Free Academy, a trustee of the Chelsea and the Dime Savings Banks, and is attorney for the Chelsea Savings Bank. Also he is a member of a number of social and business clubs and an Odd Fellow.

He married Alice A. Lathrop on September 14, 1904, and they had a daughter:

1036. Lydia Campbell, b. April 28, 1907; died May 5, 1907.

725. EGBERT HORACE ALLIS was born August 23, 1868, in Brookfield, Vt. On December 29, 1893, he married Alice Lillian Powers and is at this writing a farmer in Randolph, Vt. They have one daughter:

1037. Dorothy Powers, b. December 22, 1895.

728. TERENCE SKINNER ALLIS was born May 28, 1860, in Randolph, Vt., and lived there until the death of his mother in 1869, when he went to live with H. M. Hayden, a farmer. He obtained his education in the district schools and the State Normal School, from which he graduated in 1878. During the next year he taught school in Randolph, followed by a year in Guilford, Vt.

His next move was to Bridgeport, Conn., where he began his business career as a clerk in the clothing store of the Foster-Besse Company, but afterward moved to Ansonia, Conn., and engaged in the same line of business. In 1881 he went to Derby and formed a copartnership with J. G. Redshaw of Ansonia, under the firm name of Allis & Redshaw. At the end of ten years, during which the firm had conducted a very profitable business as clothiers, he purchased his partner's interest and has since then conducted the business alone. In addition to his store in Derby he is interested in other concerns in the same line of trade in Shelton and Winsted, Conn. In politics he is a Republican and is also a Mason and an Odd Fellow.

On August 27, 1884, he married Lottie E., daughter of Benjamin and Jane Smith of Derby, who was born December 27, 1859, and is living in Derby as this book goes to press. Their children were:

1038. Harold Watson, b. October 24, 1885; died in August, 1886.

1039. Clarence Hayden, b. April 2, 1888; *

1040. May Emily, b. December 11, 1892.

732. LEON ELISHA ALLIS was born June 11, 1863, in Brookfield, Vermont, and at this writing is living in Thetford, Vermont. He is a farmer by occupation. He is married and has two children, but detailed information is missing:

1041. Daughter.

1042. Son.

733. CHESTER DEWEY ALLIS was born September 30, 1848, in Rochester, N. Y. He was educated in the public schools of Rochester and the Holley Academy, and took a special course at Lafayette University, Easton, Pa., with the class of 1872.

Following his graduation he was for two years with A. S. Mann & Company of Rochester, N. Y., and for three or four years with the Atlantic & Great Western R. R. Company (now a part of the Erie R. R.), with headquarters in Cleveland, Ohio. His next position was with the United States Rolling Stock Company, and he was connected with its Hegeswisch (Chicago), Illinois, branch for about twenty years, eventually becoming assistant secretary.

In 1897 he accepted a position with the Elliott Car Company of Gadsden, Ala., and lived in Anniston and Gadsden, Ala. He became purchasing agent of that concern, and when it was succeeded by the Southern Car & Foundry Company he was made the purchasing and sales agent of the new company and moved to Birmingham, Ala. In 1904 he became connected with the Lathrop Lumber Company of that city, and at this writing is vice-president of that concern. He is one of the prominent members of the Presbyterian Church, and has taken the Knight Templar degree in Masonry.

On November 13, 1878, he married Mary Eleanor, daughter of Benjamin and Eleanor (Thomas) Chambers of Chambersburg, Pa., and a descendant of Benj. Chambers, a colonel in the Provincial forces. Their children were:

1043. Eleanor, b. September 4, 1879; died August 13, 1898.

1044. William Chester, b. November 25, 1882; died May 6, 1883.

1045. Chester Dewey, Jr., b. September 5, 1887; was educated in the public schools in Anniston, Gadsden and Birmingham, Ala., and the Alabama Polytechnic Institute, from which he graduated in 1909. On June 5, 1913, he married Marie Elizabeth England of Birmingham and at this writing is a farmer in Pinson, Ala.

734. JAMES WILLIAM ALLIS was born February 9, 1853, in Rochester, N. Y. He was educated in the public schools and at this writing is an accountant for the M. D. Knowlton Company of Rochester, manufacturers of paper box and shipping case machinery.

On October 18, 1879, he married Anna E. Sloan and their children are:

1046. Alfred Pells, b. October 18, 1880; a commercial traveler at this writing, living in Rochester.

1047. Anna Louise, b. January 7, 1884

742. WILLIAM F. PACKER ALLIS was born January 26, 1875, in Easton, Pa. He has always been a resident of Easton, and at this writing is secretary of the Free Press Publishing Company, general printers and publishers of the Easton Free Press.

On April 25, 1906, he married Lida C., daughter of Wilson B. Solliday of Easton, and they have one daughter:

1048. Mary Elizabeth, b. November 22, 1909.

748. FREDERICK SCOULLER ALLIS was born April 18, 1871, in Erie, Pa., and at this writing resides in Amherst, Mass. In 1893 he graduated from

Amherst College and was admitted to the Pennsylvania Bar. He practiced law in Erie until 1901, when he engaged in business in Minneapolis, Minn. In 1909 he bought a small ranch in Colorado, but came East in 1912 and became secretary of the Alumni Association of Amherst College. He is a member of the Phi Beta Kappa and Psi Upsilon fraternities.

On June 6, 1912, he married Jean, daughter of Dr. Alexander MacCoy of Overbrook, Pa. Their children are:

1049. Frederick Scouller, Jr., b. November 21, 1913.

1050. Martha Logan, b. December 17, 1916.

760. ABRAM Q. ALLIS was born November 4, 1843, in Prattsburg, N. Y. He has been a mechanic in Prattsburg for many years but is now retired from active business. On January 30, 1866, he married Cornelia S. Wilson, who died January 23, 1913. They had one son:

1051. C. Harry; *

764. GEORGE BASCOM ALLIS was born in Little Rock, Pulaski County, Ark., on November 9, 1845. He lived in Pulaski County until the year 1858, when his parents moved on to a farm in Jefferson County. When the schools were broken up on account of the Civil War he entered the telegraph service at Pine Bluff as a messenger boy, and continued in the office until he became chief operator and the town was occupied by the Federal troops under command of Col. Powell Clayton. As soon as the telegraph line between Pine Bluff and Little Rock was

rebuilt he was, upon the recommendation of Col. Clayton, placed in charge of the Pine Bluff office, under the appointment of R. C. Clowery, superintendent of the military telegraph under General Steele. He held that position during the trying times of General Steele's march to Camden and the heavy fighting on the Saline River, being required to stay in the office day and night in order to receive reports from the field and forward them to headquarters.

In 1864 he resigned from that position, and by special permission of the commanding officers the Allis and Mills families were allowed to take passage on the gunboat Naumkeag, bound for Memphis, Tenn. From there he went up the Mississippi and Ohio Rivers to New Albany, Ind., and then to Bloomington, Ill., where he attended Wesleyan University.

At the close of the war he returned to Pine Bluff and was deputy clerk and recorder for seven years. He then entered the railroad service as secretary to the general manager and paymaster. After that he engaged in the book and stationery business for a time, but at this writing is in the real estate and insurance business in Little Rock.

On October 15, 1872, he married Luella P. Hubbard, who is living in Little Rock at this writing. Their children were:

1052. Son, b. July 8, 1873; died July 19, 1873.

1053. Child, b. June 7, 1874; died June 12, 1874.

1054. Horace B., b November 23, 1875; died August 18, 1901.

1055. Hubbard, b. May 7, 1878; died December 2, 1878.

1056. George B., Jr., b. Sept. 22, 1879; died May 27, 1881.

GEORGE BASCOM ALLIS

1057. Martha C., b. May 21, 1883; is General Secretary of the Y. W. C. A., and at this writing is with the Newark, O., association.

1058. George Clifton, b September 23, 1885; is a railroad man and living in Little Rock at this writing.

1059. Hubbard Benjamin, b. October 24, 1887; *

1060. David Mills, b. January 20, 1890; married Pauline Courtney Walker of Muskogee, Okla., and is a traveling salesman as this book goes to press.

766. HORACE GREEN ALLIS was born February 3, 1855, in Little Rock, Ark., and was educated in the local schools. He was a bright, brainy, young man and rose rapidly in commercial life, his first venture being that of manager of an evening paper. He next went to the general offices of a railroad and then became owner and publisher of the "Little Rock Gazette." After that he went to St. Louis, Mo., and became cashier in one of the banks in that city, but ultimately moved back to Little Rock and became president of the First National Bank there.

He was the builder of the first electric street railroad in the city of Little Rock and the state of Arkansas, which flourished until the panic of 1892, at which time he was obliged to start out anew. He went to Alaska and spent two years locating valuable mines on Copper River, but unfortunately did not have the means to develop his claims and and was finally compelled to forfeit them. He next engaged in business in Los Angeles, Cal., and afterward in San Antonio, Texas, and at this writing is in the real estate and brokerage business in Dallas, Texas.

On December 4, 1887, he married Lou Agnes Siler, who died February 28, 1904. They had one daughter:

1061. Emma Mills, b. in 1888; married Robert W. Newell on March 16, 1904, and they have had the following children: Robert W., b. February 14, 1905, and died February 17, 1905, Paul D., b. April 13, 1906, Agnes E., b. September 14, 1908, and Francis W., b. April 20, 1911.

770. FRANK HOLCOMB ALLIS was born in Prattsburg, N. Y., August 8, 1867, and has been a farmer there all his life. On March 16, 1892, he married Hattie G., daughter of Henry and Henrietta (Carhart) Clark, who was born May 20, 1872, and is living in Prattsburg at this writing. Their children were:

1062. Henry Elbert, b. July 30, 1894.

1063. Leonard Romaine, b. October 4, 1895.

1064. Harry Francis, b. April 9, 1897; died July 18, 1898.

1065. Charlotte Henrietta, b. May 14, 1905.

771. LIZZIE MAY ALLIS was born May 27, 1863, in Prattsburg, N. Y., and obtained her early education at the Franklin Academy (Prattsburg), receiving the Regent's Diploma while there. She received the B. A. and M. A. degrees from Elmira College, Elmira, N. Y., and won the Hall essay prize and the Diven reading prize. She has taken post-graduate work at Cornell University and studied at Marburg and Berlin Universities, Germany.

Miss Allis has travelled extensively in Europe and America, having made four European tours. She has taught in Franklin Academy and in the Jacksonville Academy of

Jacksonville, Ill. For three years she was preceptress of the Susquehanna Collegiate Institute of Towanda, Pa., and for five years held a similar position in the State Normal College at Mansfield, Pa. For 13 years she was head of the Department of Modern Languages in the State College at Ames, Iowa, and at this writing is a teacher of German in the Pasadena Polytechnic High School of Pasadena, Cal.

779. EDWARD PHELPS ALLIS was born in Milwaukee, Wis., September 14, 1851, and at this writing is a scientist, residing in Mentone, France. He graduated from the Delaware Literary Institute of Franklin, N. Y., in 1867 as a civil engineer, and studied at the Antioch College of Yellow Springs, Ohio, in 1867-8, and in the Massachusetts Institute of Technology of Cambridge, Mass., in 1868-71, where he attained the highest rank ever attained there except by Ex-president Eliot of Harvard University, who had the same standing.

Following his graduation he was taken into the firm of the E. P. Allis Company of Milwaukee, and in 1889 was made vice-president. In 1887 he established what is now known as the Allis Research Laboratory and removed it to Mentone, France, in 1890, since which time he has conducted a special research in vertebrate morphology. In 1903 he received the degree of LL. D. from the University of Wisconsin, Madison, Wis., and in 1914 received the degree of M. D., honoris causa, from the University of Groningen (Netherlands).

Mr. Allis was associate editor of the Journal of Morphology and has been the author of many monographs, bulletins, etc., of a zoological and kindred nature. He is an associate in zoology of the Harvard University Museum and a member of many scientific societies in the United States, Great Britain and France, among them being the American Society of Naturilists and New York Academy of Sciences (New York), Boston Society of Natural History (Boston), Zoological Society and Society of Arts (London, England), Societi Astronomique de France, Societi Meteorologique de France, Legion d'Honeur (France) and Prix Lallemand (Paris, France), with the title Laureat de l'Institut, an honor rarely accorded to even a member of that academy. He is a fine historical scholar and a master of the French, German, Spanish and Italian languages.

In September, 1895, he married Medine Sgrena and has two children, his wife having since died:

1066. Maud, b. January 28, 1899.
1067. William Phelps, b. October 15, 1901.

781. CHARLES ALLIS was born May 4, 1853, in Milwaukee, Wis. He was educated in the public school and Markham's Academy of Milwaukee, and later in the Little Blue Academy at Farmington, Me. He began his business career with his father, Edward P. Allis, as an apprentice in 1868, serving four years in the shops. While at work he attended a night school and in 1872 entered the Little Blue Academy, graduating the following year, when he again took up his work in Milwaukee.

Mr. Allis, as secretary and treasurer of the Edward P. Allis Company, was most active in its management, the business increasing fourfold from 1889 (the year of his father's death) to 1901, when he negotiated the sale of the business to the Allis-Chalmers Company. He was the new corporation's president for the first four years of its existence, during which time the company was eminently successful.

He was vice-president and a director of the Milwaukee Trust Company until it was absorbed by the First Savings & Trust Company, and is a director of the First National Bank, a director of the First Savings & Trust Company, a trustee and member of the finance committee of the Northwestern Mutual Life Insurance Company, all of Milwaukee, and president of the Chicago Belting Company of Chicago, Illinois, which company he organized in 1890.

Mr. Allis is a great lover of art and was the first president of the Milwaukee Art Society. He is also a trustee of the Layton Art Gallery of that city and a member of a number of kindred organizations, including the Metropolitan Museum of Art of New York and the State Historical Society of Wisconsin, as well as a number of social and business clubs in Milwaukee, Chicago and New York.

On October 18, 1877, he married Sarah E. Ball, who is living in Milwaukee at this writing.

782. ERNEST ALLIS was born July 11, 1858, in Milwaukee, Wis., and was educated in the local schools and abroad, where he spent several years in study. He was a stockholder in the Edward P. Allis Company (now the Allis-Chalmers Company), and although not actively engaged in the management of its affairs he always kept well posted in regard to them. His residence was Milwaukee except for a few years when he lived in Asheville, N. C., before his death on November 9, 1894.

On February 11, 1890, he married Penelope, daughter of Orville and Katharine P. Winston, and they had one daughter:

1068. Margaret W., b. March 11, 1891; married William Benjamin Harrison, June 4, 1912, and is living in Louisville, Ky., at this writing. Their children are William Heyward, b. March 19, 1913, and Winston Pope, b. October 6, 1914.

785. LOUIS ALLIS was born December 30, 1866, in Milwaukee, Wis., where he is living at this writing. After attending the Markham Academy, a preparatory school in Milwaukee, he and his brother Frank, with a tutor, went on a nine months camping trip in the winter of 1884-5 through California in connection with their studies. They traveled from Riverside to Los Angeles, Santa Barbara, Monterey and the Yosemite Valley, camping wherever they found a good stream, and spent three or four hours a day at their books.

In September, 1885, he entered the Pennsylvania Military College at Chester, Pa., from which he graduated as a civil engineer in the fall of 1888. He then entered the employ of the E. P. Allis Company and rose from assistant shipping clerk to purchasing agent and general manufacturing assistant, which positions he held for five years. His work then became more general, and he also assumed the management of about 80,000 acres of land in the northern peninsula of Michigan which were owned by his father's estate. In 1902, after the E. P. Allis Company was sold to the Allis-Chalmers Company, he became associated with the Mechanical Appliance Company of Milwaukee, manufacturers of electric motors, and is now president of that firm.

Mr. Allis has been a director of the Central Improvement Company, developing West Allis, Wis.; director and secretary of the Cazenovia Land Company; director and secretary of the Reliance Land & Mining Company; director, secretary and treasurer of the Geneva Land & Mining Company; director, vice-president and treasurer of the Milwaukee Boiler Company.

Mr. Allis is prominent socially, has traveled abroad extensively, and is an enthusiastic golfer, having held different western championships at various times. He is a member of various clubs in Milwaukee, the Travelers Club of Paris, France, and the Societe de la Boulie, near Versailles, France. He is also extremely interested in surgery and medicine and has done benevolent work along this line.

Mr. Allis has been married twice, (first) to Carol Yates on September 17, 1890, and (second) to Louise Hegen on May 1, 1911. His children are:

By first marriage:

1069. Edward Phelps, b. August 1, 1892; graduated from Harvard University, Cambridge, Mass., in 1915, having taken his finishing preparatory course at Milton School, Milton, Mass., and at this writing is engaged in the manufacturing business with his father in Milwaukee, Wis.

By second marriage:

1070. Louis, Jr., b. April 14, 1916.

788. GILBERT ALLIS was born in Milwaukee, Wis., January 4, 1871. He was educated in the public school and the University of Pennsylvania (Philadelphia), from which he graduated in 1898 with the degree of B. S. in biology. He then lived in Paris, France, for a time and at this writing owns a ranch in Stevensville, Montana, that covers thousands of acres, where he has built a magnificent residence.

He married (first) Amber Lawlor on July 20, 1901, and (second) Mrs. Jessica S. Alward, daughter of John S. Neenah and widow of Herbert Alward. His children by the first marriage are:

1071. Gilbert, Jr.

1072. Amber, b. in 1912.

800. WILLIAM E. ALLIS was born October 6, 1884, in Syracuse, N. Y. He was educated in the public schools and Syracuse University, from which he graduated in 1906. Since then he has been engaged in engineering and fire insurance inspection work, and at this writing is special agent for the Northern Assurance Company, Ltd., of London, England, with headquarters in Syracuse.

On March 30, 1913, he married Gwladys Erskine of Mt. Vernon, N. Y. They had a son who died in infancy, and now have an adopted daughter:

1073. John Henry, b. April 12, 1914; died the same day.

1074. Anna Elizabeth, b. September 21, 1915 (adopted).

806. WILLIAM H. ALLIS was born May 20, 1850, in Philadelphia, N. Y. At this writing he in engaged in the real estate business in Aitken, Minn., and is also secretary of the Hotel Foley in that town. On October 21, 1874, he married (first) Lillie H., daughter of Albert and Harriet Anderson, who died August 11, 1907, and (second) in July, 1915, Clara M., daughter of C. A. Christensen of Aitken. His children, all by the first marriage, were:

1075. Grace Darling, b. June 22, 1879; married Walter Wilson and their children are Lillie V. and Ruth.

1076. Ethel Evaline, b. May 6, 1881; married John Wiley and their children are Pearl Dexter, Earl D. and Katherine.

1077. Alberta Luella, b. January 25, 1883; married M. D. Rowland and their children are John and Lawrence.

1078. Minnie May, b. August 16, 1885.

810. JOHN WARREN ALLIS was born May 13, 1865, in Philadelphia, N. Y. He was educated in the local schools and until 14 years of age worked on his father's farm. He then started out to make his way in the world and for the next seven years worked as clerk in a store, telegraph operator and ticket agent in a railroad office.

When he was 21 years of age he accepted a position as officeman and salesman with a concern manufacturing knit underwear, and in 1890 the firm of McAdam, Allis & Company was formed. They opened a factory in Utica, N. Y., and two years afterward incorporated as the Utica Knitting Company, with $51,000 capital. Since then the company has grown to be one of the largest of its kind in the world, now being capitalized at $2,500,000 and doing an annual business of over $5,000,000, and Mr. Allis is the vice-president and sales manager, residing in New York City. In 1888 he married Elizabeth McDermott, who is now living in New York City.

817. DEXTER HURLBUT ALLIS was born August 10, 1867, in Hatfield, Mass. He was educated in the public schools in Springfield, Mass., and the Philadelphia Dental College of Philadelphia, Pa., from which he graduated in 1887. Following his graduation he practiced his profession in the office of his uncle, Dr. J. Searle Hurlbut of Springfield, and upon the death of his uncle in 1902 assumed full charge of the business. He was a very successful dentist and at the time of his death on January 31, 1916, had one of the best practices in western Massachusetts. He was accidentally killed while inspecting the new offices he was planning to take in the Third National Bank Building.

Dr. Allis was for a time president of the Connecticut Valley District Dental Society. He was a member of the Springfield Country Club, Winthrop Club and Springfield Commandery of Knights Templar, a director of the Y. M.

C. A., and an active member of the South Congregational Church. On November 24, 1904, he married Flora May Castle and they had one daughter:

1079. Catherine Hurlbut, b. September 21, 1905.

818. EDWARD MILTON ALLIS was born in Hatfield, Mass., December 9, 1870, and lived there until six years of age, at which time the family moved to Springfield, Mass. He attended the public schools and the high school, from which he graduated in 1889, and then entered the employ of the Massachusetts Mutual Life Insurance Company. He rose from the position of clerk to agent of the company, and in October, 1905, became general agent for western Massachusetts. On April 1, 1907, he became a member of the firm of Sutton, Allis & Richards, general agents for western Massachusetts, and since the retirement of Mr. Sutton on July 1, 1911, the agency has been conducted by the firm of Richards & Allis.

Mr. Allis is very prominent in life insurance circles and is a member of the Western Massachusetts Life Underwriters Association, of which organization he was treasurer for five years and president for one year. He is actively interested in the affairs of the city, being on the Springfield Board of Trade, and is a member of the committee of management of the Y. M. C. A. He is also connected with a number of business and social clubs, among them being the Nayasset Club, Winthrop Club, Springfield Rifle Club, Springfield Fish & Game Association, and is a 32nd degree Mason and a prominent member of the Faith Congregational Church.

On October 16, 1901, he married Florence Wightman and they have had three children:

1080. Milton Wightman, b. July 8, 1902; died May 5, 1906.

1081. Jairus Hurlbut, b. July 22, 1905.

1082. Marjorie Wightman, b. December 5, 1908.

822. WILLIAM BAKER ALLIS was born June 7, 1866, in Hatfield, Mass. He attended Williams College Williamstown, Mass., and graduated in 1889, and in 1892 graduated from the Andover Theological Seminary. After leaving the seminary he was in the Andover House settlement, Boston, Mass., for a year and the following year was the assistant pastor of a Congregational church in Waltham, Mass. He next accepted a pastorate in North Conway, N. H., which he held for four years, and during three years of that time was also Superintendent of Schools.

In 1898 he became assistant pastor of the Plymouth Church, Brooklyn, N. Y., and three years afterward went to Schenectady, N. Y., as pastor of the Jay Street Congregational Church, which position he held for four years. During that time he was also chaplain of the Schenectady Fire Department and secretary of the New York State Conference of Religion.

In 1905 he moved to Mount Vernon, N. Y., and for five years was pastor of the First Congregational and Plymouth Churches. He was also Probation Officer in the City Court of Mount Vernon for a period of seven years,

EDWARD MILTON ALLIS

1905-12. For a year he was manager of the Journal of Accountancy, New York City, and at this writing is Probation Officer in the Court of Special Sessions in that city. He is also engaged as a preacher Sundays, and is writing a number of short stories for children.

On July 25, 1894, he married May Allena Pettee, who was born May 1, 1865. Their children are:

1033. Norman William, b. May 18, 1895; assistant head of the English books department of Charles Scribner's Sons, publishers and booksellers of New York, at this writing.

1084. Abbott Hastings, b. April 25, 1899; attending the Huntington School, Boston, Mass., at this writing.

823. JAMES CUTLER ALLIS was born July 21, 1866. He is a graduate of the Malden (Mass.) High School and was one of the best debaters in its literary society. He lived in Malden for 25 years and was prominent in the Malden Rifles. At this writing he is living in Whitman, Mass., and is connected with the United Shoe Machinery Company of Boston, Mass., being manager of its mailing department.

On July 17, 1912, he married Florence Adellah Ward and they have an adopted daughter:

1085. Charlotte Evelyn.

826. CLARENCE LIVINGSTON ALLIS was born November 29, 1883, in Valparaiso, Chile, and was educated in the Instituto Internacional at Santiago, Chile, until ready to enter preparatory school. He entered and graduated from the Wooster Preparatory School, Wooster,

Ohio, and in 1902 entered the University of Wooster, spending the freshman and sophomore years there.

In 1904 he entered Leland Stanford, Jr., University (California), where he spent one year on mines and mining. He then studied at Columbia University, New York City, for a year and three years afterward took special work in metallurgy at Leland Stanford University. For the past seven years he has been with the Wooster Electric Company and is secretary and treasurer of that concern at this writing.

On May 4, 1911, he married (first) Miriam Blanche Hard, and after her death he married (second) Lenore B. Hattery on March 6, 1916. His children are:

By first marriage:

1086. Clarence Livingston, Jr., b. December 9, 1912.

By second marriage:

1087. John Mather, b. February 3, 1917.

828. CHARLES ERNEST ALLIS was born July 4, 1859, in Northampton, Mass. He was educated in the local schools, and at this writing is a locomotive engineer on the Boston & Maine Railroad, living in Springfield, Mass.

He has been married twice, (first) on February 22, 1883, to Flora Belle Wood of Chicopee Falls, Mass., who died in October, 1885, and (second) on October 15, 1889, to Rose J. Morley, who is living in Springfield at this writing. There is one son by the second marriage:

1088. Ralph Morley, b. December 16, 1896.

830. WILLIAM CLINTON ALLIS was born November 30, 1866, in Northampton, Mass. He was educated in the local schools, and at this writing is a locomotive engineer on the Boston & Maine Railroad, living in Northampton. On November 11, 1896, he married Helen Johnstone Erskine, and their children are:

1089. Robert Erskine, b. June 28, 1898.

1090. Ruth Taynton, b. June 27, 1900.

832. GEORGE LINCOLN ALLIS was born August 16, 1873, in Northampton, Mass. He was educated in the public schools and at this writing is a locomotive engineer on the Boston & Maine Railroad, living in Northampton, having been connected with that road for over twenty years. At the breaking out of the Spanish-American War he enlisted in Company I, Second Massachusetts Volunteers, and his regiment reached Cuba on June 22, 1898. He took part in the battles of El Caney, San Juan and Santiago, and was mustered out on November 3, 1898.

On December 16, 1899, he married Bertha Harriette Johnson, who was born January 23, 1876. They have a daughter:

1091. Esther Johnson, b. May 6, 1902.

833. ROBERT TAYNTON ALLIS was born October 19, 1875, in Northampton, Mass., and was educated in the public schools in that city. After leaving school he held a position in the office of the Northampton

Cutlery Company, and was for several years connected with the Nonotuck Silk Company of Florence, Mass. He then accepted a government position at the Navy Yard in Portsmouth, N. H., and two years afterward became connected with the Olmstead-Quaboag Corset Company of West Brookfield, Mass. He has now been with that concern for about ten years, and at this writing is manager of the Springfield, Mass., branch, living in Springfield. On October 19, 1901, he married Madge Frey and their children are:

1092. Margaret Thompson, b. August 3, 1902.

1093. Helen Taynton, b. October 19, 1906.

1094. Elsie, b. April 1, 1909.

836. IRVING MELVIN ALLIS was born October 9, 1850, in Orwell Township, Bradford County, Pa. He was educated in the Susquehanna Collegiate Institute of Towanda, Pa., and in 1871 engaged in the drug business in Wyalusing, Pa., in which business he has since continued. On October 13, 1873, he married Julia Scoville, and they have a son:

1095. Scoville, b. September 10, 1883; graduated in 1903 from the Wyalusing High School and in 1905 from the Philadelphia School of Pharmacy. At this writing he is engaged in the drug business in Wyalusing with his father and is unmarried.

837. NED HUNTER ALLIS was born April 6, 1854, in Orwell Township, Pa. He is a graduate of the Towanda High School and studied veterinary medicine at Toronto, Canada, graduating in 1888. He then began

practicing as a veterinary surgeon in Wyalusing, Pa., and is still engaged in his profession there at this writing.

On September 20, 1888, he married Augusta E. Mitten of Herrick, Pa., who died November 3, 1916. They had two children:

1096. Paul Mitten, b. April 6, 1891; graduated from Wyalusing High School in 1907, the Wyoming Seminary in 1909, and the medical department of the University of Pennsylvania in 1914. After graduation he was an interne in the Germantown Hospital of Philadelphia for 18 months, and since then has practiced his profession in Wyalusing. He is unmarried at this writing.

1097. Helen Frost, b. February 16, 1900; is a graduate of the Wyalusing High School and at this writing is attending the Oberlin Conservatory of Music, Oberlin, Ohio.

839. FRANK ROY ALLIS was born October 21, 1869, in Orwell Township, Pa., and at this writing is a farmer and a dealer in lumber, feed and flour in Wysox, Pa. On August 28, 1895, he married Cora Elizabeth Wood, who was born June 3, 1872, in Wysox, and their children are:

1098. Cleone Wood, b. April 7, 1897; a graduate of the Rome High School and is living in Wysox as this book goes to press.

1099. Nellie May, b. February 7, 1903.

841. GEORGE GRANT ALLIS was born August 8, 1866, in Orwell Township, Pa., and at this writing is a farmer on the old homestead in Orwell. On August 7, 1888, he married Elma F. Meracle, and their children are:

1100. Earl Edwin, b. Dec. 7, 1893; married Drucie C. Lloyd on June 24, 1915, and runs a grist and feed mill on the farm in Orwell.

1101. Lile Lyman, b. November 8, 1899.

1102. Cecil Claire, b. August 1, 1901.

844. LESLIE L. ALLIS was born April 5, 1859, in South Hill (Orwell), Pa. He was a farmer in South Hill for a number of years and in 1883 moved to Smith Center, Kansas, where he engaged in the mercantile business until 1895. For a number of years afterward he was interested in the real estate business, but at this writing has retired and is living in Manhattan, Kansas.

On May 16, 1888, he married Helen, daughter of Henry Carpenter of Smith Center, and their children are:

1103. Fayette Henry, b. December 4, 1889; *

1104. Leland Carpenter, b. March 17, 1895; is living in Manhattan, Kansas, at this writing. He is a member of the First Kansas Infantry and served at the border during the Mexican disturbance in 1916.

1105. Helen Josephine, b. October 21,1896; is living in Manhattan, Kansas, at this writing.

851. MURTON E. ALLIS was born May 1, 1861, in Orwell, Bradford County, Pa., and at this writing is a farmer in New Hampton, Mo. He married Anna Pickard of King City, Mo., and their children are:

1106. Etta M.; is unmarried at this writing.

1107. Lester L., b. July 9, 1891; married Blanche Best on April 20, 1913, and at this writing is living in St. Joseph, Mo.

1108. Mary, b. in April, 1896; married Ora Day.

1109. Carl; living in New Hampton as this book goes to press.

1110. Mabel; living in New Hampton.

854. CHARLES HENRY ALLIS was born January 19, 1858. He was a farmer and merchant in Wysox, Pa., and died January 26, 1915. He married Flora M., daughter of Captain I. A. and Melissa (Meracle) Park, who died on June 10, 1915. Their children were:

1111. Manley Frank, b. December 30, 1886; a traveling salesman in Canada at this writing.

1112. Mabel, b. July 9, 1888; died June 9, 1890.

1113. Stanley Melvin, b. November 26, 1889; married Nellie Mitten on June 23, 1915, and is living in Herrickville, Pa., at this writing.

1114. Ora May, b. April 15, 1891; married Elmer Babcock.

856. MILES EARL ALLIS was born May 18, 1856, in Orwell, Pa., and at this writing is a farmer in Rome, N. Y. On January 1, 1874, he married Ida, daughter of James and Maryette (Barber) Robinson, and their children are:

1115. Fred Lewis, b. September 28, 1874; *

1116. Clayton Waller, b. April 2, 1878; *

857. JESSE BENTON ALLIS was born October 19, 1857, in Orwell, Penn., and is a farmer there at this writing. On January 24, 1885, he married Louisa, daughter of Elias Dixon of Standing Stone Township, Penn., and their children are:

1117. Loren Earl, b. January 9, 1886; *

1118. Ira Scott, b January 6, 1889; married Cecil Wheaton on February 12, 1913, and is a farmer in Orwell, Pa., at this writing.

860. GEORGE HENRY ALLIS was born June 27, 1871, in Orwell, Pa., and at this writing is a farmer in Geneva, Minn. On January 14, 1897, he married Carrie Estella, daughter of Lucius and Mary (Maynard) Gibbs of Geneva, and their children are:

1119. Marion Geraldine, b. April 25, 1899.
1120. Georgiana Belle, b. October 24, 1901.
1121. Delora Vivian, b. February 29, 1904.
1122. Claude Maynard, b. February 11, 1906.

863. NORMAN LEAD ALLIS was born April 20, 1870, in Orwell, Bradford County, Pa., and at this writing is a farmer in Rummerfield (same county), Pa. On December 16, 1897, he married Anna Bell, daughter of Harvey and Martha (Avis) Coleman of Herrickville, Pa., and their children are:

1123. Harvey Jerome, b. September 13, 1898.
1124. Jeraldine Elizabeth, b May 14, 1900.
1125. Barney Dudley, b. February 19, 1904.
1126. Percy Harrison, b. August 27, 1908.
1127. Rodney Burton, b. January 27, 1911.

866. LEWIS EUGENE ALLIS was born July 30, 1876, in Orwell, Pa., and at this writing is a manufacturer of butter and ice cream in Dushore, Sullivan County, Pa. On July 26, 1899, he married Grace Eleanor, daughter of Percy and Sarah (Spencer) Manley of Canton, Pa., and their children are:

1128. Daughter, died in infancy.
1129. Manley Lynn, b. April 20, 1907.

868. BERT SILAS ALLIS was born November 29, 1887, in Orwell, Pa., and at this writing is a farmer in Rome, Pa. On June 25, 1913, he married Florence N., daughter of John and Kathryn (Fuller) Mitten, and their children are:

1130. Kathryn Marie, b. April 15, 1914.

1131. Willema May, b. July 13, 1915.

1132. Frederick Vernon, b. November 14, 1916.

871. WILLIS EUGENE ALLIS was born May 28, 1868, in Orwell, Pa., but moved to North Platte, Neb., when a young man and in 1902 moved to Portland, Ore. At this writing he is living on a 320-acre ranch at Deer Isle, Col. On December 24, 1891, he married Laura Wilson and they have a son:

1133. Furn, b. February 10, 1900.

875. ROBERT A. ALLIS was born May 28, 1878, in Rome, Pa. He lived there for several years after his marriage, but at this writing resides in East Towanda, Pa., and is employed in the furniture factory of J. O. Frost & Sons of Towanda. On March 24, 1898, he married Maude Smith and their children are:

1134. Florence Emma, b. July 5, 1902.

1135. Kenneth S., b. August 5, 1909.

1136. Lyndon R., b. July 17, 1911.

876. WILLIAM P. ALLIS was born February 24, 1881, in Rome, Pa. He lived in Towanda and Wyalusing, Pa., for a time but at this writing is a yard

conductor for the Pennsylvania Railroad, living in Rochester, Pa. On October 27, 1900, he married Lulu Lee and their children are:

1137. Lee J., b. October 21, 1901.

1138. Virginia I., b. March 4, 1903.

1139. Eleanor E., b. December 31, 1909.

881. MURRAY G. ALLIS was born July 28, 1891, in Towanda, Penn., and was educated in the local schools. At this writing he is a chauffeur in that city. On March 24, 1911, he married Daisy Smith and they have a daughter:

1140. Gwendolyn Emma, b. November 18, 1911.

884. HENRY EUGENE ELLIS was born March 15, 1853, in Rock Island, Wis., and was educated in the local schools. He was for many years engaged in the timber and logging business, but at this writing is in the real estate business in Seattle, Wash. On December 7, 1883, he married Lillian M. Germond and their children are:

1141. Edward B., b. November 21, 1884.

1142. William G., b. April 5, 1887; is a rancher and is living in Seattle.

1143. Hubert I., b. June 28, 1889; a mining engineer in Seattle at this writing.

1144. Lelia P., b. September 29, 1891.

885. WILLIAM MARION ELLIS was born in Rock Island, Wis., September 16, 1855, and was educated in the local schools. He is living in Raymond, Wash., at

this writing and is engaged in various business enterprises. On April 27, 1886, he married Elizabeth Robinson and their children are:

1145. Clifton Marion, b. December 16, 1887.

1146. George Freeman, b. April 21, 1889.

889. HUBERT JUDD ELLIS was born May 12, 1868, in Rock Island, Wis., but was educated in Kansas, where he lived as a boy. At this writing he is engaged in the logging and towing business in Raymond, Wash. On August 12, 1901, he married Anna Johnson and their children are:

1147. Mildred Allways, b September 3, 1902.

1148. La Verna Lee, b. June 4, 1904.

898. CHARLES D. ELLIS was born August 1, 1849, in New Britain, Conn., where he is now living as a retired farmer. He married (first) on December 24, 1874, Mary J. Emerson of Brattleboro, Vermont, who died April 15, 1889, and (second) on October 14, 1891, Margaret Sloan, who is living in New Britain at this writing. His children are:

By first marriage:

1149. Howard M., b. February 8, 1889.

By second marriage:

1150. Irving E., b. December 31, 1892.

901. LOUIS PERRIN ELLIS was born September 17, 1870, in New Britain, Conn. On May 14, 1895, he married Etta Case of New Britain, and at this writing

is living in Meriden, Conn., being connected with J. E. Brown, dealer in leather goods. Their children are:

1151. Marjorie Louise, b. April 24, 1896,
1152. Carlton Case, b. September 13, 1900.
1153. Irene, b. February 16, 1904.
1154. Donald Porter, b. September 7, 1907.
1155. Winifred Mabel, b. December 2, 1910.
1156. Malcolm Judd, b. May 4, 1913.

904. ELISHA WELLS ALLIS was born December 29, 1837, and lived as a boy in Columbus, Ohio, and Huntington, Conn. He was a builder in Stamford, Conn., for many years but moved to Newtown, Conn., in 1876, where he died March 9, 1877.

Mr. Allis was a veteran of the Civil War. He enlisted on April 25, 1861, as a lieutenant in Company F, Third Regiment, Connecticut Volunteer Infantry, and was mustered into service the following month. In June he was assigned to the first brigade, first division, of McDowell's Army of the Potomac, and was engaged in the first Battle of Bull Run on July 21st. On August 12, 1861, he was discharged at Hartford by reason of the expiration of his term. He reenlisted on July 22, 1862, in Company C, 95th Regiment, Ohio Infantry Volunteers, to serve three years and took part in the following battles: Richmond, Ky., August 30, 1862, Jackson, Miss., May 14, 1863, Siege of Vicksburg, Miss., May 18 to June 22, 1863 (in which he was wounded), Siege of Jackson, July 10 to 18, 1863, and Brice's Cross Roads on June 10, 1864. He was discharged from service on August 13, 1865, at the close of the war.

On October 13, 1869, he married Lucy, daughter of John R. and Mariett (Botsford) Tomlinson, who was born October 1, 1847, and died in January, 1903. Their children were:

1157. Lucy, b. June 18, 1870; a teacher in Wallingford, Conn., at this writing.

1158. Florence, b. June 6, 1872; is a teacher in Wallingford as this book goes to press.

1159. Franklin Wells, b. November 27, 1874; graduated from Yale University, New Haven, Conn., in 1896. He then entered the service of the Columbus Telephone Company of New York and was raised to the position of general manager. At the time of the Spanish-American War he enlisted in Battery C, First Conn. Heavy Artillery, but spent the summer in camp at Niantic, Conn., and was discharged in the fall. He died on October 23, 1903, unmarried, after an illness of about two weeks.

908. SYLVESTER HILL ALLIS was born March 24, 1854, in Milford, Conn. He was educated in the public schools in Cold Spring, N. Y., and lived there until soon after his marriage. On June 9, 1875, he married Louise Davis, daughter of James N. Howell of Cold Spring. He was employed on the New York Evening Post, New York City, and resided in Brooklyn, N. Y., and lost his life from a ferryboat plying between those two cities on March 21, 1887. His wife died at Cold Spring on January 29, 1892. Their children were:

1160. Harry Sylvester, b. March 20, 1876; *

1161. Nelson Howell, b. November 9, 1879; *

910. EUGENE G. ALLIS was born August 6, 1856, in Cold Spring, N. Y. He obtained his education in the public schools of that town and during his five years apprenticeship to his father (editor of the Cold Spring Recorder) he learned the trade of printer, editor and business manager of a country newspaper. For the next three years he was employed in different newspaper offices in Massachusetts, and in 1878 purchased the Vermont Tribune of Ludlow, Vt., and became its editor and business manager. From the first the business was a success. The paper had been badly managed, but under his skillful management it became the leading news and political paper in the state.

Close attention to business and the burden of managing and editing a large paper soon began to affect his health, and he sold out his business in Ludlow and moved to New Haven, Conn., where he bought the Shore Line Times. He next went to Denver, Col., southern California and Florida, and finally Livingston Manor, N. Y. (in the Catskills), where he died August 31, 1901.

On October 8, 1879, he married Lavinia, daughter of Daniel and Ann McElroy of Cold Spring, who was born February 27, 1859, and is living in New Haven at this writing. They had two children:

1162. Raymond, b. December 12, 1884; died the same day.

1163. Marguerite, b. Feb. 6, 1886; a music teacher and contralto soloist in New Haven.

913. FERDINAND WARREN ALLIS was born November 17, 1860, in Cold Spring, N. Y. He was

No. 66. GOD OF THE NATIONS.

(The New National Hymn.)

Effective male quartet by first tenor singing alto an octave higher than written.

ANNA SKINNER CHAPMAN. F. W. ALLIS.

1. God of the na - tions, Thou! Oh, hear us, as we bow,
2. This land we love is Thine! Oh, may Thy mer - cy shine
3. Our fa - ther's God wast Thou! As then, be with us now,
4. Our coun - try's flag we love! The Blue, like that a - bove,
5. Lest we for - get we pray, Be with us day by day,

Thine aid to seek! Thine arm is ev - er strong, A - gainst the
With love and pow'r! This coun-try of the free! With love of
And guide us still! May we stand firm for right! Walk ev - er
Stands for the true! Like White, in pur - i - ty, May each heart
As in the past! O give us wis-dom, Lord! And may we

hosts of wrong! Draw near, nor tar - ry long, But help the weak!
lib - er - ty! Oh, may we, too, love Thee, Each day and hour!
in the Light! Strive hum-bly with our might, To do Thy will!
ev - er be! The Red tells you and me Of suff - 'ring too!
read Thy word! Thy strength do Thou af - ford While time shall last!

educated in the local schools and learned the trade of a printer in the office of the Cold Spring Recorder, a weekly newspaper owned and edited by his father. Desiring a wider knowledge of the printing business he left Cold Spring and gained some valuable experience in New York City, Boston, Mass., and other places, until in 1882 he settled in Hartford, Conn. He was at first connected with the Hartford Courant, but soon accepted a position with the Hartford Times, and at this writing has been in the service of that newspaper for a period of over thirty years.

In addition to being a printer Mr. Allis has acquired a general working knowledge of music, and in connection with his wife's talent as a verse writer has composed and published several songs. He is also a deacon in the Second Congregational Church of Hartford. On October 11, 1883, he married Anna Skinner, daughter of Horatio D. and Rosanna (Skinner) Chapman of East Hampton, Conn., who was born February 2, 1861. Their children are:

1164. Horatio Dana, b. July 28, 1884; *

1165. Anna Rose, b. July 6, 1886; a music teacher and church organist in Hartford at this writing.

1166. Burdette, b. Dec. 19, 1889; married Amelia G. Moseley of Hartford on May 29, 1913, and is a linotype operator for the Hartford Courant at this writing.

1167. Elizabeth Chapman, b. March 12, 1892; married Ernest H. Moseley of Hartford on August 1, 1914, where they are now living.

1168. Robert Homer, b. August 24, 1894; is living in Hartford and in the employ of the Phoenix Insurance Company.

1169. Raymond Ferdinand, b. January 15, 1897; living in Hartford and employed by the Ætna Insurance Company.

914. WILLIAM PELTON ALLIS was born January 11, 1871, in Cold Spring, N. Y. He learned the trade of a printer in his home town, and after the death of his parents attended and graduated from the Yale Business College in New Haven, Conn. He then bought out two newspapers in Groton, Conn., which he published until he moved to Hartford, Conn., and engaged in the printing business. From there he moved to New York City and was in the printing and advertising business for a time, but in 1908 settled in Cold Spring and established the Sentinel, a weekly newspaper, of which he is still the owner. At this writing he is also managing editor of the Automobile Digest & Register of New York City, with offices in Cold Spring and New York City, and resides in the former town.

On September 9, 1893, he married Sarah, daughter of Ignatz and Frances Hasenmaile of Cold Spring and their children are:

1170. Frances Elizabeth, b. July 1, 1897.

1171. Sarah Lucille, b. October 24, 1898.

1172. Agnes Houghton, b. October 9, 1902.

921. WILLIAM ELTON ALLIS was born June 12, 1853, in Shelburne Falls, Mass., and educated in the local schools. He lived for a time in Fort Dodge and for over twenty years in Council Bluffs, Iowa, and at this writing is a builder and contractor in Omaha, Neb. On October 29, 1879, he married Jennie, daughter of John C. and Mary (Smith) Watkins of Fort Dodge, Ia., who was born March 29, 1854. Their children were:

1173. Lulu Mary, b. Feb. 28, 1881; married Jerome A. Lillie, Jr., June 2, 1906, and is living in Omaha, Neb., at this writing.

1174. Laura Mae, b. February 18, 1883; married Orville Maxfield on May 20, 1903.

1175. Marguerite Cecil, b. April 18, 1892; married on July 28, 1909, Carl H. Backers.

1176. Harriet, b. July 6, 1896; died July 18, 1897.

930. EUGENE WILLIAM ALLIS was born August 3, 1854, in West Addison, Vt. On April 28, 1880. he married Clara Edwards and at this writing is a farmer in West Addison. They had a daughter:

1177. Mattie, b. April 27, 1882; died October 29, 1886.

933. EDGAR NATHANIEL ALLIS was born July 6, 1866, in Addison, Vt., and was a farmer there all his life. On October 21, 1884, he married Lucy M. Rondeau and died January 28, 1895. His widow married (second) George H. Eldridge and is living in East Middlebury, Vermont, at this writing. His two children were:

1178. Clifford Henry, b. October 31, 1886; a civil engineer and is living in Middlebury, Vermont, at this writing.

1179. Carlton Cyrus, b. April 19, 1893; is an expert mechanic, living in Bridport, Vermont, as this book goes to press.

934. GEORGE W. ALLIS was born July 6, 1844, in Baltimore, Ohio, and at this writing is a blacksmith in that town. He married (first) in October, 1866, Catherine Sullivan, who was born March 6, 1848, and died November 11, 1872; (second) on June 22, 1873,

Mary Rahley, who was born October 2, 1849, and died February 15, 1893; (third) about 1897 Jennie Fisher, who is now living in Baltimore, Ohio. His children were:

By first marriage:

1180. George, b. August 10, 1867; died the same day.

1181. Albert Thomas, b. July 4, 1868; *

1182. Sarah Jane, b. April 11, 1870; married William S. Larimer on April 18, 1890, and is living in Cooksville, Ill., at this writing.

1183. Harriet, b. February 6, 1872; died April 9, 1874.

By second marriage:

1184. Catherine, b February 14, 1875; married Mr. Jennings and is living in Athens, Ohio.

1185. Lucinda, b. April 30, 1878, married (first) Elmer Knecht and (second) Taylor Brumbaugh and is living in Fostoria, Ohio.

1186. John, b. November 25, 1882; died the same day.

1187. Emma May, b. May 9, 1884; married Roy H Widener on January 3, 1903, and is living in Lancaster, Ohio, at this writing. They have a daughter, Helen, born December 9, 1903.

1188 George Henry, b. September 20, 1886.

1189. Earl Nelson, b September 23, 1888; died Jan. 30, 1892.

1190. James, b. September 24 1890; died Nov. 20, 1890.

940. FREDERICK ALLIS was born September 1, 1848, in New Orleans, La. He lived in that city until just before the beginning of the Civil War, at which time his parents moved to St. Paul, Minn.

His preparation for college was made under private tutors in St. Paul, and after graduation from Yale University he studied law at the Columbia Law School, from which he received the degree of L. L. B. in 1872. He then spent a little over three years in Europe, including a year of study in the University of Bohn with Arthur P. Crane and John C. Benton.

Upon returning to his home he practiced law with his father until the death of the latter in 1884. Two years afterward he moved to New York City, but before leaving St. Paul he was offered an appointment by Governor Merriam of Minnesota to the bench of the District Court in that state corresponding to the Supreme Court of the state of New York. After his removal to New York his chief client for a time was Cyrus W. Field. For a time he had an office in Dobbs Ferry, then went to the Law Department of the Elevated Railway, and afterwards to the office of Martin W. Littleton. Since then he has been practicing by himself and has done considerable writing for others, chiefly on constitutional subjects. He has also published a work on the 10th amendment.

On November 11, 1875, he married Lida B. Ashton of Philadelphia, Pa., and their children are:

1191. Mary Castle, b. November 23, 1878; died August 5, 1880.

1192. Joseph Ashton, b. January 5, 1881; *

1193. Katherine Heylin, b October 4, 1883; married Audubon Tyler of New Haven, Conn., on June 20, 1914, and they have a daughter, Justine, born October 4, 1915.

945. GEORGE HENRY ALLIS was born June 10, 1848, in Coventry, N. Y. He lived in Coventry and Candor, N. Y., until about 20 years of age and then en-

gaged in the manufacture of pine lumber and shingles in Clearfield County, Pa. On April 17, 1876, he married Mary E. Leach, who was born November 23, 1837, in Seward, N. Y. Soon afterward he moved to Reynoldsville, Pa., and engaged in the manufacture of woolen goods under the firm name of Allis, Sykes & Moorehouse. He continued in that line of business until 1893, when the plant was destroyed by fire.

Mr. Allis then moved to Genesee, Pa., where he conducted a general mercantile business for four years. After that he became engaged in the shipping of farm products and continued in that line of business until his death on December 26, 1916. He was a very prominent citizen of Genesee and held the offices of town treasurer and justice of the peace. His children are:

1194. Edward T.; is unmarried and a farmer in Ellisburg, Pa., at this writing.

1195. Adella M., b June 6, 1878; married Joseph N. Dwight on December 23, 1897.

1196. Aimee Laola, b. August 12, 1882; married on February 20, 1909, Carlton W. Richmond.

947. ALBERT CALVIN ALLIS was born October 1, 1854, in Coventry, N. Y. Within a few years his parents moved to Candor, N. Y., and at the age of 18 years he engaged in the farming, milling and lumbering business in Allegany Township, Potter County, Pa. He continued in that line of business until 1885, ten years after his marriage, and then moved to Genesee, Pa., where he became the owner and manager of a hotel. In 1893 he sold

ALBERT CALVIN ALLIS

his hotel and purchased a general store, which he operated until 1902, at which time he left Genesee on account of failing health and moved to Buffalo, N. Y. At the end of three years, however, he returned to Genesee and engaged in the grocery business, but in 1914 moved back to Buffalo and is a grain dealer there at this writing. Mr. Allis was a prominent citizen of Genesee and held the offices of town treasurer and assistant postmaster.

On December 12, 1875, he married Ella M., daughter of Pardon C. and Mary M. (Jones) Reynolds of Allegany Township, Pa., who was born in Independence, N. Y., on April 9, 1855, and is now living in Buffalo. Their children are:

1197. Nora Matilda, b. January 12, 1877; married on June 24, 1900, Adelbert Whitney.

1198. Bessie Mabel, b. April 11, 1879; unmarried and living in Buffalo, N. Y., at this writing.

1199. Leah Mae, b. August 24, 1886; married James P. Shannon on January 22, 1907, and they have a daughter, Frances Mae, born July 3, 1916.

949. FRANK MARIAN ALLIS was born on August 26, 1860, in Ellisburg, Pa. He first took up the lumbering and farming business in 1880, and soon after his marriage engaged in farming near Scio, N. Y. He lived there for several years, but returned to Ellisburg to manage his father's farm, and after his father's death bought the farm and homestead from the other heirs and is residing there at this writing. He is a prominent citizen of Ellisburg and has held several town offices.

On June 30, 1880, he married Henrietta Hamilton of Scio, and their children are:

1200. Robert H , b. October 16, 1881; *

1201. William C., b. February 12, 1884; *

1202. Eleanor, b. June 20, 1886; married Frank K. Hurd on December 31, 1907, and they have a son, Myron Allis, born December 27, 1912. They reside in Ellisburg, Pa., at this writing.

1203. Ira Barber, b. November 22, 1890; *

955. WILLIAM SPENCER ALLIS was born in Coventry, N. Y., June 20, 1863. He eventually moved to Elyria, Ohio, and is a contractor there at this writing. On July 30, 1890, he married Lila C., daughter of Charles D. Gray, who was born May 11, 1862, in Brisben, N. Y., and their children are:

1204. Alfred William, b. February 9, 1892; is unmarried at this writing and living in Elyria.

1205, Spencer Franklin, b. February 19, 1898; living in Elyria as this book goes to press.

1206. Charles Gray, b. December 22, 1899; living in Elyria.

1207. Leonard Kales, b. October 15, 1901; living in Elyria.

1208. John Francis, b. June 17, 1903; living in Elyria.

956. LEONARD GUY ALLIS was born November 12, 1864, in Coventry, N. Y. He was educated in the local schools and learned the drug business in New York. In 1890 he went to Seattle, Wash., and engaged in the drug business, and until the beginning of the Spanish-American War (a period of about eight years) he was a druggist in that city.

On May 13, 1898, he enlisted in the 1st Washington Infantry, U. S. V., as hospital steward. While in Manila he was promoted to first lieutenant and assistant surgeon, and served as such until the mustering out of the regiment at San Francisco, Cal., on November 1, 1899. At this writing he is a druggist in Sawtelle, Cal., a suburb of Los Angeles.

On November 9, 1899, he married Marie E. Atwood and they have a daughter:

1209. Marie Elizabeth, b. May 7, 1902.

962. CLARENCE MORTON ALLIS was born October 23, 1858, in Charlotte, Mich. On May 28, 1888, he married Augusta, daughter of Edward Luther of South Bend, Ind., who was born March 17, 1869, and at this writing he is a barber in Chicago, Ill. Their children are:

1210. Harry, b. June 17, 1889; is married and living in St. Joseph, Mich., at this writing.

1211. Frank P., b. August 21, 1891; married and living in Los Angeles, Cal.

1212. Catherine L., b. March 12, 1893; married William Cody on September 6, 1916, and is living in Chicago, Ill., as this book goes to press.

963. IRA W. ALLIS was born June 13, 1860, in Charlotte, Mich. In 1883 he married Lizzie Harbough, and at this writing is a barber in Chicago, Ill. Their children are:

1213. Howard L., b. May 3, 1884; *

1214. Mary, b. about 1887.

964. JESSE F. ALLIS was born April 14, 1869, in Charlotte, Mich. On January 26, 1892, he married Harriet Jager, and at this writing is living in Chicago, Ill., being a foreman for Montgomery, Ward & Company of that city. They have a daughter:

1215. Frances Louise, b. November 18, 1907.

NINTH GENERATION.

965. EDWARD YOUNG ALLIS was born April 24, 1884, in Fayette, Mich., and at this writing is a farmer in Morenci, Mich. On December 21, 1905, he married Inez Boston and their children are:

1216. Gloyd E., b August 8, 1907.

1217. Katie Ellen Loretta, b. November 23, 1908.

1218. Nita J., b. March 4, 1912.

967. FLOYD V. ALLIS was born April 13, 1880, in Canastota, N. Y., and is a farmer there at this writing. He and his father, Joel Allis, are living on the 140-acre farm that was originally owned by Joel Allis (No. 139), who purchased it of the State of New York over 120 years ago. On August 15, 1906, he married Annie Laurie Bettinger, who was born August 14, 1881, and they have a daughter:

1219. Hazel E., b. August 29, 1911.

970. DARWIN F. ALLIS was born November 28, 1855, in Conway, Mass. On December 25, 1875,

he married Ida T. Rhood and is living in Conway at this writing. They have a daughter:

1220. Winifred Blanche, b. October 9, 1882; married Walter H. Barker, October 9, 1905, and they have a daughter, Dean Rhood, b. June 4, 1914.

972. CHARLES F. ALLIS was born December 3, 1852, in Conway, Mass. On March 17, 1875, he married Clara M. Boyden and was a farmer in Conway until within a short time of his death on February 9, 1917. Their children were:

1221. George Dwight, b. December 17, 1875; *

1222. Maud Winifred, b. May 3, 1877; died February 16, 1886.

1223. Bertha Loilla, b. July 3, 1879; married Albert N. Stanley in January, 1905, and is living in St. Louis, Mo., at this writing.

974. WILLIAM DICKINSON ALLIS was born August 9, 1865, in Conway, Mass., and was a farmer in that town until his death, May 1, 1917. On February 16, 1886, he married Susie R. Wood and their children were:

1224. Lula Helen, b. October 9, 1892.

1225. Ruth McKinley, b. November 13, 1896.

976. OLIVER E. ALLIS was born November 11, 1874. On June 21, 1905, he married Nellie J. Hollis and is living in Council Bluffs, Iowa, at this writing, being connected with the George A. Hoagland Lumber Company of that city. Their children are:

1226. Marian, b. September 26, 1906.

1227. Dorothy, b. November 3, 1910.

977. WILLIAM R. ALLIS was born October 15, 1876. On February 5, 1902, he married Anna Schoening and at this writing is living in Council Bluffs, Ia., being treasurer of the Home Loan Company of that city and proprietor of the White Bakery. They have had two children:

1228. Viola, b. November 10, 1902.

1229. Kathryn, b. June 14, 1908.

678. SAMUEL ALLIS was born December 18, 1879. On March 1, 1901, he married Bertha Saar and has been engaged in the real estate business in Omaha, Neb., for a number of years. They have a son:

1230. Lawrence, b. December 18, 1901.

991. RUFUS DICKENSON ALLIS was born September 16, 1876, in Conway, Mass. His early education was obtained in the public schools of Conway and was followed by special courses of study in Amherst, Mass. He has been engaged in different occupations, namely railroading, road making and the grain business, and at this writing is connected with the Montague City Rod Company of Montague, Mass., although also engaged in farming in Pelham City, Mass.

On October 20, 1909, he married Abbie L. Flagg of Bernardston, Mass., and their children are:

1231. Mary Luella, b. August 20, 1912

1232. Elinor Myra, b August 11, 1913

1233. Earle George Dickenson, b. August 11, 1913.

998. LUCIUS HOWES ALLIS was born March 9, 1886, in Whately, Mass., and is a farmer in that town at this writing. On August 15, 1906, he married Florence, daughter of Joseph and Margaret Bowman of Whately, who was born August 8, 1886. They have had the following children:

1234. Lucius Richard, b. May 22, 1907.

1235. Isabell Margaret, b January 14, 1910.

1236. Frances Augusta, b. Nov. 17, 1912; died June 9, 1916.

1237. Roger Maynard, b October 2, 1915.

1238. Esther May, b April 7, 1917.

1002. EDWARD D. ALLIS was born April 6, 1881, in Adrian, Mich. On May 4, 1916, he married Jessie L. Strang and is a farmer in Lansing, Mich., at this writing. Their children are:

1239. Lucius Charles, b. December 7, 1904.

1240. Clyde Warren, b. December 1, 1907.

1241. Leon Edward, b December 30, 1909

1242. Mary Louise, b. September 5, 1914.

1006. THOMAS WELLS ALLIS was born October 14, 1849, in Kendall, N. Y. When he was about eight years of age the family moved to Clarendon, N. Y., and he was a farmer there for several years. Afterward he was a merchant in Gaylord, Mich., until his death on February 28, 1911.

On December 31, 1874, he married Electa Irene Morse, who died October 2, 1894. They had the following children:

1243. John J., b. November 3, 1875; *

1244. George R., b. March 27, 1877; *

1245. Ava Maud, b. October 3, 1878; married Charles Ish, July 3, 1895, and they have the following children: Brice, b. June 15, 1897, John J., b September 1, 1898, Harry, b. Nov. 26, 1899, Ada Elizabeth, b. July 25, 1901, Charles B., b. February 21, 1903, Harold, b. September 23, 1904, Fay, b. July 17, 1906, and Merle A., b. Nov. 13, 1908.

1246. Ruth E., b. Dec. 3, 1885; married Avery H. Frederick on September 26, 1906, and their children are Marion E., b. July 3, 1908, and Carrie Jane, b. July 29, 1910.

1009. OLIVER JAMES ALLIS was born October 20, 1855, in Kendall, N. Y., and at this writing is a farmer in Clarendon, N. Y., in which place he has lived nearly all his life. On January 22, 1880, he married Hettie Coy and their children are:

1247. Frank C., b. January 1, 1881; *

1248. Herbert C , b. February 28, 1885; *

1249. Clement, b October 31, 1887; *

1250. May, b. Sept 2, 1889; unmarried and living in Clarendon.

1010. JAY ELIJAH ALLIS was born June 3, 1858, in Holley, N. Y., and was educated in the district school at Bennett's Corners and the Holley High School. On October 17, 1883, he married Martha A., daughter of David and Polly Balch of Medina, N. Y., and moved to Medina, where he has since lived. He has been a farmer and fruit grower all his life and is called the "Peach King." He has one son:

1251. Ray, b. Aug. 19, 1889; married Minnie E. Mosey in 1914 and is in business with his father in Medina at this time.

1011. SETH ALONZO ALLIS was born September 19, 1861, in Clarenden, N. Y., and is a farmer and large apple producer in that town at this writing. On October 13, 1886, he married Ella Smith and their children are:

1252. Truman, b. May 9, 1887; is unmarried at this writing.

1253. Lillian, b. March 1, 1897.

1012. CLARK ALLIS was born August 15, 1865, in Clarendon, N. Y., and was educated in the local schools. He was a farmer in Clarendon for a number of years, but eventually moved to Medina, N. Y., and at this writing is a farmer and extensive fruit grower in that town. He is the owner of a number of large fruit orchards, aggregating over 150 acres, and is known as the "Apple King". He is also the proprietor of a large cold storage warehouse in Medina and is vice-president of the Van Aervaur Manufacturing Company of Medina, manufacturers of milk pasteurizers.

Mr. Allis is not only a successful business man but is public spirited and actively interested in the affairs of his town and state. He is a director of the Orleans County Agricultural Society, a member of the Niagara County Farmers Club and the Western New York Horticultural Society, and was for two years president of the New York State Fruit Growers Association. In politics he is a prominent member of the Prohibition Party and in a recent election ran for lieutenant governor on that ticket. He has traveled abroad extensively and has also toured the United States, having visited nearly every state in the Union.

Mr. Allis married (first) on September 28, 1886, Alma Breed, who died May 21, 1900, and (second) on May 8, 1901, Mrs. Carrie H. Kelly. His two children by the first marriage were:

1254. Sumner, b. March 31, 1887; *

1255. Marion R., b March 26, 1888; unmarried at this writing.

1014. EDWARD L. ALLIS was born February 9, 1880, in Somerville, Mass., but has lived in Melrose, Mass., since he was two years of age. He was educated in the grammar and high schools of that city, and at the age of 20 years engaged in the electrical business. He continued in that line of business until 1907, at which time he entered the employment of the Motor Car Equipment Company of New York, Boston and Newark, and at this writing is sales manager in the Boston office.

On November 9, 1910, he married Elizabeth Jane, daughter of Robert Hunter of Highlands, N. J., who was born December 21, 1880, and their children are:

1256. Dorothy Elizabeth, b. August 28, 1911.

1257. Editha Frances, b. August 9, 1915.

1019. ADELBERT ALLIS was born May 18, 1881, at Lambs Creek, near Mansfield, Pa., and at this writing is a farmer in Mansfield. On May 18, 1904, he married Anna, daughter of William and Mary Quinn, who was born September 11, 1880, and their children are:

1258. Leo, b November 3, 1906.

1259. Allene, b. April 9, 1908.

1260. Ellsworth, b. November 28, 1909.

CLARK ALLIS

1020. WILLARD C. ALLIS was born June 10, 1874, in Evansville, Ind., and was educated in the local schools, since which time he has been connected with different manufacturing establishments. He was for twelve years with the L. & N. R. R. Company as rate-man and assistant cashier, and at this writing is cashier for the Lackawanna Steel Company of Buffalo, N. Y., which position he has held since October, 1911.

On October 20, 1905, he married Frances E., daughter of Franklin and Emma Eaton, and they are residing in Buffalo. Their children are:

1261. Willard Charles, b October 12, 1906.

1262. Albert, b. January 24, 1908.

1263. Jane Elizabeth, b. August 15, 1914.

1023. GORDON BYRON ALLIS was born September 15, 1881, in Evansville, Ind. He was educated in the public schools of Evansville, and as this book goes to press is a railroad conductor, living in that city, although he is also engaged in the real estate business. On September 18, 1912, he married Maud Irene Hubert and their two children are:

1264. Gordon Byron, Jr., b. July 2, 1913.

1265. Mary Ruth, b. September 12, 1916.

1039. CLARENCE HAYDEN ALLIS was born April 2, 1888, in Derby, Conn. His early education was obtained in the Irving Grammar School and in 1905 he graduated from the Derby High School. In September of the same year he entered the Academic Department of Yale University and graduated in 1909. After leaving college he was for two years in the employ of the Besse-Boynton Company, retail clothiers in Meriden, Conn. He then engaged in the same line of business for himself in Ansonia, Conn., and it is now conducted under the firm name of the C. H. Allis Company. He is a Mason and a resident of Ansonia.

On June 19, 1913, he married Marion Henderson Orr of Meriden and they have a son:

1266. Richard Skinner, b. January 6, 1916.

1051. C. HARRY ALLIS was born about 1873 in Prattsburg, N. Y. He is a graduate of the Detroit High School, Detroit, Mich., and is an artist by profession, dividing his time between Los Angeles, Cal., and Paris, France. On October 1, 1902, he married Letitia Torrey in Detroit and moved to France, but at this writing is located in California. Their three children were born in France:

1267. Lillian, b. August 21, 1906.

1268. Beatrice T., b. December 29, 1907.

1269. Letitia, b. November 30, 1909.

1059. HUBBARD BENJAMIN ALLIS was born October 24, 1887, in Little Rock, Ark., and was educated in the local schools. On November 17, 1914, he married Mary Jordan Buchanan and at this writing is a traveling salesman in Arkansas, Oklahoma and Texas, with headquarters in Dallas, Texas. They have a son:

1270. Charles Dickinson, b. September 27, 1915.

1060. DAVID MILLS ALLIS was born January 20, 1890, in Little Rock, Ark. He was educated in the local schools and at this writing is a traveling salesman for the American Tobacco Company, with headquarters in Little Rock. On June 15, 1915, he married Pauline C. Walker of Muskogee, Okla., and they have a daughter:

1271. Martha Elizabeth, b. May 7, 1917.

1103. FAYETTE HENRY ALLIS was born December 4, 1889, in Smith Center, Kansas, and was educated in the local schools. On May 1, 1914, he married Myrtle Oskins and at this writing is an architect in Omaha, Neb. They have a daughter:

1272. Helen E., b August 3, 1916.

1115. FRED LEWIS ALLIS was born September 28, 1874, in Rome, Pa., and obtained his education in the schools of that town. On May 1, 1898, he married Iva L. Vought and is a farmer in Orwell, Pa., as this book goes to press. They have a son:

1273. Leon, b. August 27, 1899.

1116. CLAYTON WALTER ALLIS was born April 2, 1878, in Rome, Pa. On February 20, 1897, he married Sarah, daughter of Francis Dougherty and is a machinist in Athens, Pa., at this writing. Their children are:

1274. Lyslie, b. May 29, 1908.

1275. Carlton, b. March 17, 1912.

1276. Guy E., b. July 25, 1916.

1160. HARRY SYLVESTER ALLIS was born March 20, 1876, in Cold Spring, N. Y., and was educated in the local school. He lived in Brooklyn, N. Y., for a time but is living in Stony Creek, Conn., at this writing. On June 29, 1897, he married Annie Hart and their children were:

1277. Louise, b. November 26, 1899.

1278. May, b. May 1, 1904; died October 15, 1904.

1279. Irine, b. March 26, 1908, died September 7, 1908.

1280. Nelson, b. January 20, 1909; died March 5, 1909.

1161. NELSON HOWELL ALLIS was born November 9, 1870, in Cold Spring, N. Y., and was educated in the local school. He lived in Brooklyn, N. Y., for a time but moved to New Haven, Conn., about the time of his marriage and was employed on the New Haven Union until his death on November 5, 1908. On October 31, 1901, he married Nellie Lonergan of New Haven, Conn., and their children were:

1281. Harry, b. May 22, 1903.

1282. John, b. August 6, 1905.

1164. HORATIO DANA ALLIS was born July 28, 1884, in East Hartford, Conn., but has lived in Hartford since he was a small boy. His early education was obtained in the schools of Hartford and in 1902 he graduated from Huntsinger's Business College. For a period of five years he was connected with the Ætna Life Insurance Company of Hartford, but in 1907 accepted a position with the Ætna (Fire) Insurance Company, and at this time is with the New England Department of that company.

Mr. Allis is a member of Company B, First Regiment, C. H. G. He is also a member of the Hartford Y. M. C. A., Wethersfield Rifle Club, Westbrook Gun Club, and other social and business clubs. He is actively interested in church work and is a member of the Fourth Congregational Church. In addition to the daily routine he has collected a great deal of the material used in this genealogy and is responsible for its publication.

On November 22, 1907, he married Julia A., daughter of Hector F. and Octavia (Howland) Phelps of Simsbury, Conn., born June 13, 1883. They have a daughter:

1283. Julia Octavia, b. September 7, 1909.

1181. ALBERT THOMAS ALLIS was born July 4, 1868, in Baltimore, Ohio. He was educated in the public schools and at this writing is a stationary engineer in Columbus, Ohio. In 1889 he married Mary Etta Neff of Baltimore and their children are:

1284. Fayette; died in infancy.

1285. Marie Lenore; married Mr. Curry and at this writing is living in Columbus

1286. Ruth Naoma; unmarried at this writing.

1287. Maude Irene; unmarried.

1288. Helen May; unmarried.

1192. JOSEPH ASHTON ALLIS was born in St. Paul, Minn., January 5, 1881, and lived in that city until about five years of age, when his parents moved to

New York City. He was educated at Westminster School, Dobbs Ferry, N. Y., and at this writing is a bank examiner for the New York Clearing House, residing in Upper Montclair, N. J. On June 21, 1909, he married Elizabeth L. Verreault and their children are:

1289. Frederick Ashton, b. March 21, 1910.

1290. Bayard Ashton, b. July 1, 1911.

1200. ROBERT H. ALLIS was born October 16, 1881, in Scio, N. Y. He lived in that town for many years, but eventually settled upon a farm near Ellisburg, Pa., and has been a farmer there all his life with the exception of two years he was engaged in the cheese-making business. On May 1, 1907, he married Lena M. Reynolds of Ellisburg, who died June 17, 1914. They had three children:

1291. Fred Albert, b. June 9, 1909.

1292. Glen Reynolds, b. May 11, 1912.

1293. Carl Marian, b. June 2, 1914.

1201. WILLIAM C. ALLIS was born February 12, 1884, in Scio, N. Y. He lived with his parents until 18 years of age, at which time he started working in a saw mill, and was engaged in that line of business for several years, being located in Galeton, Pa., for a time. On October 17, 1906, he married Kathryn Simonds and moved on to a farm in Ellisburg, Pa., where they are living at this writing. Their children are:

1294. Beth Loriana, b. June 2, 1908.

1295. Dorr D., b. August 1, 1911.

1296. Anna Maxine, b. April 20, 1913.

1203. IRA BARBER ALLIS was born November 22, 1890, in Scio, N. Y. On June 23, 1915, he married Mary Caroline Hurd of Ellisburg, Pa., and is a general merchandise salesman in Genesee, Pa., as this book goes to press. They have a daughter:

1297. Ruth Hyla, b. March 23, 1917.

1213. HOWARD L. ALLIS was born May 3, 1884. He was for a number of years a barber in Chicago, Ill., but at this writing is a fireman for the B. & O. R. R. On May 23, 1904, he married Grace Casher of Charlotte, Mich., and they have a daughter:

1298. Ruby, b. March 4, 1905.

TENTH GENERATION.

1221. GEORGE DWIGHT ALLIS was born December 17, 1875, in Conway, Mass. He has been a lifelong resident of that town and is a farmer by occupation. On October 16, 1907, he married Marion L. Laidley and they have the following children:

1299. Clara Elizabeth, b. January 15, 1909.
1300. Mildred F., b. July 20, 1910.
1301. Gertrude Helen, b. July 23, 1913.
1302. Charles Howard, b. March 21, 1917.

1243. JOHN J. ALLIS was born November 3, 1875, in Gaylord, Mich. On March 26, 1903, he married Mrs. Jennie B. Fox and at this writing is a farmer in Gaylord. Their children are:

1303. Walter B , b. January 15, 1904.

1304. Ward E., b. January 14, 1907.

1305. Marion Carol, b October 10, 1909.

1306. Sumner Jay, b. July 14, 1912.

1244. GEORGE R. ALLIS was born March 27, 1877, in Gaylord, Mich. At this writing he is an assistant foreman for the Buick Motor Company of Flint, Mich., and is living in Mount Morris, a neighboring town. On May 28, 1902, he married Mabel M. English and their children are:

1307. Gilbert Jay, b. August 8, 1903.

1308. Eunice Fidelia, b August 16, 1906.

1309. Viola Louise, b. June 30, 1908.

1310. Herbert, b. in 1913.

1247. FRANK C. ALLIS was born January 1, 1881, in Clarendon, N. Y. At this writing he is advertising manager of "What, When and Where in Washington, D. C.," and lives in Holley (near Clarendon), N. Y. On May 18, 1904, he married Eula Mae Bidwell and their children are:

1311. Eula Mae, b. November 1, 1907.

1312. Frank Coy, b. August 3, 1909.

1313. James Bidwell, b. October 8, 1911.

1248. HERBERT C. ALLIS was born February 28, 1885, in Clarendon, N. Y. On February 2, 1910, he married Mabel Alberts and is living in Holley, N, Y., at this writing. They have a son:

1314. Bert Albert, b. March 8, 1912.

1249. CLEMENT C. ALLIS was born October 31, 1887, in Clarendon, N. Y. He was educated in Holley, N. Y., and at this writing is a farmer in Kendall, N. Y. On September 20, 1906, he married Ida Pearl, daughter of Henry and Emma Mead, who was born April 2, 1890. Their children are:

1315. Morris Nelson, b. July 26, 1907.

1316. Albert Claud, b July 20, 1908.

1317. Irving Raymond, b. October 28, 1909.

1318. Gordon Alonzo, b. August 15, 1911.

1319. Viola Mae.

1254. SUMNER ALLIS was born March 31, 1887. On December 25, 1911, he married Jessie A. Alchin and was engaged in the apple and cold storage business with his father in Medina, N. Y., until his death on September 4, 1913. They had a daughter:

1320. Alma Elizabeth, b. January 21, 1913.

ADDENDA

55. (page 15) Jemima Allis married Eliakim Root on August 15, 1731. Their children were Joseph, b. in July, 1732, Medad, b. December 29, 1735, Jonathan, b. January 11, 1738 (died), Miriam, b November 2, 1739, Jonathan, b. June 18, 1742, and Jemima, b. June 3, 1746 (m. Ebenezer Allis, No.117).

63. (p. 25) Ebenezer Allis' first wife, Experience Warner, died in 1794 and he married (second) on March 5, 1795, Mary Ayers, widow of Joseph Locke, who died March 29, 1806. Ebenezer Allis died in 1814.

84. (page 33) Elisha Allis lived in Hatfield, Mass., for a few years after his graduation from Yale University, and was a quartermaster or government purveyor of army supplies. All that he had was placed at the service of his country and he received therefor Continental money, by the depreciation of which he found it necessary to start anew. He settled upon a farm in Williamsburg, Mass., and after living there a number of years moved to Brookfield, Vermont, where he became a prominent and influential citizen.

85. (page 21) Anna Allis married Dr Josiah Pomeroy, a surgeon in the British army, on July 5, 1774. They moved to Nova Scotia, and afterwards went back to New York State, but finally settled in Pittsfield, Mass. Their children were Nancy, Harriet and Sophia.

101. (page 24) Aaron Allis enlisted as a private in Capt. Wm. Watson's company, Col Wesson, 9th Mass., and served until April 9, 1780. In March, 1781, he enlisted as a sergeant in the 3rd Mass., Capt. Wade, Col. Michael Jackson, and was discharged at West Point, N. Y., on December 23, 1783. He was a farmer in Whately, Mass., but moved to Troy, N. Y., and was living there when he applied for and received a pension from the United States Government in 1818.

311. (page 91) Asa Allis was a farmer in Chili Station, N. Y.

323. (page 96) Samuel Allis lived in Genoa, Neb., and not Geneva.

471. (page 75) Mary Waite Allis died December 6, 1916, in East Longmeadow, Mass., age 83 years.

473. (page 136) John Mather Allis married Laura Livingston on January 2, 1883, and not June 2, 1883

508. (page 80) Ordensa H. Allis and Thomas R. Pickering had the following children: Alpha, b. June 11 1859 (died on July 4, 1873), Samuel, b. December 30, 1861, Gertrude, b. April 16, 1864, and Lynua, b. July 17, 1870.

513. (page 81) Henrietta Augusta Allis and Harry Parks had the following children: Celestia, Myron H., Silas, Burton, Lewis and William.

550. (page 85) Newton Allis died February 20, 1893. Laura Farley, his first wife, was born on August 1, 1829, and died August 6, 1871.

733. (page 177) Chester D. Allis resided in Hegewisch and not Hegeswisch, Ill.

858. (page 143) Eva Viola Allis married Lewis Brink and died March 14, 1909. They had a son, John, who was born in 1875 and married Louisa Drake.

859. (page 143) Flora Versula Allis married G. G. Wells of Herrickville, Pa., and they have two children, Laura, b. May 27, 1888, and Mabel, b. June 29, 1894.

909. (page 154) Stella Allis Adams died January 5, 1918.

923. (page 155). Eliza Allis Kron died December 19, 1916.

997. (page 169) Clarence I. Allis married Anna, daughter of Elizur F. and Lydia A. Orcutt, on May 5, 1911, and at this writing is an employe of the Nonotuck Silk Mill in Florence, Mass., where he is living.

1069. (page 188) Edward Phelps Allis married Josephine Root Dyer on November 22, 1917. He has entered the United States Army since his biography was printed and at this writing (February, 1918) is in Charlotte, N. C.

Page 188 John Watson Allis, son of Louis and Louise (Hegen) Allis, was born March 2, 1918.

1141. (page 202) Edward B. Ellis was born November 21, 1884. In 1908 he married Alice M. Sweet and they have two children, Muriel, b. August 24, 1909, and Howard Edward, b. June 23, 1914.

1143. (page 202) Hubert I. Ellis was born on June 28, 1889. In 1916 he married Grace Wells and at this writing is a mining engineer in Seattle, Wash.

1146. (page 203) George Freeman Ellis married Dora Beekman in 1915 and they have one son, George Grant, born November 27, 1916.

1166. (p. 207) Burdette Allis is a private in the Headquarters Company, 301st Infantry, U. S. A., Ayer, Mass., at this writing (March, 1918).

1171. (p. 208) Sarah Lucille Allis married Benjamin T. Hall on July 1, 1917, and they are living in Cold Spring, N. Y., as this book goes to press.

678. (page 218) This number should be 978.

INCOMPLETE LINE.

ABRAHAM ALLIS was born June 16, 1771, and died on July 30, 1852, age 81 years. He married (first) Christina———, who was born July 13, 1771, and died February 24, 1832, and (second) Laurinda Ball, widow of Erastus Palmer, who was born in 1797. Information in regard to his ancestors and his early life is missing, but at the time of his second marriage he owned and operated a grist mill at Lower Hook (near what is now Edmeston), Otsego County, N. Y. Abraham Allis is known to have had two brothers, Israel, who lived near Deruyter, N, Y., and William, who lived in Howard, Steuben County, N. Y. His children were:

By first marriage:

1. Lucy, b. February 17, 1793; died August 15, 1875.
2. Benjamin, b. November 4, 1794; *
3. Hannah, b. December 1, 1796; died March 15, 1875.
4. Solomon, b. July 22, 1799; died September 1, 1838.
5. Clarissa, b. September 20, 1804; married Franklin Spurr of Columbus, N. Y., and died February 26, 1873.
6. Welthy, b. October 9, 1807; died February 10, 1827.

By second marriage:

7. William Henry, b. September 4, 1833; *
8. Jeremiah Pratt, b. August 7, 1835; *

2. BENJAMIN ALLIS was born November 4, 1794. He married Susan Pratt and lived near Bowling Green, N. Y. A complete record of his children is missing but he is known to have had a son:

9. Abraham De Lancey; *

7. WILLIAM HENRY ALLIS was born September 4, 1833. He was twice married, first, to Emma Reece, who died January 21, 1863, and, second, to Susan Lucretia Thompson on February 22, 1864. He lived in Cleveland, Ohio, for many years and had five children:

By first marriage:

10. Frederick Elmer, b. August 6, 1861; *

By second marriage:

11. Robert James, b. February 19, 1865; *
12. Margaret Lurinda, b. June 23, 1868; married Hobart D. Hiles on May 25, 1892, and their children are William A., b. January 21, 1893, and Ruth Lucretia, b. Aug. 17, 1899. They are living in Cleveland, Ohio, at this writing.
13. William Henry, Jr., b. April 25, 1870; *
14. George Walter, b. March 11, 1875; married Mary Moore on January 12, 1901:

8. JEREMIAH P. ALLIS was born August 7, 1835. He was a carpenter and builder in Leonardsville, N. Y., until about 1878, when he moved to Plainfield, N. J., and was a draughtsman for the Potter Printing Press Company. On August 1, 1858, he married Farrie M. St. John and died December 31, 1905. Their children were:

15. Jere A., b. May 16, 1863; married Bertha E. Shannon of Lackawanna, Pa , on November 20, 1895, and is a doctor in New York City at this writing.

16. Harriet Elizabeth, b. May 26, 1876; married N. E Lewis of Plainfield, N. J., in May, 1903.

10. FREDERICK ELMER ALLIS was born on August 6, 1861, and died July 3, 1910. He was twice married, first, to Alice Oswalt, December 25, 1889, and, second, to Jennie Aitkenhead, March 21, 1901. He lived in Cleveland, O., and had two children by first marriage:

17. Vera, b. August 6, 1891.

18. Emma Rita, b. December 25, 1896.

11. ROBERT JAMES ALLIS was born on February 19, 1865. On August 9, 1888, he married May Seacoy and they are living in Cleveland, Ohio, at this time. Their children are:

19. William Pinkney, b. June 19, 1889.

20. Harold Worthington, b. January 17, 1891.

13. WILLIAM HENRY ALLIS was born April 25, 1870, and married Clara Fisher, May 15, 1890. At this writing he is a motorman, living in Galion, Ohio, and is a Knight Templar. He has a son:

21. Harry LeRoy, b. December 30, 1891.

ADDENDA (1920)

1164. (page 207) Marguerite Chapman Allis, daughter of Horatio D. and Julia A. (Phelps) Allis, was born October 20, 1918.

1167. (page 207) Ernest H. Moseley, Jr., son of Ernest H. and Elizabeth Chapman (Allis) Moseley, was born April 24, 1919. Now living in South Manchester, Conn.

1171. (pages 208 and 234) William Francis Hall, son of Benjamin T. and Sarah L. (Allis) Hall, was born September 18, 1918.

1198. (page 213) Bessie M. Allis, daughter of Albert C. and Ella M. (Reynolds) Allis, died September 23, 1918, in Buffalo, N Y., where Mr. Allis now resides.

1202. (page 214) Hyla Louise Hurd, daughter of Frank and Eleanor (Allis) Hurd, was born November 13, 1919.

1303. (page 229) Dean Hurd Allis, son of Ira B. and Mary C. (Hurd) Allis, was born August 31, 1919.

1243. (page 2)3) Carlyle Wells Allis, son of John J. and Jennie (Fox) Allis, was born March 8, 1915, and died July 28, 1916. Ruth Janette Allis, daughter of John J. and Jennie (Fox) Allis, was born March 4, 1917.

INDEX

OF

HEADS OF FAMILIES

ALLIS

ELLIS

www.ingramcontent.com/pod-product-compliance
Lightning Source LLC
La Vergne TN
LVHW020538100826
845148LV00010B/1514

* 9 7 8 1 5 9 6 4 1 4 2 6 6 *